To: Angus D.

Winning With the Scotch

Gary Lane

An Owl Book
Henry Holt and Company
New York

Henry Holt and Company, Inc.
Publishers since 1866
115 West 18th Street
New York, New York 10011

Henry Holt® is a registered trademark
of Henry Holt and Company, Inc.

First published in the United States in 1993 by
Henry Holt and Company, Inc.
Originally published in Great Britain in 1993 by
B. T. Batsford Ltd.

Library of Congress Catalog Card Number: 93-77851

ISBN 0-8050-2940-0 (An Owl Book: pbk.)

First American Edition—1993

Printed in the United Kingdom
All first editions are printed on acid-free paper. ∞

10 9 8 7 6 5 4 3 2 1

Adviser: R. D. Keene, GM, OBE
Technical Editor: Andrew Kinsman

Contents

Symbols

+	Check
++	Double check
mate	Checkmate
!	Good move
!!	Excellent move
?	Bad move
??	Blunder
!?	Interesting move
?!	Dubious move
±	Small advantage for White
∓	Small advantage for Black
±	Clear advantage for White
∓	Clear advantage for Black
+−	Winning advantage for White
−+	Winning advantage for Black
=	The position is equal
∞	The position is unclear
1–0	White wins
0–1	Black wins
½–½	Draw
Ol	Olympiad
izt	Interzonal
zt	Zonal
Ch	Championship
Corr	Correspondence
Jnr	Junior
m	Match

Preface

The Scotch is an old, established opening which has recently come back into fashion as a result of its adoption by Gary Kasparov. It offers excellent opportunities for tactical players, with lines such as the Mieses Variation leading to original and exciting positions. The Scotch Four Knights is ideally suited to the more positional player.

This book gives the current state of theory of all the major variations of the Scotch with an emphasis on the fashionable lines. The illustrative games demonstrate the critical ideas for both White and Black, and there is complete coverage of side variations for those who wish to avoid the main lines. If the main games are thoroughly absorbed then the reader will develop a good feel for the types of middlegame which can arise. It is my belief that anyone who plays the Scotch will be rewarded with rich and interesting games.

Gary Lane
March 1993

Historical Introduction

The Scotch derived its name from a correspondence game between Edinburgh and London, dating from 1826 to 1828. That game started 1 e4 e5 2 Nf3 Nc6 3 d4 Nxd4 4 Nxd4 exd4 5 Qxd4 Ne7 6 Bc4 Nc6 7 Qd5 and White went on to win after 60 moves. It is ironic that in an earlier game in that series, London played the first few moves of the opening but then branched off into a gambit line, as if they had recaptured on d4 it might now be known as the English instead of the Scotch! For those interested, the opening moves of the 1824 encounter were 1 e4 e5 2 Nf3 Nc6 3 d4 exd4 4 Bc4 Bc5 5 c3 Qe7 6 0-0 dxc3 7 Nxc3 d6 8 Nd5 Qd7 9 b4 Nxb4 10 Nxb4 Bxb4 11 Ng5 Nh6 12 Bb2 with unclear play. The first recorded mention of the Scotch (Göring) Gambit has been traced back to the Italian Ercole del Rio in 1750, and it is from this source that the London team borrowed the idea. In this volume we consider only the Scotch Game, in which White recaptures immediately on d4.

The popularity of the Scotch Game has fluctuated wildly over the last century or so. Around the end of the century it was a frequent choice despite the success of Steinitz's 4 ... Qh4 at that time. Later, attention switched to the Scotch Four Knights which was adopted by Capablanca on numerous occasions. However, eventually this developed a drawish reputation and attention turned to the Ruy Lopez.

The Scotch was then only seen occasionally up to the late 1960s when it was adopted by Radulov, Savon and Kupreichik. Although a great deal of analysis was undertaken at that time, interest faded again until the 1980s when it was often used as a surprise weapon by the Dutch Grandmaster Jan Timman.

The current wave of popularity can be traced back to the sensational fourteenth game of the Kasparov - Karpov 1990 World Championship match in Lyon. The fascinating complications of that game and the romantic nature of the Scotch Opening captured the public's imagination, and soon it was being played around the world. Kasparov has since turned to it on many occasions and many other world-class grandmasters have made important theoretical contributions. At the time of writing the future of the opening looks brighter than ever, even after more than 165 years of tournament competition with the Scotch.

1 Classical Variation: 7 ♗c4

One of the main reasons why the Scotch has come back into fashion is the spectacular results achieved by White with the 5 ♗e3 ♕f6 6 c3 ♘ge7 7 ♗c4 system, which had been neglected for decades in preference to the more forcing 5 ♘b3.

The idea of 7 ♗c4 has been known for a long time but it was previously thought that 7 ... ♘e5 and 8 ... ♕g6 was a suitable remedy, leading to equality according to an analysis by Sokolsky in the 1940s. This view was challenged in 1991 during a lecture at the Chess School of Iceland. The consequences of the line were discussed at a deep level with the result that Icelandic players enjoyed a spate of spectacular victories in Europe and the USA which aroused a great deal of interest. The basis of the new idea is that the e-pawn can be abandoned in the quest for rapid development. The theoretical debate has continued, and Kasparov has given it the "royal" seal of approval by adopting it in his own games.

Kasparov - Short
Linares 1992

1	e4	e5
2	♘f3	♘c6
3	d4	exd4
4	♘xd4	♗c5
5	♗e3	♕f6
6	c3	♘ge7
7	♗c4	(1)

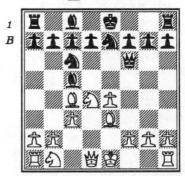

This is the beginning of the line which has revolutionized the reputation of the Scotch. White declares his aggressive intentions at the earliest opportunity by pin-pointing f7. The major alternative, 7 g3, is examined in the next chapter.

7	...	0-0
8	0-0	♗b6

Black has no time to play 8 ... a6 in order to have the option

of retreating the bishop to a7: 9
♔h1! (9 f4 d6! 10 ♔h1 ♗a7) 9 ...
b5 (9 ... d6? 10 ♘xc6 ♘xc6 11
♗xc5 dxc5 12 f4±) 10 ♗e2 ♗b7
11 f4 d6 12 ♗f3 ♘g6 (Hjartarson
– Goldin, Philadelphia 1991) 13
♘xc6! ♗xe3 (13 ... ♗xc6 14 ♗xc5
dxc5 15 e5 ♗xf3 16 ♕xf3±) 14
♘a5 ♗xf4 15 g3! ♗e5 16 ♘xb7 a5
17 ♗e2+–.

9   ♘c2!? *(2)*

The knight retreats in order
to emerge on d5 via e3. This
seems the best of an assortment of ideas:

a) 9 ♘a3 and now:

a1) 9 ... d6?! 10 ♘db5 and now

a11) 10 ... a6 11 ♘xd6 ♖d8 (11 ...
♗xe3! 12 ♘xc8 ♖axc8 13 fxe3∞
Leko – Huzman, Wijk aan Zee
1992) 12 e5! ♕g6 13 ♗xb6 cxb6 14
♕e2 ♗e6 15 ♘xb7 ♖d7 16 ♘d6
1–0 van der Wiel – David,
Mondorf 1991.

a12) 10 ... ♗a5 11 b4 a6 12 bxa5
axb5 13 ♘xb5 ♖xa5 14 ♘xc7
♕xc3 15 ♖c1 ♕e5 16 ♗b6 ♖a3 17
♘b5 ♖a6 18 ♗c7 ♘a5 19 ♗xd6+–
van der Wiel – Sarfati, Manila
Ol 1992.

a2) 9 ... ♘xd4!? 10 cxd4 d5!?

11 exd5 ♖d8 12 ♕h5 h6 13 ♖fe1
♗f5 14 ♕f3 ♖d7 15 ♘b5 ♖ad8
(Chandler – Short, English Ch
1991) 16 ♘c3 ♗xd4 17 ♗xd4
♕xd4, intending 18 ♗b5 c6! 19
dxc6 bxc6 20 ♗xc6 ♗g4 21 ♕e4
♘xc6 22 ♕xc6 ♕b4 with un-
clear chances according to
Chandler.

a3) 9 ... ♕g6 and now:

a31) 10 ♘xc6 bxc6 11 ♖e1 d6 12
♕d2 ♗b7 13 ♖ad1 h6 14 ♘c2
♖ad8 15 ♕c1 ♖fe8 16 f3 ♕f6 17
♔h1 ♘g6 18 ♗d4= Leko – van
der Sterren, Nettetal 1992.

a32) 10 ♕d2 ♘xd4 11 ♗xd4
♗xd4 12 cxd4 d5 13 exd5 ♘h3 14
f4 ♖ad8 15 ♖ae1 ♘c8 (15 ...
♘xd5? 16 ♖e5 c6 17 ♖g5+–) 16
♗b3 ♗f5 17 ♘c4 ♘b6 18 ♘xb6
axb6 19 ♖e5± Mainka – van der
Sterren, Prague 1992.

b) 9 ♗b3 and now:

b1) 9 ... d6 10 ♔h1 ♘xd4 11
cxd4 ♘c6 12 ♘c3 ♗xd4 13 ♘d5
♕e5 14 ♗xd4 ♕xd4 15 ♘xc7
♖b8 16 ♕e2 ♕f6 17 ♘d5 ♕h6 18
♖ad1 ♗e6 19 f4± Dolmatov –
Yusupov, Wijk aan Zee (10) 1991.

b2) 9 ... ♘a5 10 ♗c2 ♘c4 11
♗c1 d5 12 exd5 ♗xd4 13 cxd4
♗f5 14 ♘c3 ♗xc2 15 ♕xc2 ♘b6
16 ♕e4 ♕d6 17 ♗f4 ♕d7 18 d6
cxd6 19 a4 ♖fe8 20 ♕f3 ♘c6 21
♖fd1 ad8 22 ♕g3± J. Polgar –
Granda Zuniga, Madrid 1992.

c) 9 ♔h1?! ♖d8 (9 ... ♘a5? 10
♗d3 d5? 11 exd5 ♘xd5 12 ♕h5+–;
9 ... ♘xd4?! 10 cxd4 d5 11 ♗xd5!
♘xd5 12 exd5 ♖d8 13 ♘c3±) 10
♕h5!? h6 11 ♘d2 d5! 12 exd5
♘xd4 13 cxd4 ♗f5 14 ♕f3 ♕g6

15 ♗f4 ♛g4 16 ♛xg4 ♗xg4 17 f3! ♗f5 18 g4 ♘h7 19 d6 cxd6 20 ♖ae1∓ Kasparov - Kamsky, Tilburg 1991.

9	...	**d6**
10	**♗xb6**	**axb6**
11	**f4**	**g5!?**

A brave approach to force White to relinquish his hold on the coveted e5-square, which can then be occupied by a black knight. A less confrontational approach is 11 ... ♗e6!? 12 ♘d2 ♗xc4 13 ♘xc4 ♛e6 when White maintains a slight spatial advantage.

12	**f5**	**♘e5**
13	**♗e2**	**♗d7**
14	**c4**	

This represents another step in the quest to secure d5 for the white knights.

14	...	**g4?!**

The risky advance on the kingside is designed to create some counterplay, rather than wait for White to build up his forces. In fact, a direct approach to try and exchange one of the knights would have been more effective: 14 ... ♗a4! 15 b3 ♗c6 gives an unclear position e.g. 16 ♘c3? ♘xc4!.

15	**♘c3**	**h5**
16	**♛d2**	**♔h8**
17	**♛f4**	**♗c6**
18	**♘e3**	

Now White is on the verge of occupying d5, with the intention of 19 ♘ed5 ♗xd5 20 exd5 followed by ♘e4 and f6 with overwhelming pressure

against the overstretched black g- and h-pawns.

18	...	**♘d7?!** *(3)*

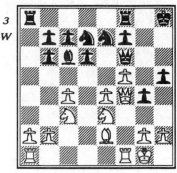

19	**♗xg4**

A startling sacrifice to open up a route to Black's king, enabling the rook and queen to create mating threats.

19	...	**hxg4**
20	**♘xg4**	**♛h4**
21	**♖f3**	**♘g6**
22	**♛e3!**	

This is the position that Kasparov had judged in his favour on move 19. Another piece is left hanging for the sake of the attack, which can only now be cut short by giving up the queen.

22	...	**♛xg4**
23	**♛h6+**	**♔g8**
24	**♖h3**	**♛xh3**
25	**gxh3!**	

White allows doubled pawns to open up the g-file in order to maintain the momentum of his attack by an eventual ♖g1.

25	...	**♘ge5**
26	**f6**	**♘xf6**
27	**♛xf6**	**♖ae8**
28	**♔h1**	

Although Black has managed to extract a rook and bishop for the queen, the vulnerability of his king is the deciding issue.

28	...	♘g6
29	h4	♖e6
30	♕g5	♖fe8
31	h5	♖e5
32	♕h6	♖xe4

A desperate response due to 32 ... ♘h4 33 ♖g1+.

33	♘xe4	♖xe4
34	♔g1	♘e5
35	♕g5+	♔h7
36	♕f5+	♔h6
37	♖f1	

The technical exercise at the moment is to prevent the black pieces from swarming around the white king.

37	...	♖e2
38	♕f6+	♔h7
39	♕g5!	♗e4

If here 39 ... ♖xb2 40 ♖xf7+ ♘xf7 41 ♕g6+ ♔h8 42 ♕f6+ ♔g8 43 ♕xb2, with a decisive advantage.

40	h6	♗g6
41	h4	♖e4
42	h5	♖g4+
43	♕xg4	♘xg4
44	hxg6+	fxg6
45	♖f7+	♔xh6
46	♖xc7	♘e5
47	♖xb7	♘xc4
48	b3	1-0

As we have seen, the quiet 7 ... 0-0 8 0-0 ♗b6 does not promise Black an equal game. The next two examples feature 7 ... ♘e5; an attempt by Black to curtail the influence of the powerful white light-squared bishop. This was originally considered to be the refutation of the whole 7 ♗c4 variation. However, after 8 ♗e2 ♕g6 9 0-0 d5 White has the twist 10 ♘h5!, giving up a pawn for a strong initiative, which has completely revived his chances.

Ehlvest – Beliavsky
Reykjavik 1991

1	e4	e5
2	♘f3	♘c6
3	d4	exd4
4	♘xd4	♗c5
5	♗e3	♕f6
6	c3	♘ge7
7	♗c4	♘e5

This move is the reason why the 7 ♗c4 line used to have a poor reputation, as the bishop is immediately forced to retreat. Sokolsky's analysis from the 1940s ran: 8 ♗e2 ♕g6 9 0-0 d5 10 exd5 ♘h3 11 ♗f3 0-0-0∓. However, Ehlvest has other ideas, as we shall see.

8 ♗e2

This is the most precise course at this juncture. White intends to force back the black knight by playing f4 and this will only really be effective if the g4-square is well covered. The 'natural' 8 ♗b3 is much less convincing: 8 ... ♕g6 9 0-0 ♕xe4 10 ♘d2 (After 10 ♗c2 ♕h4!, and 10 ♘b5 ♕c6! White has insufficient compensation for the pawn) 10 ... ♕g4! 11 ♘b5

♗xe3 12 fxe3 ♕xd1 13 ♖axd1 ♔d8 14 ♗xf7 d6 15 h3?! ♘f5 16 e4 ♘e3 17 ♘b3 a6 18 ♘d4 ♘xd1 19 ♖xd1 ♗e7-+ Meitner - Rosenthal, Vienna 1873.

8 ... ♕g6

There are no decent prospects for Black after 8 ... d5?! since the resulting tactics are in White's favour: 9 0-0 dxe4 10 ♘b5 ♗d6 11 ♗c5! 0-0 12 ♘xd6 cxd6 13 ♕xd6 ♕xd6 14 ♗xd6 ♘5c6 15 ♘d2 ♖e8 16 ♖fe1 ♗f5 17 ♖ad1 ♖ad8 18 ♘b3 h6 19 ♗b5 a6 20 ♗f1 ♘c8 21 ♗a3 ♖xd1 22 ♖xd1 ♘b6 23 ♘c5 ♘e5 24 ♘xb7 ♘ec4 25 ♘d6 ♖d8 26 ♖d4 ♗e6 27 ♗c5 ♖d7 28 ♘xc4 1-0 Steingrimsson - Malaniuk, Kecskemet 1991.

9 0-0 d5!? (4)

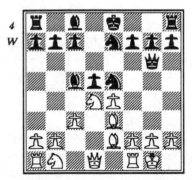

The more solid 9 ... d6 (and the risky 9 ... ♕xe4) are discussed in the next game.

10 ♘h5!

This sharp continuation has cast doubt on Black's traditional path to equality. The black queen is lured into an exposed position, allowing White to develop his pieces with gain of time at the cost of a single pawn. Other possibilities are:

a) 10 ♘b5?! ♗h3 11 ♘xc7+ (11 ♘f3 dxe4) 11 .. ♔f8 12 ♘f3 ♗xe3 13 fxe3 dxe4∓.

b) 10 ♘f4 and now:

b1) 10 ... ♗h3 11 ♗g3 h5 12 ♕a4+ ♔f8 13 ♘f3 ♘xf3+ 14 ♗xf3 h4 15 ♗xc7 ♕xg2 16 ♗xg2 h3 17 ♗g3 hxg2∓ Kopayev - Kualyachev, Ukrainian Ch 1949.

b2) 10 ...♕xe4 11 ♗g3 ♗xd4 12 ♘d2 ♕g6 13 cxd4 ♘4c6 when Black has the better chances according to Sokolsky.

c) 10 ♔h1!? and now:

c1) 10 ... dxe4 11 ♘b5! ♗b6 12 ♗xb6 ♕xb6 13 ♕d4! ♕xd4 14 cxd4 ♗g4 15 ♗xg4 ♘xg4 16 ♘xc7+ ♔d7 17 ♘xa8 ♖xa8 18 ♘c3 f5 19 f3 exf3 20 ♖xf3 ♘f6 21 ♖e1 ♘c6 22 ♖xf5 1-0 Gusakov - Radu, Corr 1978.

c2) 10 ... 0-0 (10 ... ♕xe4 11 ♘b5!) 11 ♘d2 dxe4 12 ♗h5 ♗g4 13 ♗xg6 ♗xd1 14 ♗xe4! ♗h5 15 ♘2b3 (15 ♘f5±) 15 ... ♗xd4 16 ♗xd4 ♘7c6 17 ♗c5 ♖fe8 18 ♖fe1 f5?! (18 ... f6!?) 19 ♗c2 ♖ad8 20 ♘d4 ♘xd4 21 ♗xd4± Geenen - Lacrosse, Belgian Ch 1991.

10 ... ♕xe4

If the offer of material is declined then White has excellent chances: 10 ... ♕f6 (10 ... ♕b6 11 b4!±) 11 f4! ♘c4 12 ♗f2!±.

11 ♘d2

11 ♘b5 is more forceful:

a) 11 ... ♗xe3 12 ♘xc7+ ♔d8 13 ♘xa8 ♗c5 14 ♘d2 ♕f5 (14 ... ♕h4!?) 15 ♘b3 ♗d6 16 ♗e2 b6 17 a4!± P. Lukacs.

b) 11 ... ♗d6 12 ♘xa7 (12 ♘xd6+ cxd6 13 ♗g5 ♗g4 14 ♗xg4 ♕xg4 15 ♗xe7±) 12 ... ♖xa7 13 ♗xa7 ♗d7 14 ♘d2 ♕h4 15 g3 ♕h3 16 c4! and White is slightly better according to Vladimirov.

11 ... ♕d3

This is practically forced due to 11 ... ♕h4?! 12 ♗xf7+ ♔xf7 13 ♘4f3 ♕f6 14 ♗xc5±.

12 ♘4f3 ♗d6

Black soon gets into a tangle after 12 ... ♗xe3 13 ♘xe5 ♕xd2 14 ♕f3! ♗c5 15 ♗xf7+ ♔d8 16 ♖ad1 ♕h6 17 ♗xd5!+-.

13 ♘xe5 ♗xe5 *(5)*

14 ♗c5

In return for the pawn White has active play and can gain time by chasing the black queen.

14 ... g6

The idea of shifting the king to the queenside is rather tame: 14 ... ♗f6 15 ♖e1 g6 16 ♗f3 ♗e6 17 c4 0-0-0±.

15 ♗e2 ♕f5

16 ♘f3 ♗f6

Black loses the right to castle if the bishop retreats

elsewhere, e.g. 16 ... ♗d6 17 ♗xd6 cxd6 18 ♗b5+ ♔f8 19 ♕d4±.

17	♖e1	0-0
18	♗d3	♕d7
19	♘e5	♕d8
20	♕f3	♔g7 *(6)*

21 h4!

This is designed to facilitate a clever trap. After 21 ... h5 a classic queen sacrifice is possible: 22 ♕xf6+!! ♔xf6 23 ♗d4 ♔g7 24 ♘c6+ ♔g8 25 ♘xd8 ♖xd8 26 ♖xe7 which picks up a piece.

21	...	♗xh4
22	♕f4	♗f6
23	♘f3	

Ehlvest has now completed his preliminary measures in order to threaten a knockout blow: 24 ♕xf6+! ♔xf6 25 ♗d4 mate.

23	...	♘g8
24	♗xf8+	♔xf8
25	♖ad1	

With the sacrifice of the exchange, Black has avoided an instant calamity and has two pawns to even up the material balance. However, White still has a healthy initiative and can target the fragile d5-pawn due to his well centralised rooks.

25	...	♔g7
26	c4	c6
27	cxd5	cxd5
28	♗c4	♘e7
29	♗b3	

One intriguing idea was to dispense with this safeguarding move and pursue a direct tactical course: 29 ♘g5 a5 30 ♘xh7 ♔xh7 31 ♕xf6. The best way to confront the threat would be to block access to f6 by 29 ... ♗f5 30 g4?! ♕b8!.

29	...	a5
30	♘g5	♖a6
31	♘e4	a4

The pawn on b2 is immune from capture: 31 ... ♗xb2? 32 ♕d2 ♗e5 (32 ... ♗a3 33 ♕d4++-) 33 ♘c5 ♖c6 34 ♖xe5 ♖xc5 35 ♕d4 with dual threats against the black rook and of a discovered check.

32	♗c4	♖e6
33	♕d2	♕c7
34	♘xf6	♖xf6
35	♗xd5	

White has finally won the d5-pawn since now 35 ... ♖d6 36 ♕f4 puts a stop to any hopes of pinning the bishop. To avoid the counterplay of the game, 35 ♗b5 could have been considered, with the idea of rounding up the d5-pawn later. The immediate capture allows Black to confuse matters.

35	...	♗g4
36	f3	♘xd5

37	fxg4	

If 37 ♕xd5 ♗xf3 is extremely awkward with an impending check on g3.

37	...	♕g3
38	g5	♖f4?

Black can survive after 38 ... ♖f5! 39 ♕d4+ f6 40 gxf6+ ♔h6! (40 ... ♘xf6 41 ♖e6) which is roughly equal according to Ehlvest.

39	♖f1	a3

No better is 39 ... ♖h4 40 ♖xf7++-.

40	♖xf4	♘xf4
41	♕d4+	1-0

The next game illustrates how White should react to the quieter 9 ... d6 (instead of 9 ... d5). The best reply is Ehlvest's 10 f3! which has been the subject of several recent games.

Schmittdiel - I. Sokolov
Groningen 1991

1	e4	e5
2	♘f3	♘c6
3	d4	exd4
4	♘xd4	♗c5
5	♗e3	♕f6
6	c3	♘ge7
7	♗c4	♘e5
8	♗e2	♕g6
9	0-0	d6

It is a risky venture to steal the e-pawn: 9 ... ♕xe4?! 10 b4! ♗d6 (10 ... ♗xd4 11 cxd4 and 12 ♘c3±; 10 ... ♗b6 11 c4±) 11 ♘d2 ♕g6 12 f4 ♕h6 13 ♘e4 0-0 14 ♘xd6 cxd6 15 ♕d2 ♘5c6 16 f5

♕f6 17 ♗g5 ♕e5 18 f6 ♘g6 19 ♖f5 ♘xd4 (19 ... ♕e8 20 fxg7 ♔xg7 21 ♗f6++−) 20 ♖xe5 dxe5 21 cxd4 ♖e8 22 dxe5 ♖xe5 23 ♗d3 d6 24 ♖e1 ♖xe1+ 25 ♕xe1 ♘e5 26 ♗f4 gxf6 27 ♗h6 ♗e6 28 ♕g3+ ♘g6 29 h4 1-0 Thorhallsson − Yurtaev, Hartberg 1991.

10 f3! (7)

Ehlvest's improvement on other lines normally employed at this juncture. White safeguards e4 with the aim of quick development before advancing his kingside pawns. Others:

a) 10 ♘d2?! ♗h3 11 ♗f3 0-0! 12 ♗c2 (12 ♔h1 ♗g4!) 12 ... ♖ad8 13 b4 (13 ♗xc5 dxc5∓) 13 ... ♗b6 14 ♗xb6 axb6∓ Nikovits − P. Lukacs, Hungary 1991.

b) 10 ♘b5? ♗h3 11 ♗f3 ♗xe3 12 ♘xc7+ ♔d7 13 ♘xa8 ♗f4−+.

c) 10 f4 ♕xe4 11 ♗f2! and now:

c1) 11 ... ♘d7?! 12 ♗d3 ♕d5 (12 ... ♕xf4 13 ♘b5+−) 13 c4 ♕xd4 14 ♗xd4 ♗xd4+ 15 ♖f2 ♘f6 16 h3 ♗d7 17 ♘c3 0-0-0 18 ♕c2 d5 19 ♔h2 with a clear advantage, Steingrimsson − P. Lukacs, Kecskemet 1991.

c2) 11 ... ♗xd4! 12 cxd4 ♘5g6 (12 ... ♘d7 13 ♘c3 ♕xf4 14 ♘b5 ♔d8?! [14 ... 0-0!?] 15 d5! ♕g5 16 ♖c1 ♘xd5 17 h4 ♕e5 18 ♗d4 ♕e7 19 ♗xg7+−) 13 ♘c3 ♕xf4 14 ♘b5 0-0 15 ♘xc7 ♖b8 16 ♘b5 (16 d5 b6?! 17 ♘b5 ♕g5 18 ♘xa7 ♗b7 19 ♗g3 ♘xd5 20 ♕c1 ♕e7 21 ♖e1 ♘e5 22 ♘b5 ♘f6 23 ♕g5 ♕e6 24 ♘xd6 ♘fd7 25 ♘f5 g6 26 ♗g4

♔h8 27 ♖xe5 ♘xe5 28 ♘d4 1-0 Morosevitsch − Balashov, St. Petersburg 1993) 16 ... ♘f5 (16 ... ♗d7!? 17 ♘xa7 ♕g5 18 a4 ♘f5=) 17 ♘xa7 ♗d7 18 g3= Gelfand − Beliavsky, Paris 1991.

| 10 | ... | 0-0 |
| 11 | ♘d2 | d5!? |

Black tries to seize the initiative with a central strike.

| 12 | ♔h1 | dxe4 |
| 13 | fxe4! | |

The right choice; otherwise 13 ♘xe4 ♘d5! allows the black knights to take up a commanding position in the centre.

| 13 | ... | ♕d6?! |

At the moment 13 ... f5? is ruled out by 14 exf5 ♘xf5 15 ♘xf5 winning a piece because c5 is loose. The rather artificial text move is designed to protect the bishop but merely allows White to gain time in exploiting the wandering queen. A more testing line which deserves attention is 13 ... ♗g4 14 ♗f4! (14 ♘f5?? ♘xf5 15 ♗xc5 [15 exf5 ♕h5−+] 15 ... ♘g3+ 16 hxg3 ♕h5+) 14 ... ♗xe2 15 ♕xe2 ♗d6 16 ♘b5± I. Sokolov. Also

possible is 13 ... ♘b6 14 ♗f4
♘7c6 15 ♗h5 ♕f6 16 ♘2b3 ♕e7
17 ♕c2 ♗d7 18 ♘f5 ♗xf5 19 exf5
♖ad8 20 ♗e2 ♖fe8 21 a4 a6
(Illescas – Karpov, Linares 1992)
22 ♖ad1±.

14 ♘c4 ♘xc4
15 ♗xc4

The White strategy now is
to focus attention on the weak
point at f7 by playing ♕b3 and
then to double rooks.

15 ... ♘g6
16 ♕b3 ♕d7 *(8)*

The alternatives do not
inspire confidence:

a) 16 ... ♘e5 17 ♗f4! followed
by ♗xe5 and ♗xf7.

b) 16 ... ♕e7 17 ♘f5! ♗xf5 18
exf5 ♘e5 19 f6 with a terrific
attack.

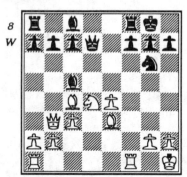

17 ♘e6!

White seizes the bishop pair
whilst opening new avenues
for attack.

17 ... fxe6
18 ♗xc5 ♖xf1+
19 ♖xf1 a6?

Black must activate his
slumbering queenside so 19 ...
b6!? was essential, although

White would still be on top.

20 ♕d1!

A nice touch, White threatens 21 ♗xe6+ ♕xe6 22 ♕d8++-,
and Black cannot afford to
exchange queens because the
white rook would then invade
the eighth rank with a winning
ending.

20 ... ♕e8
21 h4! b6
22 ♗a3 ♗d7

If instead 22 ... ♗b7 then 23
♕g4! ♗c8 24 h5 wins.

23 h5 ♘e7
24 ♕g4 ♔h8
25 h6 ♘g6?! *(9)*

It looks ugly to accept
doubled h-pawns but for good
or bad Black had to try this: 25
... gxh6 26 ♗xe6 ♗xe6 27 ♕xe6
♘g6 and the White victory is
postponed for a while.

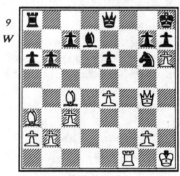

26 ♖f8+!

A nice tactic which wins the
queen – the rook is taboo to
the knight because of mate on
g7.

26 ... ♕xf8
27 ♗xf8 ♖xf8
28 hxg7+ ♔xg7

29 ♗xa6

White is clearly better and has ample time to snatch a pawn or two.

29	...	♖f4
30	♕g5	♗c6
31	♗d3	♖f7
32	e5	b5

Sokolov himself points out that installing a rook on the second rank is premature: 32 ... ♖f2? 33 ♗xg6! hxg6 (33 ... ♖xg2 34 ♕f6+!) 34 ♕e7+ ♔h6 35 ♕h4+ ♔g7 36 ♕xf2+−.

33	♔g1	♗d5
34	♗xb5	♗xa2
35	♗e8	♖f5
36	♕d8	♘xe5
37	♕xc7+	♔h6
38	♗a4	♗d5
39	♗c2	♖h5
40	♕xh7+	♔g5
41	♕g7+	1-0

The next game reveals an interesting idea, 7 ... b6, which was first introduced by Speelman. Black prepares to castle queenside and leaves his options open.

Djurhuus – Hector
Gausdal 1992

1	e4	e5
2	♘f3	♘c6
3	d4	exd4
4	♘xd4	♗c5
5	♗e3	♕f6
6	c3	♘ge7
7	♗c4	b6!?

A recent concept. Speelman was the first to play this idea which is designed to facilitate queenside castling after the fianchetto. In the middlegame Black can try and crash through on the kingside. The minus side is that the black dark-squared bishop no longer has b6 to retreat to, whilst opposite-side castling is risky if White manages to quickly mobilize his queenside pawns.

8 0-0 ♗b7 (10)

9 b4

White selects the most vigorous and sharpest method of meeting the new variation. The other continuations are:

a) 9 ♘b5 0-0-0 10 ♗xc5 bxc5 11 ♕a4 a6 12 ♘5a3 ♘e5 13 ♘d2 d5 14 ♗e2 ♕g6 15 f3 f5 16 ♖ae1 dxe4 17 ♘ac4 ♘7c6 18 fxe4 fxe4 19 ♘xe4 ♘xc4 20 ♗xc4 ♘e5 21 ♖f2 ♖he8 22 ♗f1 c4 23 ♘d2 ♗xg2 24 ♖xg2 ♖xd2 25 ♔h1! ♖xg2 26 ♗xg2 ♖f8 27 ♘h3+ ♘g4 28 ♕xc4 h5 29 ♕d5 ♔b8 30 ♗g2 ♘f2+ 31 ♔g1 ♘h3+ 32 ♔h1 ♘f2+ ½-½ Relange – Huzman, Cannes 1992.

b) 9 f4 0-0-0 10 e5 ♕h6 11

♕d2 f6 12 ♘a3 ♘xd4 13 cxd4
♗xa3 14 bxa3 (14 f5! ♕h5 15
bxa3 ♘xf5? 16 ♗e2 ♕g6 17
♗d3+−) 14 ... ♘f5 15 ♖ac1 fxe5
16 dxe5 ♗b8 17 ♘d3 ♕e6 18 ♖fe1
(18 ♗xf5 ♕xf5 19 ♖xc7 ♗xc7 20
♕d6+ ♗c8 21 ♗xb6 axb6 22 ♖c1+
♗c6 23 ♖xc6±) 18 ... ♖c8 19 a4
½−½ Chandler − Speelman,
Hastings 1991/92. Black could
have carried on with 19 ... ♘h4
and 20 ... ♕g4∓.

c) 9 ♘b3!? ♗xe3 (9 ... ♘e5 10
♘xc5 bxc5) 10 fxe3 ♕g5 11
♗xf7+ ♔d8 12 ♖f4 ♘e5 13 ♘d4
♕h6 14 ♘d2 c5 15 ♘4f3 ♘d3 16
♘c4 ♘xf4 17 exf4 ♔c7 18 e5
♘f5 19 ♗d5 ♗xd5 20 ♕xd5 ♕c6
21 ♕d3 ♖hf8 22 ♖d1 ♖ad8 23
♘g5 ♘h4 24 ♘e3 ♔b8 25 ♘d5
h6 26 ♘e4 g5 27 g3 c4 28 ♕e2
gxf4 29 gxh4 ♕g6+ 30 ♕g2 ♕h5
31 ♕f1 f3 32 ♘df6 ♕xe5 33 ♕xf3
d5 34 ♘d7++− Watson − Wells,
Walsall 1992.

9	...	♘xd4
10	cxd4	♗xb4

For the pawn, White can
gain time by attacking the
queen and dark-squared bishop.
In addition, the mobile pawn
centre is an asset.

11	a3	♗a5
12	d5	

An astute way to increase
the pressure by vacating d4 for
the bishop. The rook can only
be taken at a heavy cost: 12 ...
♕xa1 13 ♗d4 and White is
clearly better.

12	...	0−0
13	♖a2 *(11)*	

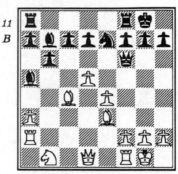

White must strive to justify
the pawn sacrifice, so it is
essential to maintain the initiative. The rook is poised to
switch across to the kingside
to lend support to a pawn rush.
To contain such advances,
Black has to try and activate
his two bishops which are
currently doing very little. It
would be a grave error for
White to launch an attack
without proper preparation: 13
f4? b5! 14 e5 (14 ♗b3 ♕xa1 15
♗d4 ♕xd4 16 ♕d4 ♗b6−+; 14
♗d4 ♗b6 15 e5 ♕h6 16 ♗xb5 [16
♗b3 ♗xd5] 16 ... ♘f5 17 ♗f2
♘e3! 18 ♗xe3 ♗xe3+ 19 ♔h1
♗xf4−+) 14 ... ♕h6 15 ♗b3 ♘f5
16 ♗f2 (16 ♗c5 d6; 16 ♗c1 ♗b6+ 17
♔h1 ♘g3+ mate) 16 ... ♕xf4 17
♕d3 ♕xe5 18 ♖a2 ♘d6 19 ♖e2
♕g5 0−1 Shirov − Agdestein,
Hastings 1991/92.

13	...	♖ae8

If Black wishes to knock the
centre then 13 ... c6 comes into
consideration, as played in
Schmittdiel − Tischbierek,
Germany 1992, which continued:
14 ♗d4 ♕g6 (14 ... ♕h6 15 ♗e3

♕g6 16 d6!) 15 f4 cxd5 16 f5
♕g5! 17 ♖f3 dxc4 18 ♖g3 ♕xg3
19 hxg3 f6 20 ♘c3 d5 with an
unclear position.

14	♖e2	♘g6
15	♗d4	♕h4
16	g3	♕h5
17	f4	

Invariably the right response
in such situations. The wave of
pawns on the kingside allows
White to build up his forces
behind the shield and deprive
the knight access to e5.

17	...	d6
18	♘d2	♗c8
19	♕c2	♗h3
20	♖ff2	

It is necessary to over-
protect f4, otherwise Black can
force a perpetual check: 20 ♖c1
♘xf4 21 gxf4 ♕g4+ 22 ♔h1
♗xd2 23 ♕xd2 ♕f3+ 24 ♔g1
♕g4+=.

20	...	♗xd2
21	♕xd2	f6
22	♖e1	♖e7
23	♗b2	

White intends to play e5 so
Black must direct his efforts to
resist this breakthrough.

23	...	♖fe8
24	♗b5	♗d7
25	♗e2	♗g4
26	♗b5	♗d7
27	♗e2	♗g4
28	♗b5	♖d8?!

In a misguided attempt to
win, Black turns down the
offer to draw by repeating
moves.

29	♖e3	♘f8

30	h3!	♗c8

The bishop is forced to
surrender its blockading role
against the white pawns due to
30 ... ♗xh3 (30 ... ♕xh3?? 31
♖h2) 31 ♖h2 ♕g4 32 ♗e2 ♕d7 33
f5+-.

31	g4	♕f7
32	♗c4	c6
33	e5	dxe5 *(12)*

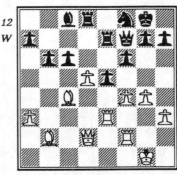

34	dxc6!	

A startling move that allows
the white queen to be taken
but at a heavy price. With this
tactical stroke White is able to
gain a material advantage which
effectively ends the game.

34	...	♖xd2
35	♗xf7+	♔xf7
36	♖xd2	exf4
37	♖xe7+	♔xe7
38	♗c3	♘e6
39	♗b4+	♔e8
40	♗d6	g5

An exchange up, the ending
is a formality for White,
especially with the bonus of a
passed pawn. The game concluded as follows: 41 ♗b8 ♘d8
42 ♖e2+ ♔f7 43 ♖c2 ♘e6 44
♗xa7 ♘d4 45 ♖c4 ♘f3+ 46 ♔f2

♘e5 47 ♖c3 f5 48 gxf5 b5 49 ♗b8 ♘c4 50 a4 ♘d2 51 ♖c2 ♘e4+ 52 ♔f3 ♗xf5 53 axb5 ♘f6 54 ♖c5 ♗e4+ 55 ♔f2 g4 56 ♗xf4 ♘d5 57 c7 1–0.

We have so far seen that Black has yet to find a suitable route to equality against 7 ♗c4; neither 7 ... 0–0, 7 ... ♘e5 nor 7 ... b6 are fully satisfactory. Even worse for Black is the immediate 7 ... ♕g6 which practically loses by force, as the following game shows.

Ivanchuk – Gulko
Reykjavik 1991

1	e4	e5
2	♘f3	♘c6
3	d4	exd4
4	♘xd4	♗c5
5	♗e3	♕f6
6	c3	♘ge7
7	♗c4	

Apart from 7 g3 (considered in the next chapter) White has exhausted the possibilities at this stage:

a) 7 ♗e2 d6 (or 7 ... d5 8 0–0 0–0 9 ♘xc6 ♕xc6 with an equal game according to Euwe) 8 0–0 a6 9 f4 0–0 10 ♔h1 ♘g6 11 ♕d2 ♖e8 12 f5 ♘f8 13 ♗g5 ♕e5 14 ♘xc6 bxc6 15 f6 with an unclear position in Konguvel – Tan, Calcutta 1992.

b) 7 ♕d2 d5! 8 ♘b5 ♗xe3 9 ♕xe3 0–0! 10 ♘xc7 ♖b8 11 ♘xd5 ♘xd5 12 exd5 ♘b4! 13 cxb4 ♕xb2 14 ♕c3 ♖e8+ 15 ♔d1 ♕xf2

16 ♕d2 ♘g4+ and Black is slightly better according to Bilguer.

c) 7 f4 ♘xd4 8 cxd4 d5 9 ♘c3 dxe4 (9 ... 0–0!?) 10 d5 ♘f5 11 ♗c5 ♘ce7 12 ♗b5+ c6 13 dxc6 bxc6 14 ♘d5!± (suggested by Brat).

d) 7 ♘c2 ♗xe3 8 ♘xe3 ♕e5 and now:

d1) 9 ♘d2 d5! 10 exd5 ♘xd5 11 ♘dc4 ♘xe3 12 ♘xe3 ♗e6∓ Sveshnikov – Korchnoi, USSR Ch 1973.

d2) 9 ♕f3 0–0 10 ♗c4 d6 11 ♘d2 ♗e6 12 0–0 ♕g5 13 ♕e2 ♘g6 14 g3 ♗h3 15 ♖fe1 ♘ce5 16 ♔h1 ♘xc4 17 f4 ♕c5 18 ♕xc4 ♕xc4= Tartakower – Tarrasch, Vienna 1922.

e) 7 ♘d2? ♘xd4 8 e5 ♘c2+! 9 ♕xc2 ♕xe5 winning a pawn, Czerniak – Trifunovic, Belgrade 1954.

f) 7 ♗b5 a6 8 ♗xc6 (8 ♗a4?! ♘e5 9 ♕e2 ♘7g6∓ Randiir – Keres, Parnu 1947) 8 ... bxc6 9 0–0 0–0 10 ♘d2 d6 11 ♕f3= Roch – Kiovan, Budapest 1970.

7	...	♕g6?!

This is rarely played for reasons that will soon become obvious. An experiment with 7 ... ♘xd4!? occurred in Schmitt-diel – Romanisin, Groningen 1991, and Black was lucky to salvage equality: 8 cxd4 ♗b4+ 9 ♘c3 ♗xc3+ 10 bxc3 0–0 11 0–0 ♕c6 12 ♗d3 d5 13 ♕c2 ♕g6 14 exd5 ♗f5 15 ♗xf5 ♘xf5 16 ♖fe1 ♖ad8 17 ♗f4? ♘xd4! 18 ♕xg6 fxg6 19 ♗xc7 ♖d7 20 ♖ad1 ♖xc7

21 ♖xd4 ♖xc3=.

    8   ♘xc6   ♕xc6 *(13)*

No better is 8 ... ♗xe3 9 ♘xe7 ♕xg2 10 ♖f1 with a clear advantage.

    9   ♗xf7+!

The bishop is temporarily given up to wreck the kingside and deny Black the opportunity to castle.

    9   ...   ♔xf7
    10   ♕h5+   ♘g6

A slight improvement is possible: 10 ... g6 11 ♕xc5 ♕xe4, but ultimately White remains on top.

    11   ♕f5+   ♔e8
    12   ♕xc5   ♕xe4 *(14)*

    13   ♘d2

White is certainly better

with a lead in development and the opposing king stranded in the middle of the board. There is no point in Black snatching the g-pawn as this would merely open up another avenue for White's rooks: 13 ... ♕xg2 14 0-0-0!.

    13   ...   ♕c6
    14   ♕h5   d6
    15   0-0   ♗e6
    16   ♗d4   ♔d7
    17   f4

Now that White has whisked the king to safety and given the bishop its most influential square on the a1-h8 diagonal, he is well set to disrupt the co-ordination of the black forces. The f-pawn is used as a battering ram with the immediate threat of 18 f5, forking the defensive pieces.

    17   ...   ♘e7
    18   f5   ♗xf5
    19   ♖ae1

The attraction of winning two pieces for a rook is somewhat tarnished after 19 ♖xf5 g6! 20 ♕g5 ♘xf5 21 ♗xh8 ♖xh8 and Black is still hanging on. The text brings White's last piece into the main arena.

    19   ...   g6 *(15)*
    20   ♖xe7+!

The culmination of White's campaign. The rook is given up as part of a combination which will exploit the position of Black's king in the centre.

    20   ...   ♔xe7
    21   ♕g5+   ♔d7

27	♕xb7	♖d8
28	♖f1	♕xd2
29	♕xc7+	♘d7
30	♗f6+	♔e6
31	♕c4+	1-0

Conclusion

The lines with 7 ♗c4 present a real danger to Black. The ease with which Kasparov defeated Short in this line demonstrates what a force it can be, even at the very highest level. The most interesting defence is 7 ... b6 which leads to very double-edged positions. If Black manages to secure equality then the complexities surrounding the sub-variation Watson – Wells will require further investigation. In any case, clearly 7 ♗c4 is an ideal winning weapon at all levels of play and is worth studying in some detail.

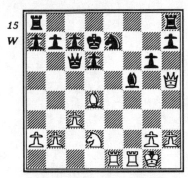

22 ♗xh8 ♕b6+

This is tantamount to resignation since Black remains a piece down with only vague chances of obtaining a few pawns in compensation. However, the alternative is not very attractive either: 22 ... ♖xh8 23 ♖xf5! gxf5 24 ♕g7+ ♔e6 25 ♕xh8+–.

23	♗d4	♕xb2
24	g4	♗e6
25	♖b1	♕xa2
26	♕b5+	♔e7

2 Classical Variation: 7 g3

White's possibilities in the Classical Variation are not restricted to 7 ♗c4; in the last few years another discarded idea has been successfully revived, 7 g3. This seventh move used to be dismissed by the footnote 7 ... d5=, although one can find some examples from the 1970s with the continuation 8 ♗g2 dxe4 9 ♘b5, when the resulting complications favour Black. However, Sveshnikov has recently pioneered 9 ♘d2 on the international scene, a move which makes this variation a fully viable alternative to the more common 7 ♗c4.

Sveshnikov – Yurtaev
Podolsk 1990

1	e4	e5
2	♘f3	♘c6
3	d4	exd4
4	♘xd4	♗c5
5	♗e3	♕f6
6	c3	♘ge7
7	g3	

White prepares to fianchetto the bishop; a safer and less complex variation than 7 ♗c4.

| 7 | ... | d5 (16) |

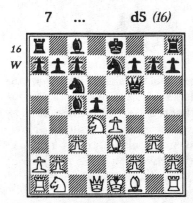

Black must challenge in the centre if he wishes to stand any chance of achieving equality. Other replies allow the latent power of White's quiet system to be revealed:

a) 7 ... d6 8 ♗g2 and now:

a1) 8 ... ♘e5 9 h3 ♗d7 10 ♕e2 g5!? 11 ♘d2 ♘7g6 (Honfi – Knezevic, Majdanpek 1976) 12 ♘2b3 ♗b6 13 0-0-0±.

a2) 8 ... ♗d7 9 0-0 ♘e5 10 h3 ♘c4 11 ♗c1 ♘c6 12 ♕e2 (12 ♘e2!?) 12 ... ♘4e5 13 ♗e3 ♗b6 14 ♘d2 0-0 (½-½ Pazos – Spassky, Dubai Ol 1986) is slightly better for White.

b) 7 ... ♘xd4 8 cxd4 ♗b4+ 9 ♘c3 0-0 10 ♗g2 ♕a6 11 ♕b3! ♗a5 12 d5 ♘g6 13 ♗d4 ♖e8 0-0-0± Dubinsky – Grabczewski, Moscow 1973/74.

c) 7 ... 0–0 8 ♗g2 d6 9 0–0 ♘e5 (9 ... ♕b6 10 ♘a3 ♕g6 11 ♘c4 ♘xd4 12 cxd4 f5 13 ♘xb6 [13 e5!?] 13 ... axb6 14 f3 ♔h8 15 ♕c2= Bus – Ong, Oakham 1992) 10 h3 ♘c4 11 ♗c1 ♘c6 12 ♘e2 and now:

c1) 12 ... ♖e8 (12 ... a5!?) 13 ♘f4 a6 14 b3 ♘4e5 15 ♘a3 ♘e7 16 ♘c2 c6 17 ♘d4± Klovan – Pioch, USSR 1974.

c2) 12 ... ♕g6 13 ♔h2 ♕h5 14 ♕e1! ♘4e5 15 ♘f4! ♘f3+ 16 ♗xf3 ♕xf3 17 b4 (17 ♘d2 ♘e5) 17 ... ♕b6 18 ♗b2 g5 19 ♘d2 ♘e5 20 ♕c1+- Tseitlin – Milicevic, Kragujevac 1974.

8 ♗g2 dxe4

The main alternatives, 8 ... ♘xd4, 8 ... ♘e5 and 8 ... ♗xd4, are examined in the illustrative game Salov – Karpov.

9 ♘d2!?

The old line, 9 ♘b5, is dubious and despite a recent attempt to revive it, the conclusion that Black emerges with the better game has not been seriously brought into doubt. For example:

a) 9 ... ♗d6?! 10 ♘d2 and now:

a1) 10 ... ♗e5 11 ♘xe4 ♕g6 12 0–0 a6 13 ♘d4 0–0 14 ♘xc6 ♘xc6 15 ♘c5 ♗d6 16 ♕a4 ♕h5 17 ♘xb7 winning, Dubinsky – Ivanov, Moscow 1973/74.

a2) 10 ... ♕e5 11 ♘xd6+ ♕xd6 12 ♘xe4 ♕g6 13 0–0± Zhuraviev – Semenyuk, Vilnius 1974.

b) 9 ... ♗xe3! 10 ♘xc7+ ♔f8 11 fxe3 (or 11 0–0 ♖b8 12 fxe3 ♕e5 13 ♕b3 f5 with an unclear position, Sveshnikov – Geller, Sochi 1976) 11 ... ♖b8 12 ♘d5 and now:

b1) 12 ... ♕g5 13 ♘f4 ♕c5 14 0–0 g5 15 ♘h5 ♗e6 with complications favouring Black, Klovan – Romanishin, Odessa 1974.

b2) 12 ... ♕e5 13 ♘xe7 ♔xe7 14 ♘d2 ♖d8 15 0–0 ♗e6 16 ♕e2 f5 17 ♘b3 ♗xb3 18 axb3 g6 19 g4 ♖f8 20 ♖f4 ♖f6 21 gxf5 gxf5 22 ♕h5 h6 23 ♖af1 ♖bf8 24 ♔h1 ♔d6 25 ♕h4 ♘e7 26 ♖4f2 ♘d5 27 ♖d2 ♔c7 28 ♕f2 f4 29 exf4 ♘xf4 30 ♕g3 e3 31 ♖d5 ♕e7 32 ♖b5 b6 33 ♖a1 ♔b8 34 ♗f3 ♖g6 35 ♗g4 ♕e4+ 36 ♕f3 ♕xf3+ 37 ♗xf3 ♘d3 38 ♗g2 e2 0–1 Izeta – Lakunza, San Sebastian 1991.

9 ... ♕b6

The other replies give White all the chances:

a) 9 ... ♘xd4 10 ♘xe4 ♕c6 11 0–0! ♕b6 12 cxd4 0–0 13 ♘c5 ♕g6 14 ♘xb7 ♗xb7 15 ♗xb7 ♖ab8 16 ♗g2 ♖fd8 17 ♕a4± P. Delaney – Wallace, Mulcahy 1978.

b) 9 ... ♗xd4 10 cxd4 and now:

b1) 10 ... ♗f5?! 11 ♘xe4 ♕g6 12 ♘c3! 0–0 (12 ... ♗d3?! 13 d5 ♘e5 14 ♕a4+ c6 15 ♗d4 ♘c4 16 0–0–0±) 13 0–0 ♖fd8 14 ♕a4 ♗c2?! 15 ♕a3 ♘f5 16 ♘d5! ♖d7 17 ♕c3 ♘xe3 18 fxe3 ♕d3 (18 ... ♗e4? 19 ♘f4 ♕f5 20 ♗h3+-) 19 ♕e1 ♕b5 20 ♕f2 ♗g6 21 e4± Honfi – Kluger, Hungary 1976.

b2) 10 ... 0–0 11 ♘xe4 ♕g6 12

0-0 ♗e6 13 ♘c5 ♗d5 (Kupreichik - Parma, Dortmund 1975) 14 ♘xb7!±.

10 ♘xe4 ♕g6
11 0-0

It is sensible to get the king to safety. The sortie 11 ♘b5?! is dubious on account of White's exposed central king position; Sveshnikov - Balashov, Moscow 1989, continued: 11 ... 0-0 12 ♗xb6 ♗h3!! 13 ♘f6+ ♕xf6 14 ♗xh3 cxb6 15 0-0 ♖ad8 16 ♕e2 ♕h6 17 ♗g2 ♖d2 18 ♕e4 a6 19 ♘a3 b5∓.

11 ... ♗g4
12 ♕a4 0-0
13 ♘c5! *(17)*

A tremendous move; the knight leaps to an influential square since after 13 ... ♗xc5 14 ♘xc6 ♘xc6 15 ♗xc5 White regains the piece, emerging with a pair of commanding bishops.

13 ... ♘e5
14 ♗f4 ♗xc5
15 ♗xe5 ♕h5?!

A somewhat better defence is afforded by 15 ... c6 16 ♖ae1, when White has to settle for a slightly better game. The text aims to take the initiative by offering a pawn in exchange for active play.

16 ♗xc7 ♖ac8
17 ♗a5

It seems strange to allow the bishop to be stuck on the edge of the board but this is only a temporary measure. The 'natural' 17 ♗f4 was what Black planned for: 17 ... ♘g6 18 ♗e3 ♘e5 with tactical chances of exploiting the light squares based upon ... ♗xd4 and ... ♘f3+.

17 ... ♘d5
18 ♘b3 ♗f3!
19 ♗xf3 ♕xf3
20 ♘d4

Now that the influential bishop on g2 has been exchanged, White must endeavour to utilise the extra pawn before his draughty king comes under attack. If 20 ♖ae1 (20 ♖ad1? ♘e3!-+) 20 ... b6 21 ♘xc5 ♖xc5 22 ♗b4 ♘f4 23 gxf4 ♕g4+ 24 ♔h1 ♕f3+ with perpetual check.

20 ... ♕f6
21 ♕d7 ♘f4
22 ♕xb7 ♗xd4
23 cxd4 ♘e2+
24 ♔g2 ♕xd4
25 ♖fd1

The situation has become somewhat clearer after the flurry of exchanges. White is a clear pawn up and once the knight is ejected from e2, the bishop can be rehabilitated on c3 with control of the a1-h8 diagonal. Black must try to prevent the expansion of White's queenside pawns, while searching for a way to control the a8–h1 diagonal to harass the white king.

25 ... ♛a4
26 ♗e1 ♖fe8
27 ♖d7?!

The lure of occupying the seventh rank proves far too strong. A calmer approach, blocking the h1–a8 diagonal, was the key to success: 27 ♛b3! ♛xb3 (27 ... ♛e4+ 28 ♛f3±) 28 axb3 ♖c7 29 ♖d2 intending f3 and ♗f2 when White is slightly better according to Sveshnikov.

27 ... ♖c6!

White had missed this surprising move which abandons the f-pawn in return for counterplay against the white king.

28 ♖xf7 ♛e4+
29 f3 (18)

18
B

No better was 29 ♖f3 ♘f4+! 30 gxf4 ♖g6+ winning the queen.

29 ... ♘f4+!

Suddenly Black's forces

stream around the white king.

30 gxf4

Not 30 ♖xf4 ♖c2+ 31 ♔h3 ♛xb7–+.

30 ... ♖c2+
31 ♔h3

White has no choice in the matter as other replies lead to instant disaster:

a) 31 ♔h1 ♛xe1+ 32 ♖xe1 ♖xe1 mate.

b) 31 ♔g3 ♛g6+ 32 ♔h3 ♛g2+ 33 ♔h4 ♛xh2+ 34 ♔g5 ♖g2+ 35 ♔f5 ♛h5 mate.

31 ... ♛e6+
32 f5 ♛xf7
33 ♛xf7+ ♔xf7
34 ♗c3 ♖ee2
35 ♖d1! ♖xh2+
36 ♔g3 h5

Sveshnikov considers that 36 ... g5 37 fxg6+ ♔xg6 was Black's best winning try as the black king avoids being cut off on the back rank.

37 ♖d7+ ♔e8
38 ♖xa7 g5
39 fxg6 ♖cg2+
40 ♔f4 ♖xg6
41 a4

The connected passed pawns offer White good practical chances. Black will be unable to run the h-pawn to promotion since his rooks will be tied down on the queenside. The game concluded as follows: 41 ... h4 42 a5 h3 43 a6 ♖e2 44 ♖a8+ ♔d7 45 a7 ♖a6 46 ♘d4 h2 47 ♖h8 ♔c6 48 ♖h5?! (48 b4 ♔b5 49 ♗c5 ♖a1 50 ♔f5 ♖ea2 51 a8♛ ♖xa8 52 ♖xh2±) 48 ... ♖e8

49 ♔g3 ♖a4 50 ♗f2 h1(♕) 51 ♖xh1
♖g8+ 52 ♔h2 ♖h8+ 53 ♔g2
♖g8+ 54 ♔f1 ♖a1+ 55 ♗e1 ♖xa7
56 ♔f2 ♖f7 57 ♖h6+ ♔d5 58
♖h5+ ♔c4 59 ♖h4+ ♔d5 60 ♘c3
♖gf8 61 ♖d4+ ♔c5 62 ♖d3 ♖e8
63 ♘d2 ♖b8 64 b4+ ♔c4 65
♖c3+ ♔d4 66 ♖a3 ♖b5 67 ♘e3+
♔c4 68 ♘c5 ♖b8 69 ♖e3 ♖h8 70
♖e4+ ♔d3 71 ♖d4+ ♔c3 72 ♔g3
♖h1 73 f4 ♖f1 ½-½.

Instead of 8 ... dxe4, Black
can also follow a quieter plan,
8 ... ♘xd4, which has been
played by Anatoly Karpov
amongst others. This variation
almost equalises for Black, but
accurate play by White can still
make things very difficult for
his opponent.

Salov - Karpov
Reggio Emilia 1991/92

1	e4	e5
2	♘f3	♘c6
3	d4	exd4
4	♘xd4	♗c5
5	♗e3	♕f6
6	c3	♘ge7
7	g3	d5
8	♗g2	♘xd4

Karpov adopts a plan of
liquidation with the idea of
eventually isolating the white
d-pawn. Apart from 8 ... dxe4,
discussed in the previous game,
Black has several other possibilities:

a) 8 ... ♘e5!? 9 0-0 ♗g4 10 f3
♗d7 11 ♘d2 ♗b6 12 a4 a5 13 h3
♕g6 14 ♔h2 dxe4 15 ♘xe4 0-0
16 f4 ♘c4 17 ♗c1 ♘f5 18 ♕d3
♘xd4 19 cxd4 ♘d6 20 g4 f5 21
♘c5! ♗c8 22 ♗f3= Campora -
Gouveia, Buenos Aires 1991.

b) 8 ... ♘xd4 9 cxd4 dxe4 10
♘c3 0-0 11 ♘xe4 ♕g6 12 0-0
and now:

b1) 12 ... ♗e6 13 ♘c3 (not 13
♘c5 ♗d5 14 ♖c1 ♗xg2 15 ♔xg2
♘f5!∓ Kupreichik - Parma,
Dortmund 1975) 13 ... ♖ad8 14
♕a4 ♘d5 15 ♘xd5 ♗xd5 16
♗xd5 ♖xd5 17 ♕b3= Timmer-
man - Pliester, Amsterdam
1982.

b2) 12 ... ♘c5?! 13 ♘c3 ♘xc3
14 bxc3 ♗f5 15 ♗f4 ♖ac8 16 ♖e1
♖fd8 17 ♕a4± Zhuraviev -
Ostrovsky, Rostov-on-Don
1975.

9	cxd4	♗b4+	*(19)*

This line of play used to be
frowned upon, as White
generally managed to exploit
his space advantage in the
middlegame. The alternative
approach gives White slight but
persistent pressure: 9 ... ♗b6 10
exd5 ♘f5! 11 0-0 0-0 12 ♘c3
♗xd4 13 ♘e4 ♕b6 (13 ... ♕e5 14

♘f4 ♕e7 15 g4+−) 14 ♘xd4
♘xd4 15 ♖c1 ♗f5 16 ♖c5!? ♗xe4
17 ♕xd4 ♗xg2 18 ♔xg2 ♖ad8 19
♕c4 ♕xb2 20 ♖xc7 b5 21 ♕c6!
♕xa2!? 22 d6 ♕c4 (22 ... b4 23
d7 a5 24 ♖e1+−) 23 ♕xc4 bxc4
24 d7 (Nunn − Smagin, Bundesliga 1990/91) 24 ... f5=.

10	♘c3	♗xc3+
11	bxc3	dxe4
12	♗xe4	*(20)*

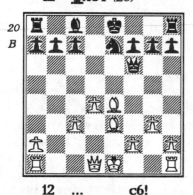

12   ...   c6!

The point of Karpov's play is
revealed, as now the white
light-squared bishop is blunted.
The alternatives are inferior:

a) 12 ... ♕e6 13 ♕d3 ♘d5 14
♗g2 ♘xe3 15 ♕xe3 ♖b8 16 ♔d2!
♕xe3+ 17 fxe3 ♔e7 18 c4 h5?!
(18 ... ♖d8!?) 19 e4 h4 20 e5 ♖h6
21 ♘f3 b6 22 g4 ♖g6 23 ♖hg1
♖g5 24 ♖ge1 ♘a6 25 ♔c3 ♖d8 26
a4! ♘c8 27 a5 f5 28 axb6 axb6
29 ♖a7+− Campora − Rubinetti,
Buenos Aires 1986.

b) 12 ... ♗h3 13 ♖b1 ♕e6 14
♕d3 ♖d8 15 ♖xb7 0−0 16 ♖xa7
f5 17 ♘f3 ♘d5 18 ♕c4 f4! 19
gxf4 ♔h8 20 ♗xd5 ♖xd5 21
♕xc7 ♕g6 22 ♔d2 ♖b5 with an
unclear position according to

Botterill and Harding. There is
plenty of room for improvement in this analysis, for example 13 ♕h5! ♕e6 14 ♗xb7
♖b8 (14 ... ♖d8 15 ♕e5±) 15 ♘f3
intending g4±.

| 13 | 0−0 | 0−0 |
| 14 | a4 | |

A preliminary measure to
prevent the black queenside
pawns from ever advancing. If
White turns his attention solely
to the queenside to keep the
c8-bishop at bay, then Black
has a comfortable game: 14 ♕b1
h6 (14 ... ♗f5 15 ♗xf5 ♘xf5 16
♕xb7 ♘xe3 17 fxe3 ♕e6 with an
unclear position) 15 a4 b6
intending ... ♘f5∓.

14	...	♗f5
15	♗g2	♖ad8
16	♕b3	♖d7
17	c4	♖fd8

Consistent and best according to Karpov himself:

a) 17 ... ♗e6 18 ♖ad1 ♖fd8 19
♖d2±.

b) 17 ... ♗g4 18 d5 ♘f3 19
♗xa7 ♗xg2 20 ♔xg2 cxd5=.

| 18 | h3 | |

This is to prevent ... ♗g4-f3
since Black would have problems if he could manage to
exchange White's prominent
light-squared bishop: 18 ♖fd1
♗g4 19 ♖d2 ♗f3.

18	...	h5
19	♖fe1	♕g6
20	a5	♗e6
21	♖ad1	*(21)*
21	...	b5!?

A clever way to simplify

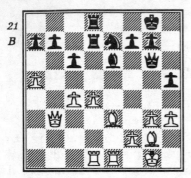

21
B

matters and steer the game towards a drawn outcome. If Black wishes to invite complications then 21 ... h4 is also playable: 22 g4 f5 23 f3 ♕f7 24 ♗f1 with an unclear position.

22 axb6   axb6
23 ♕b4

After 23 ♕xb6 ♗xc4 Black can exchange bishops via d5 and emerge with a good knight against a bad bishop.

23 ...   b5
24 cxb5   ♘d5
25 ♕c5   cxb5
26 ♕xb5!

Even though this loses the exchange, White has calculated far enough to see that Black cannot profit by it.

26 ...   ♘c3
27 ♕d3   ♘xd1
28 ♕xg6   fxg6
29 ♖xd1   ♗d5
30 ♗xd5+   ♖xd5
31 h4

With no pawn breaks available, Black can make no progress.

31 ...   ♔f7
½–½

Conclusion

The variation with 7 g3 is a steady continuation which avoids the highly theoretical main lines associated with 7 ♗c4 and still provides many pitfalls for the unwary black player. However, with best play it is doubtful whether White can achieve anything more than an equal position. Perhaps 7 g3 is most effective as a surprise.

3 Classical Variation: Other Lines With 5 ♗e3

So far we have only discussed the variation following 5 ... ♕f6 in the Classical Variation. In this chapter we look at Black's two main alternatives, 5 ... ♘b6 and 5 ... ♘xd4, both of which promise White good chances if he continues with natural developing moves.

Sveshnikov – B. Ivanovic
RSFS – Crna Gora 1987

1	e4	e5
2	♘f3	♘c6
3	d4	exd4
4	♘xd4	♗c5
5	♗e3	♗xd4?!

It is quite unusual for Black to relieve the pressure in the centre so early but White still needs to know how to deal with such a situation. In order to avoid the main lines of 5 ... ♕f6, Black players have also frequently tried 5 ... ♘b6 in recent practice:

a) 6 ♘f5!? ♗xe3 7 ♘xe3 ♘f6 8 ♘c3 0–0 9 ♗d3 ♖e8 10 0–0 ♘b4 11 f4 c6 12 e5! ♕b6 13 exf6 ♕xe3+ 14 ♔h1 ♘xd3 15 ♕g4! g6 16 cxd3 d5 17 ♕h4 ♕d4 18 ♖ae1 ♗f5 19 ♖e5 ♔h8 20 ♖fe1 ♖xe5 21 ♖xe5 ♕xd3 22 h3 h5 23 ♘e2 ♖g8 24 ♘g3 g5 25 ♕xh5+ ♔h7 26 ♖xg5 ♖xg5 27 ♕xg5+– Forgarasi – Szabolcsi, Budapest 1992.

b) 6 ♘c3 and now:

b1) 6 ... ♘ge7 7 g3 0–0 8 ♗g2 d6 9 ♘xc6 (9 0–0 ♘xd4 10 ♗xd4 ♘c6 11 ♗xb6 axb6 12 ♘d5± Sveshnikov – Kharitonov, Sochi 1987) 9 ... bxc6 10 ♕d2 ♗e6 11 0–0 ♕b8! 12 ♘a4 ♗xe3 13 ♕xe3 ♕b5 14 b3 c5 15 f4 ♘d7 16 ♖fe1 ♖ae8 17 ♘c3 ♕b4 18 ♘e2 ♘c6 19 ♕d3 a5 20 a4 ♕b7 21 ♘c3± Watson – Adams, English Ch 1991.

b2) 6 ... d6 and now:

b21) 7 g3 ♘f6 8 ♗g2 0–0 9 ♘xc6 bxc6 10 ♗xb6 axb6 11 0–0 ♖a5!? 12 f4= Sveshnikov – Tseitlin, Budapest 1989.

b22) 7 ♘d5 ♘f6 8 ♘xb6 axb6= Mieses – Lasker, St. Petersburg 1909.

b23) 7 ♗e2 ♘f6 8 ♕d2 ♘g4 9 ♗xg4 ♗xg4 10 f3 ♗d7 11 ♘d5 0–0 12 0–0–0= Spielmann – Tarrasch, Breslau 1912.

b24) 7 ♗c4 ♘f6 8 ♘xc6 bxc6 9 ♗g5 0–0= Mieses – Spielmann, Regensburg 1910.

b25) 7 ♕d2!? ♘f6 8 f3 0–0 9

0-0-0 ♗d7 10 g4 ♘xd4 11 ♗xd4 ♗c6 (11 ... ♕e7!?) 12 h4 ♘d7 13 g5 ♗xd4 14 ♕xd4 ♘b6 15 ♘h3! ♕e7 16 f4 ♖ae8 17 ♖de1 ♗d7 18 h5 ♗xh3 19 ♖xh3 f6 20 g6 h6 21 ♖he3 c6 22 a4 ♘c8 23 ♘e2 1-0 Estrin - Shapovalov, Corr 1974. The knight heads for f5 or e6 with a crushing position.

6   ♗xd4   ♘f6

This is an attempt to improve upon previous games in which Black exchanged in the centre, allowing White a free rein. After 6 ... ♘xd4 7 ♕xd4 Black can play:

a) 7 ... ♕g5 8 ♘c3 c6 9 h4 ♕h6 10 g4 ♕g6 11 e5 when White has complete control of the centre, Alekhine - Andersen, Chicago 1933.

b) 7 ... ♕f6 8 e5 ♕b6 9 ♕xb6 axb6 10 ♘c3± Tartakower - Schwarzmann, 1929.

7   ♘c3   0-0 *(22)*

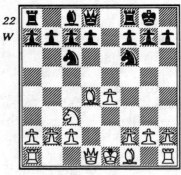

8   ♗xf6
White quickly disposes of the knight on f6, which is fundamental to Black's opening strategy of undermining e4. In his analysis of the game, upon which these notes are based, Sveshnikov reveals his opponent's intentions: 8 ♗e3 ♖e8 9 ♗d3 d5 10 exd5 ♘b4 with an unclear position, e.g. 11 ♗c4 ♘g4 or 11 ♗b5 ♗d7 12 a3 ♘bxd5!.

8   ...   ♕xf6
9   ♕d2

A quiet move maintaining White's spacial advantage. Sveshnikov prepares to castle queenside with a basic plan of f4 and ♗c4 or ♗d3.

9   ...   d5!?
Black is not willing to resign himself to a passive game, so he gives up a pawn to create active play.

10   exd5   ♖e8+
11   ♗e2   ♘d4

Of course, 11 ... ♗g4 12 f3 easily rebuffs the pin.

12   0-0 *(23)*
The situation has changed now that White has the extra pawn, so queenside castling is no longer desirable: 12 0-0-0? ♘xe2+ 13 ♘xe2 ♕xf2 14 ♘d4 ♕xd2+ 15 ♖xd2 with an equal game.

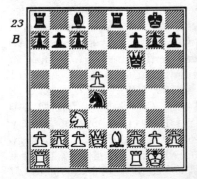

12 ... ♗h3?!

This direct method of attack is a misguided attempt to end the game quickly. A more critical way forward for Black is 12 ... ♘xe2+ 13 ♘xe2 ♕xb2 14 ♘d4 which gives White a small advantage, according to Sveshnikov, due to the strong central knight, which limits the scope of the opposing bishop, and the possibility of bringing a rook to the open b-file.

13 f4!

A stereotyped move would have allowed Black to unleash a winning series of tactics:

a) 13 ♔h1? ♖xe2! 14 ♘xe2 ♗xg2+ 15 ♔xg2 (15 ♔g1 ♘f3+) 15 ... ♕f3+ 16 ♔g1 ♘xe2+ and Black is clearly better.

b) 13 gxh3? ♖xe2 14 ♕d3 (14 ♘xe2 ♘f3+) 15 ... ♘f3+ 15 ♔g2 ♘h4+ when the white kingside has been shattered.

13 ... ♕b6

After 13 ... ♕g6 White must still play accurately to avoid a calamity:

a) 14 ♗d3? ♘e2+! (14 ... ♖e2? 15 ♗xg6 ♖xd2 16 ♗e4 with the idea of ♖f2±) 15 ♕xe2 ♖xe2 16 ♗xg6 ♖xg2+ 17 ♔h1 ♖xg6∓.

b) 14 ♖f2! ♖xe2 15 ♕xd4 (15 ♘xe2 ♘f3+−+) 15 ... ♖xf2 16 ♕xf2 ♗f5 17 ♖e1± ♗xc2? 18 ♕xa7!+−.

14 ♔h1 ♘xe2
15 ♘xe2 ♗g4
16 ♘g3

White has emerged from the opening phase with the better game. His extra pawn is a significant factor since Black only has temporary control of the e-file in compensation.

16 ... ♖e3

If 16 ... h5, intending ... h4 to force the knight to relinquish control of e2, then White can go on the offensive: 17 f5! h4 18 ♕g5± hxg3?? 19 f6 g6 20 ♕h6 followed by mate.

17 ♖ae1 ♖ae8
18 h3 ♘d7
19 ♔h2 *(24)*

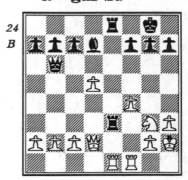

Sveshnikov shows great mastery in his handling of this stage of the game. The key is to slowly improve one's position while awaiting the right moment to exchange pieces.

19 ... g6

Black understandably gives the king an escape hole to avoid any future tactics involving back-rank mate as, for example, in the following sequence: 19 ... ♖xe1 20 ♖xe1 ♕xb2 21 ♖xe8+ ♗xe8 22 ♕e3 ♕b5 (22 ... ♗a4 23 ♕xa7+−; 22 ... ♗b5 23 ♕xa7 h6 24 ♕xb7+−) 23 c4! ♕a4 (23 ... ♕d7 24 ♕xa7) 24

♕e5 c5 25 ♘f5 f6 26 ♕e7 ♗f7 27 d6+−.

20	♖xe3	♕xe3
21	♕b4	♕b6
22	♕xb6	axb6
23	♔g1	

White has successfully managed to enter an ending with the d5-pawn still intact, and maintains excellent chances of victory. The ultimate aim is to create a passed pawn, but the immediate priority must be to reduce the effectiveness of the opposing rook.

23	...	h5
24	♔f2	h4
25	♘e2	♗b5
26	♖e1	♖e4
27	♔f3	

The lure of forking the remaining pieces is rightly rejected: 27 ♘c3? ♖xf4+ 28 ♔e3 ♖f1 with good chances of a draw.

27	...	f5
28	b3	♗e8
29	♔f2	♔f8
30	♖d1	♗e7
31	♖d4	♖xd4
32	♘xd4	

Black's only chance was to hold onto the rook in hope of a swindle. Now the extra pawn together with influential knight is a lethal combination.

32	...	♔d6
33	c4	b5
34	♔e3	bxc4
35	bxc4	♗f7
36	♘b5+	♔c5
37	♘xc7	♔xc4
38	d6	1–0

Conclusion

The early alternatives 5 ... ♘xd4 and 5 ... ♗b6 do not offer real chances of equality. These harmless continuations only really have merit for their surprise value. The best course of action for Black in the Classical Variation is 5 ... ♕f6 6 c3 ♘ge7, as in the first two chapters.

4 Classical Variation: 5 ♘b3

The most common alternative to the fashionable 5 ♗e3 is the solid 5 ♘b3 with which White hopes to create a space advantage and prevent the freeing ... d5. With precise play Black should survive the opening stage but there a number of subtle traps which might catch out an unprepared opponent.

van der Wiel – Gulko
Amsterdam 1987

1	e4	e5
2	♘f3	♘c6
3	d4	exd4
4	♘xd4	♗c5
5	♘b3	

White intends to molest the bishop and strive for a territorial advantage.

5	...	♗b6
6	a4	

Gaining space on the queenside and applying direct pressure to the bishop. The immediate 6 ♘c3 is considered in the illustrative game Atkinson – Brander later in this chapter.

| 6 | ... | a5?! *(25)* |

Of course, Black needs to create a hole on a7 for his

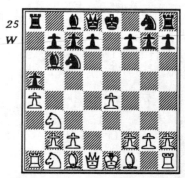

25
W

bishop but this is not the correct way of implementing this plan as the a5-pawn often becomes a vulnerable target. More reliable methods of meeting the threat to the bishop are 6 ... a6, and 6 ... ♕f6 7 ♕e2 a6, which are featured later in this chapter.

| 7 | ♘c3 | |

The superficially attractive 7 ♘a3 intending to exchange the bishop allows Black to equalize without difficulty: 7 ... ♘f6! 8 ♘c4 (8 ♗d3 d5!) 8 ... d5 9 ♘xb6 cxb6 10 exd5 ♕xd5 11 ♕xd5 ♘xd5 12 ♗d3 0-0 13 0-0 ♘db4= van der Wiel – Matera, Lone Pine 1979.

| 7 | ... | d6 |

At this point Black has sometimes deviated but White

should still be able to maintain a slight advantage:

a) 7 ... ♕f6 8 ♕e2 ♘ge7 and now:

a1) 9 ♗e3 and now:

a11) 9 ... ♘b4 10 0-0-0 0-0 11 f4 (11 g3 ♗xe3+ 12 ♕xe3± Parma) 11 ... d5 12 e5 ♗xe3+ 13 ♕xe3 ♕g6 14 ♖d2 b6± Musil - Ilievsky, Yugoslav Ch 1968.

a111) 9 ... ♗xe3 10 ♕xe3 0-0 11 0-0-0 d6?! 12 ♘b5! ♘e5 13 f4 ♘g4 14 ♕d2 ♗d7 15 h3 ♗xb5 16 ♗xb5 ♘h6 17 g4 1-0 Benko - Risselen, Malaga 1969.

a2) 9 ♘d5 ♘xd5 10 exd5+ ♘e7 11 h4! h6 12 g4 d6 13 ♗g2 ♗d7 14 c3 0-0-0 15 ♗e3 ♗xe3 16 fxe3 ♕e5 17 0-0-0± Stupina - Viner, USSR 1978.

b) 7 ... ♘ge7 8 ♗g5 f6 9 ♗h4 0-0 10 ♕d2 d6 11 0-0-0 ♗e6 12 f4 (12 ♘d5! is a suggestion by Keres) 12 ... ♕e8 13 ♗f2 ♗xf2 14 ♕xf2 ♕f7± Radulov - Westerinen, Raach 1969.

8	♘d5	♗a7
9	♗b5	♗d7
10	0-0	♘e5

The attempt to oust the dominant knight at d5 fails to work: 10 ... ♘ce7 (10 ... ♘ge7 11 ♗g5!) 11 ♕g4! ♘g6 (11 ... c6 12 ♕xg7 ♘g6 13 ♘f4+-) 12 ♕xd7+ ♕xd7 13 ♘xc7++-.

11 ♗d2! *(26)*

White boldly allows the knight and bishop to be forked in return for a strong initiative. This new idea is a clear improvement on the older continuation: 11 ♗xd7+ ♕xd7 12

♗e3 ♗xe3 13 ♘xe3 ♘f6 14 ♖e1 0-0 15 ♘d5= Letelier - Bronstein, Mar del Plata 1960.

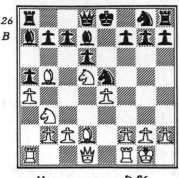

11 ... ♘f6

If Black were to take up the gauntlet of White's opening novelty then the game would come to an abrupt halt. For example: 11 ... c6 12 ♗xa5 b6 (12 ... ♕h4 13 ♘c7+ ♔e7 14 ♗b4+-; 12 ... ♗xf2+ 13 ♖xf2 ♖xa5 14 ♘xa5 ♕xa5 15 ♘c3 cxb5 16 axb5+-) 13 ♗c3 and now Black may try:

a) 13 ... cxb5?! 14 f4 ♘g6 (14 ... bxa4 15 fxe5 axb3 16 e6!+-) 15 ♗xg7 h6 16 f5 ♖h7 17 fxg6 ♖xg7 18 gxf7+ ♖xf7 19 ♕h5 ♗e6 20 ♘d4+-.

b) 13 ... f6 14 ♗xe5! fxe5 (14 ... dxe5?! 15 ♗c4 cxd5 16 ♕xd5 ♘h6 17 ♖fd1+-) 15 f4! cxd5 (15 ... exf4 16 ♘d4; 15 ... cxb5 16 fxe5 intending ♕f3+-) 16 fxe5 with a clear advantage according to van der Wiel.

12	♗xa5	♘xd5
13	exd5	

The simplest reply, but White could also investigate another treatment of the position: 13 ♗xd7+ ♕xd7 (13 ... ♔xd7?! 14 ♕xd5 ♕h4 [14 ... ♔c8!?] 15 ♕xb7 ♘g4 16 ♕xc7+ ♔e6 17 ♕c4+ ♔e7 18 h3+-) 14 ♕xd5 c6 15 ♕d1 0-0 with advantage to White (van der Wiel).

13 ... ♗xb5
14 axb5 0-0

No better is 14 ... ♕d7 15 b6! ♗xb6 16 ♗xb6 ♖xa1 17 ♕xa1 cxb6 18 f4 ♘g6 19 ♕a8+ ♕d8 20 ♖e1+ ♘e7 21 ♕xb7+-.

15 ♗c3 ♕g5?

A pawn down, Black activates his queen in a futile bid for compensation. In fact, every possibility leaves White in a superior position:

a) 15 ... ♕d7? 16 ♗xe5 dxe5 17 c4.

b) 15 ... ♖e8 16 h3.

c) 15 ... ♕h4 16 ♗d4! ♗xd4 17 ♕xd4.

16 ♖xa7! *(27)*

Suddenly, White unveils a tactical trick to destroy Black's lingering hopes.

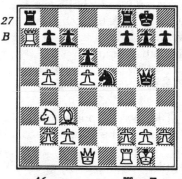

27
B

16 ... ♖xa7
17 f4 ♕h6
18 ♕d4!

White chooses to pile on the pressure, although 18 fxe5 would also be enough to guarantee victory in the long term.

18 ... ♘g4
19 h3 ♖aa8
20 hxg4 ♖fe8

The threat of mate on g7 severely reduces Black's options and White can easily use his material advantage to provoke further kingside concessions.

21 ♘d2 ♖e2
22 ♘e4 1-0

Black resigned in view of the threat of 23 g5 ♕g6 24 f5+- e.g. 22 ... f6 23 ♘g3+-.

Instead of 6 ... a5, most Black players prefer the more solid 6 ... a6. However, even this is not bereft of pitfalls for the unwary, as the following game shows.

S. Arkell - Gallagher
Hastings 1987/88

1	e4	e5
2	♘f3	♘c6
3	d4	exd4
4	♘xd4	♗c5
5	♘b3	♗b6
6	a4	a6
7	♘c3	d6

Here 7 ... ♕f6 would transpose after 8 ♕e2 to the variation 6 ... ♕f6 7 ♕e2 a6 8 ♘c3 which is discussed in the game Djurovic - Rajic. Also worthy of consideration are:

a) 7 ... ♘ge7 and now:

a1) 8 ♗g5 and now:

a11) 8 ... 0–0?! 9 ♘d5 ♗a7 10 ♘f6+! gxf6 11 ♗xf6 ♕e8 12 ♕h5 ♘d8 13 ♕h6 ♘e6 14 0–0–0 ♗xf2 15 ♖d3 ♘g6 16 ♖h3 ♗h4 17 ♖xh4 ♘xh4 18 ♕xh4 1–0 Botterill – Thomas, British Ch 1974.

a12) 8 ... f6 9 ♗h4 0–0 10 ♕d2 d6 11 0–0–0 ♗d7 12 f4 ♕b8 13 ♘d5 ♘xd5 14 exd5 ♘e7 15 a5 ♗a7 16 ♗d3 b6 17 ♖he1 ♖e8 18 ♖e2±.

a2) 8 ♕e2 0–0 9 ♗g5 d6 10 ♘d5 ♗a7 11 0–0–0± Pasman – Unzicker, Beer-Sheva 1984.

a3) 8 g3 d6 9 ♗g2 0–0 10 0–0 f5 11 ♘d5 ♗a7 12 a5 fxe4 13 ♗xe4 ♗f5 14 ♖a4 ♕d7 15 ♗e3 ♗xe3 16 ♘xe3 ♗xe4 17 ♖xe4 ♖ad8 18 c3 ♘f5 19 ♘d5= Hort – Unzicker, Bundesliga 1990/91.

b) 7 ... ♘f6 8 ♗g5 d6 and now:

b1) 9 a5!? ♗a7 10 ♗e2 ♗e6 11 0–0 h6 12 ♗h4 g5 13 ♗g3 h5 14 h3± Agzamov – Ivanov, USSR 1974.

b2) 9 ♕e2 h6 10 ♗h4 ♘d4 11 ♘xd4 ♗xd4 12 ♕d2 ♗e5 (12 ... ♗a7? 13 ♘d5) 13 ♗d3 ♗e6 14 f4 ♗xc3 15 ♕xc3 ♘xe4 16 ♗xd8 ♘xc3 17 ♗xc7 ♘d5 18 ♗xd6 ♖d8 19 ♗e5 f6 20 f5 and White is slightly better according to Botterill and Harding.

8   ♗e2   ♘f6
9   0–0   ♗e6?! *(28)*

A more logical move is 9 ... h6, ruling out any threat of ♗g5.

10   ♘d5!   ♗xd5
Black has little choice but to

28
W

trade off minor pieces, otherwise his position would deteriorate even further:

a) 10 ... ♗a7 11 ♗g5 ♗xd5 12 exd5 ♘e5 13 c4±.

b) 10 ... ♘xe4 11 ♘xb6 cxb6 12 ♘d4 ♘xd4 13 ♕xd4 ♘f6 14 ♗f4 d5 15 ♕b4 and White is better according to Susan Arkell.

11   exd5   ♘e7
12   c4

Maintaining the strongpoint at d5. It is easier for White to form a plan in this position since her space advantage enables easy mobilization behind the pawn shelter. Having given up the bishop pair Black faces a difficult task as there are no obvious targets in the opposing camp.

12   ...   0–0
13   ♘d4   h6
14   ♖a3!

The rook is poised to swing across to the kingside to aid the impending assault. This is a regular feature of lines involving an advance of the a-pawn and is often overlooked by the opponent.

14	...	♛d7
15	♖f3 *(29)*	

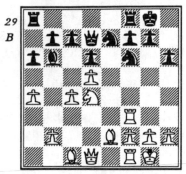

The threat of 16 ♗xh6 gxh6 17 ♖xf6 is transparent, but Black is forced to further disrupt his piece formation to deal with it.

15	...	♘e4
16	♖f4	♘g5

If 16 ... ♘c5 17 b3! and Black's forces are congested on the queenside while White is well placed to conduct a lethal attack.

17	h4	♘h7
18	♗d3	

Now White's control of the b1-h7 diagonal becomes an important issue. Black must try to block it while White can even consider the direct approach of ♗b1 and ♛c2 to add to the pressure.

18	...	♘g6
19	♗f5	♛e7

After 19 ... ♛d8? 20 ♗xg6 fxe6 21 ♘e6 White wins.

20	♖e1	♘e5
21	♗b1	♗xd4
22	♖xd4	

White has to be careful to avoid the diabolical trap 22 ♛xd4? ♘f3+! 23 ♖xf3 ♛xe1+-+.

22	...	♛d7
23	♛c2	f5
24	♖f4 *(30)*	

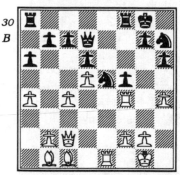

Now that White has managed to force a concession with 23 ... f5, this weak point is attacked by the roving rook.

24	...	♖ae8
25	♖e3	

A necessary precaution in view of the dangerous 25 ... ♘f3+.

25	...	♘g6

The f-pawn must fall whatever precautionary measures are taken: 25 ... g6 26 h5 ♘f6 27 hxg6 ♘e4 28 f3 and Black is busted.

26	♖xf5	♖xe3
27	♗xe3	♘f6

The grim reality of Black's position has become somewhat clearer. He is a pawn down and facing an attack based on the two powerful bishops. The immediate problem is that 27 ... ♘xh4 is well met by 28 ♖f4! g5 29 ♛xh7+ ♛xh7 30 ♗xh7++-.

28	h5	♘e5

29 ♗d4   ♖e8
30 f3

This further restricts the activity of the knights and prepares a future g4 to safeguard the h5-pawn.

30 ...   b6
31 b4   ♘xc4
32 ♖xf6!

A crushing response to Black's idea of 32 ♕xc4 ♖e1+ 33 ♔h2 ♖xb1. Now after 32 ... gxf6 33 ♕g6+ is decisive.

32 ...   ♖e1+
33 ♔f2   ♖xb1
34 ♖g6   1-0

In order to avoid a pin on the king's knight after 8 ... ♘f6, Black often develops this piece on e7 instead. This idea has been played by the former World Champion Mikhail Tal, amongst others, as we see in the next game.

B. Ivanovic – Tal
USSR 1979

1 e4   e5
2 ♘f3   ♘c6
3 d4   exd4
4 ♘xd4   ♗c5
5 ♘b3   ♗b6
6 a4   a6

The adventurous 6 ... ♕h4 is flawed as the queen can be rebuffed with gain of tempi. After 7 ♕e2 Black may play:

a) 7 ... ♘f6 8 a5 ♘d4 9 ♘xd4 ♗xd4 10 ♖a4! (10 c3 ♗c5 11 b4 ♗e7 12 ♘d2± Michel - Mengar-

ini, St. Martin 1991) 10 ... ♗c5 11 ♖c4 d6 12 e5+- Estrin - Berezin, USSR 1953.

b) 7 ... d6 8 a5 ♗g4 9 ♕d2 ♗c5 10 ♘b5 ♘ge7 11 ♘xc5 dxc5 12 0-0 0-0 13 c3 ♗e6 14 ♘a3± Damjanovic - Kolarov, 1964.

7 ♘c3   d6
8 ♗e2

White's other possibilities do not make much of an impression:

a) 8 ♘d5 ♗a7 9 ♗e2 ♘f6 10 0-0 (10 ♗g5? ♗xf2+ 11 ♔f1 ♘xd5! 12 ♕xd5 f6 is slightly better for Black according to Keres) 10 ... ♘xd5 11 exd5 ♘e5 12 ♘d4 0-0 (Pfleger - Keres, Tallinn 1973) 13 ♗e3=.

b) 8 ♕e2 ♗e6 9 ♗e3 ♗xe3 10 ♕xe3 ♗xb3! 11 cxb3 ♘f6 12 ♗c4 0-0 13 0-0 ♘b4 14 ♖ad1 ♕e7 15 ♕d2 a5 16 ♖fe1 ♖fe8 17 f3 ♖ad8 18 ♕f2 c6 19 ♖e2 ♖d7 20 ♕b6 ♕d8 21 ♕xd8 ♖exd8 22 ♖ed2 d5 23 exd5 ♘bxd5 24 ♗xd5 ♘xd5 ½-½ Botterill - Perkins, British Ch 1974.

c) 8 a5 ♗a7 9 ♗e2 h6 10 0-0 ♘f6 11 ♔h1 0-0 12 f4 ♖e8 13 ♗f3 ♗e6 14 ♖a4 ♗d7 15 h3 ♖b8 16 ♔h2 ♘e7 17 ♖a1 ♘g6 18 g3 ♗c6 19 ♕d3 ♘f8 20 ♗d2 ½-½ Ljubojevic - Portisch, Amsterdam 1981.

8 ...   ♘ge7 *(31)*

Black can also try the relatively untested 8 ... ♕h4!? 9 0-0 ♘ge7 10 a5 ♗a7 11 ♖a4 (11 ♘d5!?) 11 ... ♘e5 12 ♘d4 ♗d7 13 ♖a3 0-0= Zihitenev - Lhagkva, Moscow 1972.

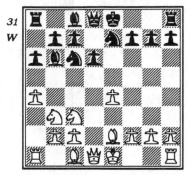

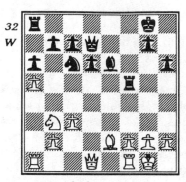

9	♗g5	♗e6
10	a5	♗a7
11	♘d5	

White increases the pressure by advancing his knight, exploiting the pin.

| 11 | ... | h6 |

The most accurate continuation. After the weaker 11 ... ♗xd5?! 12 exd5 ♘e5 13 c4 White has much the better position with play similar to the main game S. Arkell – Gallagher.

12	♗e3	♗xe3
13	♘xe3	0-0
14	0-0	♕d7
15	c3	

White now embarks on a plan of moving the other knight into the centre to try and curtail ... f5. By including the move c3 White keeps the option of playing cxd4 if Black were to exchange on d4, increasing his central control.

| 15 | ... | f5 |

Also possible is the preliminary 15 ... ♖ae8, in order to avoid the game continuation.

| 16 | exf5 | ♘xf5 |
| 17 | ♘xf5 | ♖xf5 *(32)* |

| 18 | ♘d4! | |

This fine pawn sacrifice is the only way for White to gain the initiative.

| 18 | ... | ♘xd4 |

Black declines the offered material in view of the activity that White's pieces would enjoy, and in particular the influence of the white bishop when the light-squares around the king are so weak. For example: 18 ... ♖xa5 19 ♖xa5 ♘xa5 20 ♘xe6 ♕xe6 21 ♖e1! ♕f7 (21 ... ♖e8? 22 ♗c4!+-) 22 ♗h5 ♕b3 23 ♕f3 (with the idea of h3 and ♖e7) 23 ... ♘c6 (23 ... ♖f8?? 24 ♕xf8+ ♔xf8 25 ♖e8 mate) 24 ♕f5, intending 25 f4, when White stands better since the black queen must control f7, e.g. 24 ... ♕xb2 25 ♕f7+ ♔h8 26 ♖e8+ ♖xe8 27 ♕xe8+ ♔h7 28 ♗g6 mate.

19	♕xd4	♖d5
20	♕e4	c6
21	♖fe1	

White chooses to contest the control of the e-file now that Black has temporarily staked a claim on the d-file.

21	...	♗f5
22	♕f4	g5

In his desire to complicate matters Tal goes astray. This pawn lunge tries to limit the damage of the impending ♗c4 but fails to help. The alternative was also unattractive, however: 22 ... ♔h8 23 ♗c4 ♖c5 24 b4 ♖e5 25 ♖xe5 dxe5 26 ♕xe5 winning a pawn. The long-term drawback of 22 ... g5 is that the black king is exposed.

23	♕g3	♔h7
24	h4	gxh4

Also very unpleasant was 24 ... ♖g8 25 ♗c4 gxh4 26 ♕xh4 ♖g4 27 ♖e7++−.

25	♕xh4	♖e8
26	♘h5!	♗g6
27	♗xg6+	♔xg6 (33)

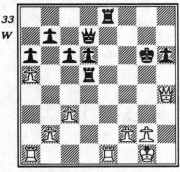

33
W

28 f4!

A timely advance to prevent 28 ... ♖de5, after which the doubled rooks would offer reasonable drawing chances.

28 ... ♖d3

If 28 ... ♖f5 then White is able to infiltrate the heart of Black's camp: 29 ♖xe8 ♕xe8 30 ♖e1 ♕d7 31 ♖e7 and 32 ♕g4++−.

29	f5+!	♔h7
30	♕h5	

The attack has rapidly become decisive. With the help of the f-pawn White is able to take control of the e-file and simultaneously threatens 31 ♕g6+.

30	...	♖xe1+
31	♖xe1	♖g3
32	f6	1–0

Instead of 6 ... a5 or 6 ... a6, Black can also delay the defence of his bishop by launching a counter-attack with 6 ... ♕f6. Of course, after 7 ♕e2 Black still has to make a decision about his bishop but the addition of the two queen moves leads to sharper play as White usually attempts to use the e-file for an early attack but cannot immediately bring his king's bishop into play.

Djurovic – Rajic
Novi Sad Open 1988

1	e4	e5
2	♘f3	♘c6
3	d4	exd4
4	♘xd4	♗c5
5	♘b3	♗b6
6	a4	♕f6

This queen move is Black's most active choice here.

7 ♕e2 a6 (34)

Black's alternatives are less attractive:

a) 7 ... a5 8 ♘c3 ♘ge7 9 ♗e3 and now:

a1) 9 ... ♘b4 10 0-0-0!? 0-0 11 g3 ♗xe3+ 12 ♕xe3 d6 13 ♗g2 ♗e6 14 ♘d4 ♘ec6 15 f4± Johansson – Jansson, Corr 1969.

a2) 9 ... ♗xe3 10 ♕xe3 0-0 11 0-0-0 d6 12 ♗e2 ♗e6 13 f4 ♗xb3 14 cxb3± Prandstetter – Hernandez, Cienfuegos 1983.

b) 7 ... ♘ge7 8 a5 ♘d4 9 ♘xd4 ♗xd4 10 c3 ♗c5! (10 ... ♗e5 11 g3 c6 12 ♗g2 0-0 13 0-0 d5 14 a6! bxa6 15 exd5 ♘xd5 16 ♘d2 ♗c7 17 ♘e4±) 11 e5!? ♕c6 12 ♘d2 a6± Damjanovic – Barczay, Tallinn 1969.

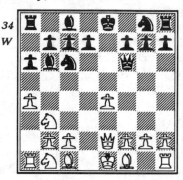

8	♘c3	♘ge7
9	♘d5	♘xd5
10	exd5+	♘e7
11	a5	♗a7
12	h4	*(35)*

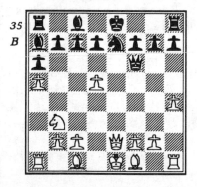

This is one of the most crucial positions in the theory of the Scotch. The White plan is based upon an aggressive advance of his kingside pawns, using his space advantage to manoeuvre his pieces to their optimum squares. Usually White will develop his queen's rook via a4, although this does have the drawback that the white king will remain in the centre. Clearly Black's counterplay will revolve around the exposed white d5-pawn, particularly if White advances on the kingside without adequate preparation.

12   ...   h6

To prevent 13 ♗g5. Other moves are risky for Black:

a) 12 ... 0-0? 13 ♗g5 ♕xb2 14 ♗xe7 ♖e8 15 ♔d1! d6 16 ♘f6 ♖xe2 17 ♘xb2 ♖xf2 18 ♘d4+– Barczay – Sapi, Budapest 1964.

b) 12 ... d6 13 ♖a4! and now:

b1) 13 ... ♗d7? 14 ♖f4 ♗f5 (14 ... ♕e5 15 ♖e4 ♕f6 16 ♗g5) 15 g4 0-0 16 gxf5+– Bastrikov – Formin, USSR 1955.

b2) 13 ... 0-0 14 ♖f4 ♗f5 15 g4 ♖ae8 16 gxf5 (16 ♔d1 ♕e5 17 ♕xe5 dxe5 18 ♖xf5 ♘xf5 19 gxf5+– Bebchuk – Bakulin, USSR 1963) 16 ... ♘xd5 17 ♖e4 ♗xf2+ 18 ♔d1 ♘e3+ 19 ♗xe3 ♖xe4 20 ♕xf2 ♕xb2 21 ♘d3+– van der Wiel – Ree, Hilversum 1987.

b3) 13 ... ♕f5 14 ♖e4! ♗xf2+ 15 ♔d1 ♕xd5+ 16 ♘d2 ♗f5 17 c4! (17 ♖xe7+ ♔f8 18 ♕xf2 ♔xe7 19 ♗e2

♔f8 20 ♖f1 ♗g6 21 ♘f3 ♕f5∓
Pantazi - Balshan, Ybbs 1968) 17
... ♕c5 (17 ... ♕xa5 18 ♖xe7+ ♔f8
19 g4+-) 18 ♖xe7+ ♔d8 19 ♖e4
(intending 20 ♖f4 and b4) 19 ...
♗xe4 20 ♘xe4 ♕d4+ 21 ♔c2
♖e8 22 ♕xf2 ♕xe4+ 23 ♘d3 ♕c6
24 ♕xf7 ♕xg2+ 25 ♔c3 h6 26
♖f1 b5 27 ♗g6 ♕g3+ 28 ♖f3
♕e1+ 29 ♘d2 b4+ 30 ♔c2 b3+ 31
♖xb3 ♖e7 32 ♕f8+ 1-0 Stoica -
Orlowski, Poland 1970.

b4) 13 ... ♘f5 14 g4 ♗g6 15 h5
0-0-0 16 ♗g2 ♖he8 17 ♘e3 and
White is slightly better according to Kaikamdzhozov.

c) 12 ... ♕d6 13 ♗g5 (13 ♖a4!
0-0 [13 ... ♕xd5 14 ♖e4] 14 ♘f4)
13 ... h6 14 ♘d2 ♕xd5 15 0-0-0
♕e6 16 ♕f3 ♕f6 17 ♕g3 ♗xf2 18
♕xc7 ♘d5 19 ♕c4 ♕e6 20 ♖h3
0-0 21 g4! with good play on
the kingside, Timofeyeva -
Dmitrieva, USSR 1958.

13 ♘d2

This is currently the most
topical continuation. The main
alternative, 13 ♖a4, has ex-
perienced bouts of fluctuating
popularity but does not appear
to set Black as many problems
as 13 ♘d2:

a) 13 ... ♕f5? 14 ♖f4 ♕xd5 15
♖e4 ♗c5 16 ♘xc5 ♕xc5 17 ♘d2!
♕xc2 (17 ... ♕d6 18 ♖h3 ♔d8 19
♖d3 ♕f6 20 ♗c3+-) 18 ♖xe7+
♔d8 19 ♖e3 ♕xb2 20 ♗c3 ♕b1+
21 ♕d1 1-0 Botterill - Bellinger,
London 1973.

b) 13 ... ♔d8!? 14 g4 (14 ♖f4!?)
14 ... ♖e8 15 ♖e4 ♕g6 16 ♗g2?!
f5! 17 h5 ♕f7 18 gxf5 d6 19 0-0

♘g8 20 ♖xe8+ ♕xe8 21 ♖xe8+
♔xe8∓ (White's pawns are
weak) Hultquist - Wikstrom,
Corr 1973.

c) 13 ... 0-0 14 g4 and now:

c1) 14 ... ♕d6 15 g5 ♕xd5 (15 ...
h5 16 ♗g2 ♘xd5 17 0-0 ♕c6 18
♖e4 and White is winning
according to Botterill and
Harding; 15 ... ♘xd5 16 ♗g2) 16
♕xe7! ♕xh1 17 gxh6 ♕g1 18
♖f4+-.

c2) 14 ... d6 15 g5 ♕e5 (15 ...
♕f5! 16 ♗g2 ♘xd5 17 ♘d4 ♕e5
18 ♕xe5 dxe5 19 ♗xd5 ♗xd4 20
c3 which Botterill and Harding
assess as equal) 16 ♖e4 ♕xd5 17
c4 ♕c6 18 ♖g1 ♘g6 19 gxh6 ♘f5
20 ♗g2 ♕a4 21 h5 ♕xb3 22 hxg6
♗xg6 23 hxg7 ♔xg7 24 ♘d2 ♕a4
25 ♗c3+ f6 26 ♖e7+ ♖f7 27
♗xf6++- Bebchuk - Sazonov,
USSR 1962.

c3) 14 ... ♘xd5 15 g5 ♕d8!? 16
gxh6 ♖e8 17 ♖e4 ♖xe4 18 ♕xe4
♕e7 19 ♕xe7 ♘xe7 20 hxg7 d6!
(20 ... ♔xg7? 21 ♖g1+ ♔h8 22
♗c4 gives White a winning
advantage according to Botterill
and Harding) 21 ♘d3 ♗f5 22 ♘e3
♗xd3 23 cxd3 ♘f5 24 ♔d2
(Hultquist - Kretschmar, Corr
1982) 24 ... ♗xe3+=.

13 ... 0-0

The absolute test of White's
plan is to snatch the b-pawn: 13
... ♕xb2 14 ♖h3 ♕xc2 15 ♖c1 (15
♖a4!? Brat) 15 ... ♕f5 16 ♘b4
♗xf2+ 17 ♔d1 ♕xd5+ 18 ♖d3 ♕e6
19 ♕xf2± (Black only has
remote chances of mobilizing
his pawns in any endgame)

Klein – Ahman, Corr 1973. It might be more prudent to play 16 ... d6 17 ♖xc7 ♗d7 with an unclear position according to Botterill and Harding. However, White should be able to make use of his tremendous lead in development.

Another idea for Black is queenside castling after the sequence 13 ... d6 14 ♗c3 ♕f4, as considered in the next game, Djurovic – Fercec.

14 ♗c3 ♕d6?
15 0-0-0

Now White has excellent attacking chances; he can menacingly push forward his g-and h-pawns, while the rest of his pieces are well co-ordinated to force a path through to the king. In contrast, Black has grave difficulties developing, and is forced to capture the hot d-pawn.

15 ... ♘xd5
16 ♖xd5!

A wonderfully direct concept; White eliminates the knight, relying on the strength of the dark-squared bishop to undertake a mating attack.

16 ... ♕xd5
17 ♕g4 g6

The obvious 17 ... f6 fails to 18 ♗c4+-.

18 ♕f4 ♔h7
19 ♗d3 *(36)*

White dominates the whole board. The threat of 20 h5 forces Black into a desperate and ultimately futile barrage of

checks which only postpone the inevitable.

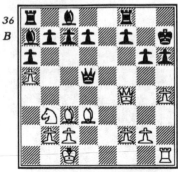

19	...	♕xg2
20	♕f6	♕xh1+
21	♔d2	♗e3+
22	fxe3	♕h2+
23	♔d1	♕h1+
24	♔d2	♕h2+
25	♔c1	♕g1+
26	♗f1	♕xe3+
27	♔b1	♕xc3

Now that the checks have run out, Black is obliged to give up his queen.

28	bxc3	d6
29	♘d4	♗g4
30	♗c4	c5
31	♗xf7	1-0

Having seen the power of White's attack after the careless 13 ... 0-0 14 ♗c3 ♕d6, we can now move on to a look at Black's best defence, 13 ... d6 14 ♗e3 ♕f4, as in the next game.

Djurovic – Fercec
Novi Sad Open 1988

1	e4	e5
2	♘f3	♘c6

3	d4	exd4
4	♘xd4	♗c5
5	♘b3	♗b6
6	a4	♕f6
7	♕e2	a6
8	♘c3	♘ge7 *(37)*

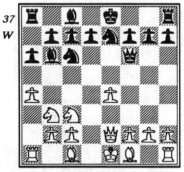

37
W

9 ♘d5

This is the most accurate move in this position as after 9 a5 White can only hope for a transposition at best:

a) 9 ... ♗a7 and now:

a1) 10 ♘d5 transposes to the main game after 10 ... ♘xd5 11 exd5+ ♘e7.

a2) 10 ♗e3 ♗xe3 11 ♕xe3 d6 (11 ... 0-0 12 ♗d3 d6 13 0-0 ♗e6 14 ♘d2 ♖ad8 15 f4 ♕h6! 16 ♕f2 f5 17 g3 ♘b4!∓ Musil - Donner, Busum 1968) 12 0-0-0 0-0 13 ♗e2 ♗e6 14 ♘d5 ♗xd5 15 exd5 ♘e5 16 f4 ♘5g6 17 g3 ♖fe8 18 ♕f2 ♘f5 19 ♗d3 ♘e3 20 ♖d2 ♖e7 21 ♕f3 ♖ae8 22 c3 ½-½ Ljubojevic - Karpov, Bugojno 1980.

a3) 10 h4 ♘d4 11 ♘xd4 ♗xd4 12 ♖h3 d6 13 ♗g5 ♕e5 14 ♖g3 ♗e6 15 f4 ♕c5 16 ♗xe7 ♔xe7 17 f5 ♗c4 18 ♕f3= Nechaev - Matseak, Kirghizian Ch 1966.

b) 9 ... ♘d4 10 e5 ♕g6 11 ♘xd4 ♗xd4 12 ♖a4 ♗xc3+ 13 bxc3 0-0∓ Neishtadt - Golubev, USSR 1955.

9	...	♘xd5
10	exd5+	♘e7
11	a5	♗a7
12	h4	h6
13	♗d2	

Apart from 13 ♖a4 (see the notes to the previous game) White has also experimented with the aggressive-looking 13 g4, although it appears that White cannot really hope for more than equality with this:

a) 13 ... 0-0?! 14 g5 ♕f5 15 gxh6 ♗xf2+? 16 ♕xf2 ♕e4+ 17 ♕e3 ♕xh1 18 ♕xe7+- Skegina - Postnikova, USSR 1963.

b) 13 ... ♕d6! 14 ♗d2 ♕xd5 15 ♖h3 ♕e6 16 ♗e3 d6 17 0-0-0 0-0 18 ♕d2 ♗xe3 19 ♖xe3 ♕g6 20 g5 hxg5 21 hxg5 ♕xg5 22 ♗d3 ♘g6 (after 22 ... ♘f5! Black is slightly better according to Aronin) 23 ♖h1 ♗d7 24 ♔b1 ♗c6 25 ♖eh3 f6 (25 ... ♕xd2?? 26 ♖h8+ ♘xh8 27 ♗h7 mate) 26 ♕xg5 fxg5 27 ♗xg6 ♗xh1 28 ♖xh1 ♖xf2 ½-½ Padevsky - Reshevsky, Tel Aviv 1964.

Harmless is 13 ♖h3 (13 ♗g5? hxg5 14 hxg5 ♕xf2+!-+) 13 ... d6 14 ♖g3 0-0 15 c4 ♗d7∓ Sefc - Beni, Prague 1956.

13	...	d6
14	♗c3	

Here 14 ♖a4 is tame as 14 ... ♗f5 cancels out any attacking notions, e.g. 15 g4 ♗xc2 16 ♗c3 ♕xf2+-+ or 15 ♗c3 ♕g6 16 ♔d1=.

14 ... ♛f4 *(38)*

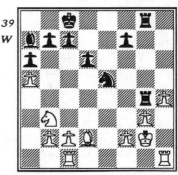

15 g3

Keres considered the position to be equal based on the variation 15 ♗xg7 ♖g8 16 g3 (16 ♗c3 ♗d7=) 16 ... ♛xf2+ 17 ♛xf2 ♗xf2+ 18 ♔xf2 ♖xg7=. However, 15 g3 completely changes the situation, for when the g7-pawn falls Black cannot capture one of White's kingside pawns and has to settle for the d-pawn, leaving White with a clear pawn majority on the kingside.

15 ... ♛g4
16 ♛xg4 ♗xg4
17 ♗xg7 ♖g8?!

Black sacrifices a pawn in order to activate the rook, but this plan is ineffectual. Although 17 ... ♖h7 looks uncomfortable for Black it is essential, although White still enjoys the brighter prospects: 18 ♗d4 ♗f3 19 ♖g1 ♗xd4 (19 ... ♗xd5 20 ♗d3!±) 20 ♘xd4 ♗xd5 21 ♗h3! ♘c6 22 ♘xc6 ♗xc6 23 ♔d2 f6 24 ♖ae1+ ♖e7 25 ♖xe7+ ♔xe7 26 ♖e1+ ♔f7?! (26 ... ♔f8 27 ♔d3 ♖e8 28 ♖xe8+ ♔xe8 29 ♔d4

with a slight edge to White due to his superior pawn structure) 27 ♘g4 ♗e8 (27 ... ♖d8 28 ♘h5+ ♔f8 29 ♖e6+−) 28 ♘h5+ ♔f8 29 ♖xe8+ ♖xe8 30 ♗xe8 ♔xe8 31 ♔e3 ♔e7 32 g4 ♔e6 33 ♔f4 b6 34 axb6 cxb6 35 c4 b5 36 cxb5 axb5 37 ♔e4 b4 38 ♔d4 f5 39 g5 1-0 Hertel - Bruckel, Corr 1988.

18 ♗xh6 ♘xd5
19 ♗h3 ♘b4
20 ♖c1 0-0-0
21 ♗d2

Black enjoys an initiative, but it is only temporary and White quickly consolidates. Although his king still lies in the centre there is enough time to shuffle it to safety via f1-g2.

21 ... ♘c6
22 ♗xg4+ ♖xg4
23 ♔f1 ♘e5
24 ♔g2 ♖dg8 *(39)*

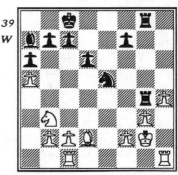

25 ♖h3!

It is necessary to mobilize the kingside pawns. For this purpose the rook on h3 is ideally placed, guarding g3 and maintaining support for the h-pawn.

25 ... f5

26	f3	♖c4
27	h5	f4
28	h6	♗e3
29	h7	♖h8
30	♗xe3	fxe3
31	f4	♘g4
32	♔f3	

It is not necessary to calculate the exact consequences of giving up the h-pawn for the e-pawn, since White's passed connected pawns have a clear road to promotion.

32	...	♘f6
33	♔xe3	♖xh7
34	♖xh7	♘xh7
35	♔d3	d5
36	♘d2	♖a4
37	♖h1	

The game now more or less runs its course; White's rook chases the black knight to a passive position and then he is ready to advance his passed pawns to their queening squares.

37	...	♘f6
38	♖h6	♘e8
39	♖h7	♘f6
40	♖f7	♘h5
41	b3	

Now 41 ... ♖d4 is met by 42 c3 after which the rook must leave the fourth rank and White can play g4 in safety.

1–0

Although White invariably follows 4 ... ♗c5 5 ♘b3 ♗b6 with 6 a4 he does occasionally try to do without this move, although Black should be able

to achieve an equal game without too many difficulties, notwithstanding the result of the next game.

Atkinson – Brandner
Arnhem 1989

1	e4	e5
2	♘f3	♘c6
3	d4	exd4
4	♘xd4	♗c5
5	♘b3	♗b6

Instead 5 ... ♗b4+ is worthy of attention, disrupting White's development. After 6 c3 ♗e7 White may play:

a) 7 g3 ♘f6 8 ♗g2 0–0 9 0–0 ♖e8 10 f4 d6 11 h3 ♗f8 12 ♘1d2 g6 13 ♘d4 ♗g7 14 ♔h2± Grotkov – Tarasov, Agler 1969.

b) 7 ♘d4 ♗f6 8 g3 ♘ge7 9 ♗g2 0–0 10 0–0 d6 11 ♘a3 ♗d7 12 h3 ♘xd4 13 cxd4 c5 (Radulov – Keres, Budapest 1970) 14 ♗e3 ♘c6 15 ♘c2=.

c) 7 ♗f4 d6 8 ♘1d2 ♘f6 9 ♗e2 0–0 10 0–0 ♖e8 11 ♖e1 ♗f8 12 ♗f1 g6 13 ♕c2± Pfleger – O'Kelly, Montilla 1973.

d) 7 c4!? ♘f6 8 ♘c3 0–0 (8 ... ♗b4 9 ♗d3±) 9 ♗e2 ♖e8 10 f3 a5 (B. Ivanovic – Petrosian, USSR 1979) 11 0–0 a4 12 ♘d4 ♗c5 13 ♗e3±.

e) 7 f4 d6 8 ♗d3 and now:

e1) 8 ... ♗h4+!? 9 g3 ♗f6 10 ♗e3 h5 11 h3 g5 12 ♕d2 gxf4 13 gxf4 ♘ge7 14 ♘a3 ♗h4+ 15 ♗f2 ♘g6 16 ♔d1 ½–½ Hübner – Spassky, Linares 1985.

e2) 8 ... ♘f6 9 ♕c2 0–0 10

♘1d2 ♖e8 11 0-0 ♗f8 12 ♘f3± Santo Roman - Kharitonov, Royan 1988.

Instead of 6 c3, White can also play 6 ♘d2 a5!? 7 a3 ♗e7 8 a4 ♘f6 9 ♘c3 0-0 10 ♗b5 d5 11 exd5 ♘b4 12 0-0 ♗g4 13 ♗e2 ♗xe2 14 ♕xe2 ♘xc2 15 ♖ad1 ♘b4 16 ♕b5 ♘bxd5 17 ♘xd5 ½-½ Smirin - Khalifman, USSR 1990.

Less good is the timid 5 ... ♗e7?! 6 g3 ♘f6 7 ♗g2 0-0 8 0-0 ♖e8 9 h3 a5 10 a4± Bastrikov - Bannik, USSR 1952.

6 ♘c3

Naturally, even after this move White can still seek to transpose into other lines by an early a4, but usually this move indicates a desire to avoid the well-trodden main lines. Not so good is 6 c4?! d6 7 ♘c3 ♕h4! 8 g3 ♕f6 9 c5 dxc5 10 ♗e3 ♘ge7 11 ♘xc5 0-0 12 ♗g2 ♘e5∓ Estrin - Furman, USSR 1950.

6 ... ♘ge7 (40)

As we have seen earlier in this chapter (with a4 and ... a6 already played), Black's most reliable means of development is this knight move, avoiding the pin which might follow an early ... ♘f6. The alternatives are:

a) 6 ... ♘f6 7 ♗f4 (7 ♗g5 d6 8 ♕d2 h6 9 ♗e3 0-0 10 0-0-0 ♕e7 11 f3 ♗xe3 12 ♕xe3± Radulov - Matanovic, Helsinki 1972) 7 ... d6 8 ♕d2 and now:

a1) 8 ... ♗e6 and now:

a11) 9 0-0-0 h6?! 10 ♗b5 ♘h5 11 h4 ♕f6 12 ♗e3 ♗xe3 13 ♕xe3 0-0 14 g3 ♕g6 15 g4! and White is better as the g-pawn cannot be taken due to ♖dg1, Seeliger - Kapic, Corr 1984.

a12) 9 ♗b5 a6 10 ♗xc6+ bxc6 11 0-0 0-0 12 ♖ad1 ♗c4 13 ♖fe1 ♘g4 14 ♘d4 ♕f6 15 ♗g3 ♘e5 16 b3 ♖fe8 17 ♘a4!± Seeliger - Florian, Corr 1984.

a2) 8 ... ♘g4 9 ♗g3 ♗e6 10 ♘d5 ♗xd5 11 exd5 ♕e7+ 12 ♗e2 ♘ce5 13 0-0-0 ♘xf2 14 ♗b5+ c6 15 dxc6 bxc6 16 ♗xe5 0-0 17 ♗xd6+- Doncevic - Besada, Geneva 1985.

a3) 8 ... ♕e7 9 0-0-0 h6 10 ♘d5 ♘xd5 11 exd5 ♘e5 12 ♗b5+ ♔f8 13 ♖he1 ♕f6 14 ♗e3 ♗g4 15 f3 ♗d7 16 f4 ♗xb5 17 fxe5 dxe5 18 ♕b4+ 1-0 Doncevic - Labbude, Geneva 1985.

a4) 8 ... 0-0 9 f3 ♘e5 10 0-0-0 ♘g6?! (10 ... ♖e8!?) 11 ♗g3 ♖e8 12 h4! h5 13 ♔b1 ♗d7 14 ♕g5!? ♘f8 15 ♗c4 ♗e6 (Doncevic - Kavalek, Bundesliga 1985/86) 16 ♗e2 ♘8h7 17 ♕f4 ♘d7 18 ♘d5±.

b) 6 ... d6 7 ♗e2 ♗e6 8 0-0 ♘f6 9 ♗g5 h6 10 ♗h4 g5 11 ♗g3 d5 12 exd5 ♘xd5 13 ♘e4 ♘f4 14 ♗xf4 gxf4 15 ♖e1 ♘d4 16 ♗c4! f3 17 ♘xd4 ♕xd4 18 ♗xe6 fxe6 19 ♕xf3 0-0-0 20 a4 ♖hf8 21 ♕h3 ♖f5 22 ♕xh6 ♖e5 23 c3 ♕d3 24 ♕h7 1-0 Castro - Shapiro, St. Martin 1991.

c) 6 ... ♕f6 7 ♕e2 ♘ge7 8 ♗e3!? (8 ♘d5 ♘xd5 9 exd5+ ♘e7 10 h4?! [White lacks the potential lateral development

of his queen's rook here] 10 ...
h6 11 c4 ♕g6 12 ♗d2 ♕g4= Roth
– Matanovic, Vienna 1986) 8 ...
♘d4 9 ♕d2 ♘xb3 10 axb3 ♗xe3
11 ♕xe3 ♘c6 12 ♘d5 ♕xb2 13
♖d1 0–0 14 ♗d3 ♘d4 15 0–0 ♘e6
16 e5 ♔h8 17 ♗xh7 1–0 Chiburdanidze – Malaniuk, Kusadasi
1990.

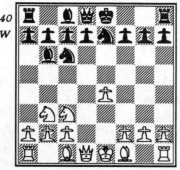

7	♗e2	d6
8	0–0	0–0
9	♗g5	

It is necessary to activate the
bishop in order to diminish the
effect of ... f5. The careless
9♘a4?! allows Black to open the
f-file and rapidly marshal his
forces towards the kingside:
9 ... f5 10 ♘xb6 axb6 11 exf5
♘xf5 12 ♗f3 ♕f6 13 c3 ♗e6 14
♗e4 ♕f7 15 ♗c2 ♗c4 16 ♖e1 ♘h4
17 ♗e3 ♗d5 18 ♕b1 ♘xg2! 19
♗xh7+ ♔h8 20 ♗g6 ♕f3 21 ♘d2
♕g4 22 f3 ♘f4+!! 0–1 Mathe –
Yakovich, Kecskemet 1991.

9	...	f6
10	♗h4	♘g6
11	♗g3	a6

The bishop is given an escape square in case of ♘a4.

| 12 | ♔h1 | f5 |

| 13 | exf5 | ♗xf5 (41) |

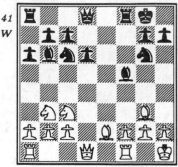

| 14 | ♘d5 | ♗a7 |

A roughly equal position has
arisen in which White's greater
freedom of movement is
counterbalanced by Black's play
on the f-file. White now connects his rooks as quickly as
possible but he lacks any real
weaknesses to attack unless
Black mishandles things.

15	♕d2	♔h8
16	♖ae1	♕d7
17	♗h5	♘ce5?!

A careless move which cedes
White a lasting initiative. Black
aims to block the e-file but
this simply encourages the
white f-pawn to advance. Although the pawn on f4 blocks
the white bishop on g3, this is
a secondary factor relative to
his control over the e-file.
Much more satisfactory was
the solid 17 ... ♖ae8.

| 18 | f4! | ♘c6 |

An embarrassing move to
have to make, but Black cannot
afford to lose control of the
e7-square, e.g. 18 ... ♘g4 19
♗xg6 ♗xg6 20 ♖e7 ♕d8 21 ♖xc7

♘e3 22 ♕c3! winning.

19	♖e2	♘ge7
20	♘xe7	♘xe7
21	♖fe1	♘g8
22	♘d4	

A remarkable transformation has occurred since the last diagram. White has seized control of the e-file and now brings his offside knight into the battle for the e6-square.

22 ... ♗g4?!

Under pressure, Black prefers to trade bishops rather than allow it to be exchanged for the knight.

23	♗xg4	♕xg4
24	♘e6	♖f6

It is pointless to try and preserve the c-pawn: 24 ... ♖f7 25 ♘g5 ♖ff8 26 ♕d5 ♕h5 27 ♕xb7+-.

25	♘xc7	♖c8
26	♘d5	♖h6
27	♕d3	

White easily defends against the threat of 27 ... fxg3.

27	...	♕h5
28	♘e7	♘xe7
29	♖xe7	♗f2 (42)

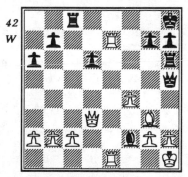

30 ♕c3!

In a tense situation, White finds a surprising way of neutralising Black's activity, using the weakness of his opponent's back rank to create mating threats.

30	...	♖g8
31	♖1e2	♗xg3
32	♕xg3	♕b5
33	c3	♖f6
34	♕e3	♕d5
35	a3	g5
36	♕e4	

With an extra pawn and mobile rooks, White is happy to settle for the ending.

36	...	♕xe4
37	♖7xe4	gxf4
38	♖f2	♖gf8
39	♖f3	♖8f7
40	♔g1	♔g7
41	♔f2	♖f5
42	♖d4	♖7f6
43	♖fd3	

The weakness of Black's pawn formation finally tells.

1-0

Conclusion

The main lines of the 5 ♘b3 line are far from harmless for Black unless he is well prepared against them. Black's best course is to follow the game B. Ivanovic - Tal as both 6 ... a5 and 6 ... ♕f6 are risky ways of meeting 6 a4. The variation 6 ♘c3 is much less dangerous as Black has many more options than in the 6 a4 variations.

5 Classical Variation: 5 ♘f5

This is practically the Dutch Grandmaster Jan Timman's patent variation as he is one of the few top-class players who plays it regularly, with excellent practical results. Black is forced to disrupt his formation in defending against the threat to the g7-pawn, after which White relocates his knight to e3 in order to occupy the important d5-square. Of course, these knight manoeuvres do take several moves to carry out and Black may be able to use this time to create counterplay.

Timman – Smyslov
Bugojno 1984

1	e4	e5
2	♘f3	♘c6
3	d4	exd4
4	♘xd4	♗c5
5	♘f5 (43)	
5	...	g6

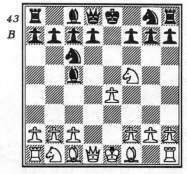

After this move the knight is forced to retreat immediately and Black can get on with the job of developing his pieces. However, the dark squares around the black king are now permanently weak as the bishop is not able to take up its natural outpost on g7. If White can infiltrate these squares then Black's position will quickly fall apart. It is perhaps curious that no one has yet dared to test Timman with an old analysis given by Steinitz in *Modern Chess Instructor* which runs 5 ... d5 6 ♘xg7+ ♔f8 7 ♘h5 ♕h4 8 ♘g3 ♘f6 9 ♗e2 ♘e5 10 h3 ♖g8 with an initiative for Black. Practical examples of this variation tend to be in Black's favour: 5 ... d5 6 ♘xg7+ (6 exd5? ♗xf5 7 dxc6 ♗xf2+!-+) 6 ... ♔f8 7 ♘h5 (7 ♕xd5 ♕xd5 8 exd5 ♘b4-+; 7 exd5 ♔xg7 8 dxc6 ♗xf2+; 7 ♘f5 ♗xf5 8 exf5 ♕h4) 7 ... ♕h4 8 ♘g3 ♘f6 and now:

a) 9 ♕d2? ♘g4 10 ♕xd5

♗xf2+ 11 ♔e2 ♘f6!-+ Ivanovic - Pinter, Plovdiv 1979.

b) 9 ♗e2 ♘e5 10 ♗e3 ♗xe3 11 fxe3 ♖g8 12 ♖f1 ♕xh2 13 ♖xf6 ♕xg3+ 14 ♔d2 ♘g4 15 ♗xg4 ♖xg4 0-1 Prudhomme - Jacobs, Cappelle la Grande 1989.

On this evidence it is probably best to leave the g-pawn alone: 6 ♘c3! ♗xf5 (6 ... dxe4?! 7 ♘xg7+ ♔f8 8 ♕xd8+ ♘xd8 9 ♘xe4±) 7 exf5 d4 8 ♘e4 with an unclear position.

Another major alternative for Black is 5 ... d6 when White probably does best to decline the offer of the pawn:

a) 6 ♘xg7+ ♔f8 7 ♘h5 (7 ♘f5 ♗xf5 8 exf5 ♕h4∓) 7 ... ♕h4 8 ♘g3 ♘f6 (8 ... ♕f6!? 9 ♕d2 h5 10 ♕f4 h4 11 ♘e2 h3 12 ♘bc3 ♘b4 13 ♔d1 ♗xf2∓ Yakovich - Barle, Berne 1992) 9 ♗e2 ♘e5 and now:

a1) 10 f3? and now:

a11) 10 ... ♘eg4? 11 fxg4 ♘xe4 12 ♕d5! f5 13 ♖f1 ♘f6 14 ♖xf5± Timman - Handoko, Zagreb 1985.

a12) 10 ... ♖g8 11 ♔d2 (11 ♕d2 ♖xg3 12 ♕h6+ ♕xh6 13 ♗xh6+ ♖g7; 11 ♔f1!? ♖xg3 12 ♕e1 ♘h5 13 ♘c3 ♕h3!-+) 11 ... d5 12 ♘c3 ♗e6 intending ... ♖d8∓.

a13) 10 ... ♘h5! 11 ♔d2 (11 ♕d2 h6!∓) 11 ... ♘xg3 12 hxg3 ♕xg3∓.

a2) 10 ♕d2 ♗xf2+!∓.

a3) 10 b4 ♗xb4+ 11 c3 ♗c5 12 ♗a3 ♘xe4 13 ♗xc5 ♘xc5∓ Timman - Borm, Netherlands 1985.

a4) 10 ♘c3 ♘fg4 11 ♗xg4 ♘xg4 12 ♖f1 ♖g8 13 ♘a4 ♘xh2 14 ♘xc5 ♘xf1 15 ♔xf1 ♖xg3 16 fxg3 ♕h1+ 17 ♔f2 ♕xd1 18 ♗h6+ ♔e7 19 ♖xd1 dxc5 20 ♗f4 ♗g4 ½-½ Timman - Karpov, Brussels (exhibition game) 1988.

b) 6 ♘e3 and now:

b1) 6 ... ♕f6 7 ♘c3 ♗e6 (7 ... ♘ge7 8 ♗d3 transposes to the main game) 8 ♗e2 (8 ♗d3!?) 8 ... ♘ge7 9 0-0 0-0 10 ♔h1= Schulz - Herbrechtsmeir, Bundesliga 1984/85.

b2) 6 ... ♘f6 7 ♘c3 0-0 8 ♗d3 ♘e5 9 0-0 c6 10 ♘a4 ♗b4 11 f4 ♘xd3 12 cxd3 b5?! (12 ... d5! 13 a3! ♗e7 14 e5 ♘e8∞) 13 ♘c3 ♖e8 14 ♕f3 ♗c5 15 ♔h1± Wu Xibin - Thorsteins, China 1985.

The final alternative, 5 ... ♕f6, is discussed in the next illustrative game.

6 ♘e3 ♘f6
7 ♘c3 0-0

Black chooses to delay moving the d-pawn in order to keep his options open. In Ivanovic - Plachetka, Naleczow 1979, Black played the immediate 7 ... d6 without success: 8 ♗d3 ♖e6 9 0-0 ♘e5 10 ♗e2 ♕d7 11 ♔h1 ♘eg4 12 ♘ed5 c6 13 b4+-.

8 ♗d3 ♖e8
9 0-0

Although White has not yet revealed his middlegame intentions, he can clearly hope to develop an attack with ♘ed5, ♔h1 and f4 as Black has no way of freeing his game.

9 ...   ♘e5

It is surprising to find that this identical position arose in a master game soon after the opening was first introduced. On that occasion Black chose a weaker path, and White's attack developed automatically: 9 ... ♗d4?! 10 ♘ed5 ♘xd5 11 ♘xd5 d6 12 c3 ♗g7 13 f4 ♘e7 14 f5! gxf5 15 ♗g5 fxe4 16 ♗xe4 ♕d7 17 ♗xh7+ ♔xh7 18 ♕h5+ ♔g8 19 ♕xf7+ ♔h8 20 ♘f6 1–0 Wayte – Ranken, Edinburgh 1877.

10 ♔h1   d6

Exchanging the bishop with 10 ... ♘xd3 would only strengthen White's centre. The game Savon – Ivkov, Wijk aan Zee 1972, continued 11 cxd3 ♗f8 12 f4 d6 13 ♕f3 and White eventually pushed forward the kingside pawns with an advantage.

11 ♗e2   ♘c6?!

In view of the impending f4, Black chooses to relocate the knight immediately, but chooses the wrong square. A better course of action is 11 ... ♘ed7! 12 f3 a6 13 a3 ♗f8 14 b4 ♗a7 15 ♗c4 c6 16 ♕d3 ♗e6 17 ♗xe6 ♘xe6 with equal chances, Handoka – Smejkal, Zagreb 1985.

12 f3

The strongpoint at e4 is reinforced in order to free the white pieces which are defending it.

12 ...   ♘d4

In Timman – Gligoric, Bug-

ojno 1984, Black played more cautiously: 12 ... a6 13 ♗d2 ♘d4 14 ♗c4 c6 15 f4 ♘b5 ½–½.

13 ♗c4   a5? *(44)*

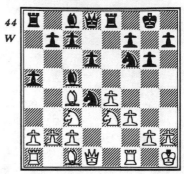

This is too casual; Black should take steps to defend the f7-square with 13 ... ♗e6, when the position is roughly equal.

14 ♘g4!

A marvellous conception which offers Black the chance to split the white pawns in order to open access to the f-file. After 14 ... ♘xg4 the weakness of the kingside dark squares becomes apparent: 15 fxg4 ♗e6 (15 ... ♘e6 16 ♕f3!) 16 ♘d5 ♔g7 17 ♕d2 with excellent attacking chances.

14 ...   ♗e6
15 ♗g5   ♘xg4

Black has no choice but to seek salvation in giving up the queen for an assortment of pieces. However, Timman conducts the technical phase of the game with real efficiency.

16 ♗xd8   ♘e3

If 16 ... ♗xc4 17 fxg4 ♗xf1 18 ♗f6+–.

17 ♕c1   ♗xc4

18	♕xe3	♘xc2
19	♕d2	♘xa1 *(45)*

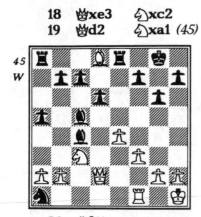

20 ♗f6!

Now that White menaces 21 ♕h6 Black is forced into inferior simplifications. This is much stronger than the routine 20 ♖xa1 ♖axd8 when the black rooks retain their coordination.

20	...	♖e6
21	♖xa1	♖xf6
22	b3	♗e6
23	♘a4!	♗a3

Black cannot improve on the game continuation by 23 ... ♗b4 as 24 ♕b2 ♖f4 25 a3 would leave the bishop and rook awkwardly placed.

24 ♕c3 ♖f4

It is wrong to allow the rook to be pinned: 24 ... ♔g7? 25 g4 h6 26 h4 g5 27 f4!+-.

25	g3	♗b4
26	♕d3	♖f6
27	a3	b5

An audacious way of continuing the situation. This is clearly a better course than 27 ... ♗c5 28 ♘xc5 dxc5 29 ♕c3 ♔g7 30 g4+- with similar play to the previous note.

28	axb4	axb4
29	♔g2	bxa4
30	♕d4	♗xb3

Black gives up the rook in a frantic attempt to utilize the passed queenside pawns. White has no more problems after 30 ... ♔g7 31 ♖xa4 ♖xa4 32 bxa4 c5 33 ♕a1 c4 34 ♕d4 when the white a-pawn decides the game.

31	♕xf6	a3
32	♕d4	c5
33	♕xd6	♖c8
34	♕d2	♗e6
35	f4	h6
36	g4	♗xg4
37	f5!	

In clinical fashion, White locks the bishop out of the game.

37	...	♖e8
38	♕xh6	gxf5
39	h3	1-0

Another way of dealing with the threat to the g-pawn created by White's fifth move is the response 5 ... ♕f6, though Timman's handling of the white pieces in the following games shows a model treatment of this variation.

**Timman – Hübner
Sarajevo (3) 1991**

1	e4	e5
2	♘f3	♘c6
3	d4	exd4
4	♘xd4	♗c5
5	♘f5	♕f6

This move is also considered satisfactory for Black as it defends the g-pawn and activates the queen.

   6   ♘c3   ♘ge7 *(46)*

In Salazar - Benko, Buenos Aires 1991, Black tried a bizarre plan: 6 ... ♘ce7?! 7 ♘e3 c6 8 ♗d3 d5 9 exd5 ♕b4 10 0-0 ♗xc3 11 bxc3 ♗d7 12 ♖b1 cxd5 13 ♖xb7 ♕c6 14 ♖b3 ♘f6 15 ♗a3 ♘c8 16 ♖e1 ♔d8 17 c4 ♖e8 18 cxd5 ♘xd5 19 ♗b5 ♕b7 20 ♗xd7 1-0.

   7   ♘e3   **0-0**
   8   ♗d3

Timman opts for the same set up as used in his game against Smyslov in the previous illustrative game. Prior to this game, practical experience had been largely confined to the continuation 8 g3 ♘e5 9 f4 ♘5g6 10 ♗g2 c6 11 0-0 d5 12 ♔h1! ♗xe3 13 ♗xe3 dxe4 14 ♕c1! ♗f5 15 ♘xe4 ♗xe4?! (15 ... ♕e6!? =) 16 ♗xe4 ♖fe8 17 ♖e1 b6 18 c3 ♘f5 19 ♗f2 when White is much better due to his powerful pair of bishops, Ljubojevic - Karpov, Montreal 1979.

   8   ...   ♘e5
   9   ♗e2   ♘5g6
   10   g3

The knight is prevented from invading at f4 and White prepares to drive it back with h4-h5.

   10   ...   **d6**
   11   h4   ♖e8
   12   h5   ♘f8 *(47)*

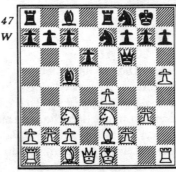

   13   ♖h4!

An astounding idea; White gives up the right to castle kingside in order to bring his rook into a position where it can harass the black queen. Suddenly White's space advantage takes on menacing proportions.

   13   ...   **c6?!**

A more flexible approach is 13 ... a6 in order to leave an escape square on a7 for the bishop. Less good is 13 ... ♘c6?! 14 ♗b5 a6 15 ♗a4 ♗e6 16 ♖f4 ♕d8 17 ♘f5 ♗xf5 18 ♖xf5 ♖e5 19 ♗g5 ♕e8 20 ♔f1 ♖xf5 21 exf5 ♕e5 22 ♕g4 ♖e8 23 ♖d1 b5 24 ♗f4 ♕f6 25 ♘d5 ♕xb2 26 f6 g6 27 hxg6 hxg6 28 ♗b3 ♖e6 29 ♕h4 ♘d7 30 ♘e7+ 1-0 Hernandez–Guerrero – A. Lopez, Mexico 1992.

14 ♘a4   ♕d4

Timman himself points out that preserving the important bishop by 14 ... ♗b4+ is not sufficient to solve Black's problems: 15 c3 (15 ♗d2!?) 15 ... ♗a5 16 ♖f4 (16 b4 ♗c7 with an unclear position) 16 ... ♕e6 (16 ... ♕h6 17 ♘c4+–) 17 ♗g4±.

15 ♘xc5   ♕xc5?

It was essential to recapture with 15 ... dxc5 although 16 ♘c4 intending ♗e3 is still better for White.

16 ♘c4!   ♖d8

The weakness of the d-pawn caused by Black's thirteenth move becomes apparent. If 16 ... d5 then White pursues the queen: 17 ♗e3 ♕b5 18 a4 ♕a6 19 ♘d6 ♕a5+ 20 ♗d2+–.

17 ♗e3   ♕b5
18 a4   ♕a6
19 b4

The last outlet for the beleaguered queen is closed down. Now White threatens both 20 ♘b6 and 20 ♘xd6.

19 ...   d5 *(48)*

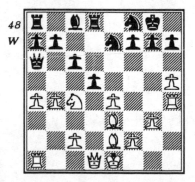

20 ♘b6

Timman nets the queen for two pieces but there was a quicker way to win: 20 ♗c5! ♖d7 (20 ... ♖e8 21 ♘d6+–) 21 ♘e5+–.

20 ...   ♕xb6
21 ♗xb6   axb6
22 exd5   ♘f5
23 ♖f4   ♖xd5
24 ♗d3

White now has the simple plan of exchanging as many pieces as possible in order to maximise the power of his queen.

24 ...   g6
25 hxg6   hxg6
26 ♖e4   ♗e6
27 ♕d2   ♘d4
28 ♕c3   c5

It is imperative for Black to block the a1–h8 diagonal; otherwise the opposing rooks will double on the h-file with excellent mating chances.

29 bxc5   bxc5
30 ♗c4   ♖h5
31 ♗xe6   ♘fxe6
32 ♖h4   ♖f5

Black's best practical chance is to keep the pieces on and create tricks based on the exposed white king.

33 ♔f1   ♖f3
34 ♕b2   ♖e8
35 ♖e1   ♖e7
36 a5   ♖d7
37 ♔g2   ♖f5
38 ♖eh1   ♘g5
39 a6

The pawn is taboo due to 39

... bxa6 40 ♕b8+ ♔g7 41 ♕h8 mate, so it becomes a passed pawn and finishes the game.

40	c3	♘df3
41	♖f4	1–0

Conclusion

The 5 ♘f5 variation indicates that White wants a fight right out of the opening and is therefore ideally suited to players such as Timman who have a confrontational style. Black's most promising course of action is 5 ... d6 which leads to very unclear play. This is an ideal choice for investigation.

6 Classical Variation: 5 ♘xc6

This solid variation has always enjoyed a rather dour reputation although recently the Russian Grandmaster Smagin has chosen it on a regular basis. White hopes to exploit the damage to Black's pawn structure after ... bxc6, but it is doubtful whether he really has any advantage after the intermediate move 5 ... ♕f6!.

Smagin – Gligoric
Yugoslavia 1991

1	e4	e5
2	♘f3	♘c6
3	d4	exd4
4	♘xd4	♗c5
5	♘xc6	

White releases the tension, steering the game away from the heavily analysed main lines.

5 ... ♕f6!

The threat of mate in one allows Black to develop with ease.

6 ♕d2

This is White's most combative choice here; although the queen's bishop is blocked White can rapidly activate his other forces and can harass the enemy queen. Other defences against the mate allow Black an easy game:

a) 6 ♕f3 bxc6 7 ♗c4 ♕xf3 8 gxf3 d6=.

b) 6 ♕e2 bxc6 7 ♘c3 a5 8 ♗e3 ♗a6 9 ♕d2 ♗xe3 10 ♕xe3 ♗xf1 11 ♖xf1 ♘e7= Barczay – Lengyel, Kecskemet 1968.

c) 6 f4 and now:

c1) 6 ... ♕xc6?! 7 ♘c3 ♘f6 8 ♗b5 ♕e6 9 ♕e2 0–0 10 e5 ♘d5 11 ♘e4 ♗e7 12 0–0+– Larsen – Brinck-Claussen, Copenhagen 1979.

c2) 6 ... dxc6 7 ♘c3 and now:

c21) 7 ... h5 8 ♕d3?! (8 f5!?) 8 ... ♗g4 9 h3 ♖d8 10 e5 ♕h4+! 11 g3 ♕e7 12 ♕e4 ♘f6 13 ♕g2 ♗f5 14 ♕e2 ♘d5 15 ♘xd5 cxd5 16 ♗g2 0–0 17 g4 ♕h4+ 18 ♔d1 ♗e4! 19 ♗d2 ♕g3 20 ♗xe4 dxe4 21 ♔c1 ♖xd2–+ Hekuriani – Sturua, USSR 1982.

c22) 7 ... ♘h6! 8 ♕f3 ♕h4+ 9 g3 ♗g4 10 ♕g2 ♕h5 11 ♗e2 0–0–0 12 h3 ♗xe2 13 ♕xe2 ♕g6 14 g4 ♖he8 15 ♗d2 ♘f5!! 16 0–0–0 (16 gxf5 ♕g3+ 17 ♔f1 ♖d2!–+; 17 ♔d1 ♗e3–+) 16 ... ♘g3–+ Barczay – Romanishin, Dortmund 1982.

6 ... bxc6 (49)

An interesting recapture, which is motivated by a desire to play a later ... d5 and contest the centre. Of the two alternatives, 6 ... dxc6 is a solid choice whilst Smagin's 9 b4 may cast some doubt on the viability of the queen recapture:

a) 6 ... dxc6 and now:

a1) 7 ♗d3 ♗e6 8 ♘c3 0-0-0 9 ♕e2 ♗d4 10 ♗d2 ♘e7 11 f4 ♖he8 12 e5 ♕h4+ 13 g3 ♕h3 14 0-0-0 f6 15 exf6 gxf6 16 ♖de1 ♘f7 17 ♕f1 ♕h5 18 f5 ♗e5 ½-½ Smagin - Mainka, Prague 1992.

a2) 7 ♕f4!? ♗e6 8 ♘c3 ♕e7 9 ♗e3 0-0-0 10 ♗e2 ♘f6 11 0-0 ♖he8 12 ♕g3 ♗xe3 13 ♕xe3 ♔b8 14 a3?! (14 ♖ad1 =) 14 ... ♗c8 15 ♗d3 ♘g4 16 ♔g3 (Chaplin - Lane, Fourmies 1992) 16 ... g5, intending to station the knight on e5 ∓.

b) 6 ... ♕xc6 7 ♗d3 ♘f6 8 0-0 0-0 9 b4! (9 ♕f4 b6 = Wade - J. Littlewood, Rhyl 1969) 9 ... ♗d4 10 c3 ♗b6 11 c4! ♗d4 12 ♘c3 a5 (12 ... ♗xc3? 13 ♕xc3 ♘xe4 14 ♕c2!) 13 ♗b2 ♖e8 (13 ... axb4 14 ♘d5 ♕c5 15 e5! ♗xb2 16 ♘xf6+ ♔h8 17 ♕xb2 ♗xf6 18 ♖fe1±) 14

b5 ♕d6 15 ♖ad1 ♕e5 16 h3 c5 17 ♘a4 ♗xb2 (Smagin - Hjartarson, Bundesliga 1991) 18 ♘xb2 intending f4 gives White the superior chances due to his space advantage.

7	♗d3	♘e7
8	0-0	0-0
9	♘c3	

The quiet 9 ♔h1 to facilitate a swift f4 represents an important alternative: 9 ... d5 10 ♘c3 ♗d4 11 exd5 cxd5 12 ♘b5 ♗e5 13 f4 ♗d6 14 ♘xd6 ♕xd6 15 f5 f6 16 ♕f4 ♕xf4 17 ♗xf4 (17 ♖xf4 ♘c6 18 ♗e3= Iv. Markovic - Si. Popov, Yugoslavia 1991) 17 ... ♗xf5 18 ♗xc7 ♗xd3 19 cxd3±.

9	...	♘g6

More logical is 9 ... d5, when 10 ♔h1 transposes to the previous note.

10	♔h1	a5?!

It was not essential to provide a retreat square for the bishop on a7 against ♘a4. In order to meet White's e5-breakthrough Black should play 10 ... d6 (10 ... ♘e5 11 ♗e2 with the idea of f4±) 11 f4 ♗b6 when White has slightly the better chances.

11	f4	d6 (50)
12	e5!	

White plays a well-known trick in such positions based on the knight occupying e4.

12	...	♕h4

After 12 ... dxe5 Black's game would swiftly fall apart: 13 ♘e4 ♕e7 14 f5 ♘f4 15 f6 gxf6 16 g3 ♘d5 (16 ... ♘h5 17 ♕h6 ♗g4 18

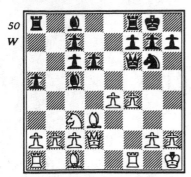

♘g5+-) 17 c4+-.

13	♘e4	♗b6
14	exd6	♗f5
15	♕c3	

White could also call Black's bluff: 15 dxc7 ♗xc7 16 ♕f2! which leaves Black struggling to find compensation for the pawn.

15	...	cxd6
16	♕xc6	♖ab8
17	♗d2	♖fd8 *(51)*

18 ♗e1!

White has adjusted well to the changed circumstances and continues in an energetic manner. More casual moves would allow Black to generate some counterplay: 18 ♗c3 ♘e7 19 ♕a4 (19 ♕c4? d5) 19 ... d5 20 ♘g3 ♗xd3 21 cxd3 d4 22 ♗d2 (22 ♗xa5? ♖a8) 22 ... ♘d5 intending to invade on e3.

18	...	♕e7
19	♗c3	♘h4

Otherwise 20 ♘f6+ gxf6 21 ♗xf5 wrecks the kingside.

20	♖ae1	♕d7
21	♕d5	♕e6

Instead 21 ... ♗e6 would meet with a hostile response: 22 ♕h5 ♘f5 23 ♘f6+ gxf6 24 ♗xf6 ♗d4 25 ♕g5+ ♔f8 26 ♗xf5 ♗xf6 27 ♕xf6 ♗xf5 28 ♕h8 mate.

22	♘f6+!	gxf6
23	♖xe6	fxe6

Black's game is hopeless.

24	♕c6	♔f7
25	♖e1	♗xd3
26	cxd3	f5
27	d4!	1-0

Conclusion

Although 5 ♘xc6 has the advantage of avoiding the theory of 5 ♗e3 or 5 ♘b3 it is not really testing enough. Black should be able to reach equality after 5 ... ♕f6 6 ♕d2 dxc6.

7 Scotch Four Knights

The Scotch Four Knights is a positional approach by which White postpones the confrontation until the middlegame. From White's point of view, the main line is quite easy to follow as his plans will be similar regardless of Black's response. Black should be able to achieve equality but if he plays too passively his position can deteriorate in an almost imperceptible fashion.

**Salgado Allaria – Nunez
Corr 1986–88**

1	e4	e5
2	♘f3	♘c6
3	d4	exd4
4	♘xd4	♘f6
5	♘c3	*(52)*

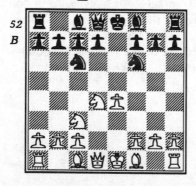

This is the starting point of the Scotch Four Knights.

    5   ...   **♗b4**

Black's alternatives do not really promise anything more than surprise value:

a) 5 ... ♗c5 6 ♗e3 ♗b6 and now:

a1) 7 ♗e2 d6 and:

a11) 8 0–0 0–0 9 ♘xc6 bxc6 10 ♗g5 ♕e7 11 ♔h1 h6 12 ♘h4 g5?! 13 ♗g3 ♘xe4 14 ♘xe4 ♕xe4 15 f4 ♕d4 16 ♗d3 f5 17 fxg5 hxg5 18 ♕h5 ♕f6 19 ♗e1! ♗d4 20 ♗d2 ♗xb2 21 ♖ae1 ♗e5 22 ♖xe5!? dxe5 23 ♗xg5 ♕f7 24 ♕h6 ♗e6? (24 ... ♕e6!) 25 ♖f3 f4 26 ♘f6! 1–0 Klovan – Razuvayev, USSR 1974.

a12) 8 ♕d2 ♘g4 (8 ... 0–0 9 0–0–0 ♖e8 10 f3 ♗d7 11 g4±) 9 ♗xg4 ♗xg4 10 h3 ♗d7 11 0–0–0 0–0 12 ♖he1±.

a2) 7 ♘xc6 bxc6 8 e5 ♗xe3 9 exf6 ♗h6 10 ♕e2+ ♔f8 11 fxg7+ ♗xg7 12 0–0–0 ♕g5+∓ Bikhovsky – Lilienthal, Moscow 1958.

b) After 5 ... ♘xe4?! 6 ♘xe4 ♕e7 play might continue:

b1) 7 ♗e2? ♕xe4 8 ♘b5 ♗b4+ 9 c3 ♗a5 10 0–0 0–0∓ Obuchowsky – Matsukewitsch, USSR 1976.

b2) 7 f3 d5 and now:

b21) 8 ♗f4? dxe4 9 ♘b5 exf3+ 10 ♔f2 ♘e5–+.

b22) 8 ♘xc6 bxc6 9 ♕e2 dxe4 10 ♕xe4 ♕xe4+ 11 fxe4 ♗d6 12 ♗c4 ♔e7=.

b23) 8 ♗b5 ♗d7 9 ♗xc6 bxc6 10 0–0 dxe4 and now:

b231) 11 ♖e1 0–0–0 12 ♖xe4 ♕f6 13 ♕f1 (Handoko – Hecht, Thessaloniki Ol 1984) 13 ... ♗c5 offers equal chances.

b232) 11 fxe4! g6 (11 ... 0–0–0 12 ♕d3!±) 12 ♗e3 ♗g7 13 ♘b3! 0–0? 14 ♗c5+–.

6   ♘xc6

Not to be trusted is 6 ♗g5?! h6 7 ♗h4 g5 8 ♘xc6 bxc6 9 ♗g3 ♘xe4 10 ♕d4 ♗xc3+ 11 bxc3 0–0!∓.

6   ...   bxc6
7   ♗d3   d5
8   e5?!

An unusual continuation which has been featured in a number of correspondence games, but is not often seen in over-the-board tournament play. This might be due to its potentially highly complicated nature (after 8 ... ♘g4 9 ♗f4 d4) or simply because Black has a reasonably comfortable route to simplification (8 ... ♘g4 9 ♗f4 f6). Certainly to be avoided is 8 0–0? ♗xc3 9 bxc3 dxe4 10 ♖e1 0–0 and White remains a pawn down as taking on e4 would lose a piece after the queens are exchanged. The normal continuation, 8 exd5, is considered in the other games

in this chapter.

8   ...   ♘g4
9   ♗f4   d4?! (53)

Black boldly takes up the challenge leading to extremely double-edged play.

a) 9 ... f6! 10 h3 (10 exf6 0–0!) 10 ... ♘xe5 11 ♗xe5 fxe5 12 ♕h5+ ♔f8 13 ♕xe5 ♗d6 (13 ... d4?! 14 0–0–0 dxc3? 15 ♕f4+ and 16 ♕xb4++–; 13 ... ♕e8 14 ♕xe8+ ♔xe8 15 0–0∞) 14 ♕h5 (14 ♕e2! is a suggestion of Gligoric's) 14 ... ♕f6 15 0–0 g6 16 ♕h6+ ♔f7 17 ♘e2 ♗d7 18 c3∓ Davie – Gligoric, Dundee 1967.

b) 9 ... ♗c5 10 0–0 g5?! 11 ♗g3 h5 12 ♗e2! and White is slightly better according to van Scheltinga.

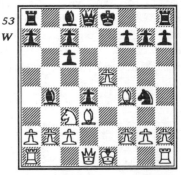

53
W

10   ♕f3!

A swashbuckling idea which sets up a violent attack. It is useless to attempt to save the piece: 10 a3? dxc3 11 axb4 cxb2 12 ♖b1 ♕d4–+.

10   ...   dxc3
11   0–0–0   cxb2+

Black unveils a prepared improvement over the standard 11 ... ♕d5, which leads to remarkable complications: 12 ♘e4 ♛xa2 13 ♗xc6+ ♔f8 14 ♖d8+ ♔e7 15 ♘g5+ f6 16 exf6+ gxf6 17 ♖e1+ ♗e6 18 ♖d7+ ♔f8 19 ♘h6+ ♘xh6 20 ♛xf6+ ♘f7 21 ♖xf7+ ♗xf7 22 ♛xh8+ ♗g8 23 ♛f6+ ♗f7 24 ♛h8+ ½-½ van Scheltinga - Cortlever, Amsterdam 1954. However, White has a significant improvement: 18 ♖xe6+ ♛xe6 19 ♖d7+ ♔f8 20 ♛xg4!! cxb2+ (20 ... ♛xg4 21 ♗h6+ ♔e8 [21 ... ♔g8 22 ♘d5+] 22 ♖g7+ ♔d8 23 ♖xg4 cxb2+ 24 ♔b1 ♖b8 25 ♗g7 ♖e8 26 ♘xf6+ ♗e7 27 ♘xe7+ ♔xe7 28 ♖e4+ ♔f7 29 ♖xe8 ♖xe8 30 ♗xe8+ ♔xe8 31 ♔xb2 winning, according to Velickovic) 21 ♔b1 ♛xg4 22 ♘h6+ ♔e8 23 ♖g7+ ♛d7 24 ♖xd7 ♗e7 25 ♖xc7+ ♔f7 26 ♗xa8 ♖xa8 27 ♘e3 ♔e6 28 ♖xa7 ♖xa7 29 ♘xa7 ♗d6 30 h3 ♗e5 31 ♗c5 f5 32 ♘a3 ♗d4 33 f3 h5 34 ♗xb2 ♗f2 35 g4 1-0 Furmston - Poletayev, Corr 1967.

12 ♔b1   ♘xf2 *(54)*

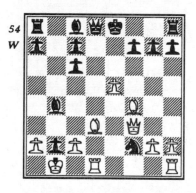

This is the real point of Black's play - by giving back the piece he plans to buy time

to whisk his king to safety. For example: 13 ♛xf2 ♛e7 14 ♘e4 (14 ♖hf1 ♗e6 15 ♘e4 0-0 16 ♗xc6 ♖ad8∓) 14 ... ♘d7 15 ♖hf1 0-0!? 16 ♛g3 with an unclear position.

13 ♗e4!

Having already given up a knight White disdains the capture on f2 in order to sacrifice another exchange! In this way he manages to capture on c6 with his bishop before Black can find time to castle.

13 ...   ♘xd1
14 ♗xc6+   ♗d7
15 ♖xd1   0-0

There is nothing to be gained by giving up the queen as Black's exposed king would make his king indefensible: 15 ... ♖b8 16 ♖xd7 ♛xd7 17 ♛d5 ♖d8 18 e6! (18 ♗xd7+ ♖xd7 19 ♛a8+?! [19 ♛b5!?] 19 ... ♔e7 20 ♛xh8?? ♗c3-+) 18 ... ♛xc6 19 ♛xc6+ ♔e7 20 ♛xc7+ and White is winning according to Morgado and Salgado Allaria.

16 ♖xd7

The rook takes up a powerful position on the seventh rank, where it strengthens the chances of a direct assault on the king. White's initiative would be quickly dissipated in the ending which would arise after 16 ♗xa8 ♛xa8 17 ♛xa8 (17 ♖xd7 ♛xf3 18 gxf3 ♗a3! 19 ♖d3 ♗e7 20 ♔xb2 ♖d8=) 17 ... ♖xa8 18 ♖xd7 ♗a3! 19 ♖d3 ♗e7 20 ♔xb2 ♖d8=.

16 ...   ♛c8
17 ♛g4   ♖d8 *(55)*

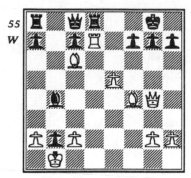

18 e6!

The culmination of White's strategy: the pawn is immune due to mate on g7.

18	...	♖xd7
19	exd7	♕d8
20	♗xa8	♕xa8
21	♗xc7	♘e7
22	♕d4	♘d8
23	♕e5!	1-0

Much more commonly seen than 8 e5 is 8 exd5, which is regarded as the main line of the Scotch Four Knights. In the next game Black follows a long-established plan but runs into a prepared improvement.

Salov – Nunn
Wijk aan Zee 1991

1	e4	e5
2	♘f3	♘c6
3	♘c3	♘f6
4	d4	exd4
5	♘xd4	♗b4

On this occasion the standard position has arisen from a Four Knights move order.

| 6 | ♘xc6 | bxc6 |

7 ♗d3

A sensible measure as the bishop will be well placed after Black plays ... d5. Other paths give Black at least equality:

a) 7 ♕d4 ♕e7 8 f3 and now:

a1) 8 ... c5 9 ♕f2 0-0 10 ♗d2 d5 11 0-0-0= Levenfish.

a2) 8 ... ♗c5 9 ♕d3 ♖b8 10 ♗d2 d5 11 0-0-0∓ Bondarevsky – Smyslov, USSR 1944.

b) 7 ♗d2 0-0 8 ♗d3 d5 9 f3 dxe4 (or 9 ... ♗xc3 10 ♗xc3 dxe4 with an equal game according to Keres) 10 ♘xe4 ♘xe4 11 fxe4 ♗c5= Alekhine – Alexander, Margate 1937.

7	...	d5
8	exd5	cxd5
9	0-0	0-0
10	♗g5	♗e6 (56)

The major alternative, 10 ... c6, is analysed in later games in this chapter.

11 ♘e2 h6

The alternatives are examined in the game Rigo – Zysk.

12 ♗h4 ♗d6

The pin can be blocked although this is not good enough for equality: 12 ... ♘e7 13

♘d4 ♗g4 14 f3 ♗d7 15 ♘f5±
Plater – Drieciotowski, Poland
1957.

13 ♘d4

A quick pawn rush on the
kingside fails to make any
headway: 13 f4?! ♗c5+ 14 ♔h1
♗g4 15 h3 ♗xe2 16 ♕xe2 ♖e8 17
♕f3 ♖e3 18 ♗xf6 ♖xf3 19 ♗xd8
♖xf1+ 20 ♖xf1 ♖xd8∓ Alex-
ander – Smyslov, England –
USSR 1954.

13 ... c5

The bishop can also retreat,
offering a level game: 13 ... ♗d7
14 ♘f5 ♗xf5 15 ♗xf5 ♖b8 16 b3
♗e5 17 ♖b1 ♕d6 18 ♗g3 ♗xg3 19
hxg3 ♖fe8= Rossetto – Bolbo-
chan, Mar del Plata 1956.

14 ♘xe6

This is a major improvement
on the old line: 14 ♘f5 ♗xf5 15
♗xf5 ♗e5 16 c3 ♖b8 17 f4 ♗c7 18
b3 ♕d6 19 ♕f3 ♖fe8 20 ♖ad1
d4∓ Alexander – Kluger, Amsterdam Ol 1954.

14 ... fxe6
15 ♕e2 e5 *(57)*

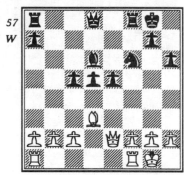

16 ♗g6!

After this move it becomes
clear that White has the better
chances. Now that ... ♖e8 is
ruled out White can set about
undermining the central pawns.
Less clear is 16 c4 e4 17 ♗c2
♕b8!.

16 ... ♖b8

Very often in this variation
Black strikes at b2 with his
rook in this way. However, in
this particular circumstance
Black would have been better
served by 16 ... c4!? 17 b3 cxb3
18 axb3 ♕c7 when White's
advantage is minimal.

17 c4!

The queen now protects b2
while the pawn thrust under-
mines the black pawn centre,
which does not have a firm
base.

17 ... e4
18 ♖ad1 ♕c7
19 ♔h1

With the intention of 19
♗xh2 20 g3 trapping the bishop.

19 ... dxc4
20 ♗xf6

White has a pleasant choice
here: 20 ♗xe4 g5 21 ♗g3 ♗xg3
22 hxg3 ♔g7±.

20 ... ♖xf6
21 ♗xe4 ♗e5
22 ♕xc4+ ♔h8
23 b3 *(58)*

The extra pawn ensures
White the advantage, although
there are still a few obstacles
to overcome before victory can
be secured. White is aided by
the weakness of the light
squares around the black king
which offer him various mating

58
B

possibilities. Black's chances for a draw rest on the exchange of the major pieces to reach an opposite-coloured bishop ending, which would prove very difficult to win.

23	...	♖bf8
24	♕e2	♘d4
25	f3	♕e5
26	g3	♖e8
27	♕d3	

As all the entry squares have been blocked, White can afford to spend some time improving the position of his pieces. The immediate threat is 28 b4 which would severely undermine the bishop on d4.

27	...	♖d6
28	♖d2	h5
29	♖e2	h4
30	gxh4	

There is no immediate reason for White to remove the support of his well-established bishop on e4. Black might conjure up some counterplay after 30 f4?! ♕f6 31 ♕f3 ♖de6.

| 30 | ... | ♖h6 |
| 31 | f4 | |

Now that Black's rook is offside White is able to advance the f-pawn in safety as it would take Black too long to organize his rooks on the e-file.

31	...	♕f6
32	♕f3	♖xh4
33	♘d3	♖f8

Not 33 ... ♖xe2?? 34 ♕a8+.

| 34 | ♕g3 | ♕h6 |

If the pawn is snatched off, Black pays a heavy penalty: 34 ... ♖xf4? 35 ♕h3+ ♕h6 36 ♖xf4 ♖xf4 37 ♕c8++-.

35	♕g6	♖h3
36	♕xh6+	gxh6
37	♘c4	

White still enjoys a significant edge thanks to the extra pawn. Clearly 37 ... ♖e3 38 ♖g2 would leave Black in great difficulties but he makes a serious mistake.

| 37 | ... | ♘e3? |
| 38 | ♔g2 | 1-0 |

In the next game we again see how dangerous White's initiative can be if Black makes even the slightest positional error.

Rigo – Zysk
Budapest 1985

1	e4	e5
2	♘f3	♘c6
3	♘c3	♘f6
4	d4	exd4
5	♘xd4	♗b4
6	♘xc6	bxc6
7	♗d3	d5

This is an automatic choice

in tournament practice to challenge White's hold on the centre. The alternatives are more passive but are fairly sound:

a) 7 ... 0–0 8 0–0 ♖e8 and now:

a1) 9 ♕f3 ♗d6 10 ♘f4 ♗xf4 11 ♕xf4 d6 12 ♖ae1 ♕e7= Radulov – Planinc, Vrsac 1971.

a2) 9 ♗g5 h6 10 ♗h4:

a21) 10 ... g5?! 11 ♗g3 d6 (11 ... ♗xc3 12 bxc3 ♘xe4 13 ♕h5 ♔g7 14 ♗xe4 ♖xe4 15 f4!+−) 12 e5 dxe5 13 ♗xe5 ♘g4 (13 ... ♖xe5 14 ♗h7+!) 14 ♗g3 f5 15 h3 ♘f6 16 f4± Pomar – Ljubojevic, Las Palmas 1974.

a22) 10 ... d6 11 f4 ♗b7 12 ♔h1 (12 ♕f3!?) 12 ... ♗xc3 13 bxc3 c5 (Puc – Planinc, Ljubljana – Portoroz 1973) 14 ♖e1±.

b) 7 ... d6 and now:

b1) 8 0–0 ♘g4 9 ♗e2 ♕h4 10 ♗xg4 ♕xg4∓ Schlechter – Lasker, Nuremberg 1896.

b2) 8 ♗g5 h6 9 ♗h4 ♕e7 10 0–0 0–0 11 f4 ♕e6= Wade – Gereben, Monte Carlo 1967.

8	exd5	cxd5
9	0–0	0–0
10	♗g5	♗e6

It is incorrect for Black to immediately double White's pawns. This, and Black's other moves, are considered elsewhere in this chapter (Lautier – I. Sokolov and Estevez – Rivera).

11 ♘e2

Not as popular is 11 ♕f3 ♗e7 12 ♖ae1 ♖b8 and now:

a) 13 ♖e5? ♖xb2 14 ♘b5 c5 15

♗c1 ♖b4 16 ♗d2 ♖a4 17 ♘c3 ♖a3 18 ♘b5 ♖a6 19 ♘d4 ♖d6 20 ♘f5 ♗xf5 21 ♕xf5 ♘e4 22 ♕f4 ♗f6 23 ♖e1 ♗xe5 24 ♗xe5 ♖b6 25 ♕g4 ♕g5 26 ♕xg5 ♘xg5 27 h4 ♘e6 28 ♖e3 f6 29 ♗g3 ♘d4 0–1 A. Thomas – Lane, Paignton 1981.

b) 13 ♘d1 c5 14 ♗f5 ♖b6∓ Ekstrom – Euwe, Hastings 1945/46.

11 ... ♗d6?! (59)

Black points the bishop towards the kingside, harbouring attacking ambitions, but this is not an accurate choice. We have already discussed 11 ... h6 in the previous game and there are several other playable alternatives:

a) 11 ... ♗e7 12 ♘f4 and now:

a1) 12 ... ♕d6 13 ♖e1 ♖ab8 14 ♕f3! h6 15 ♘xe6 fxe6 16 ♗f4 ♕b6 17 ♕h3± Czerniak – Ed. Lasker, Vienna 1951.

a2) 12 ... ♗g4 13 f3 (13 ♕d2!?) 13 ... ♗c8 and now:

a21) 14 ♗xf6!? ♗xf6 15 ♘xd5 ♗xb2 16 ♖b1 with an unclear position.

a22) 14 ♕e1 h6 15 ♗xh6 gxh6 16 ♕h4 ♔g7 17 ♖fe1 (Bebchuk – Baranov, Rostov 1957) 17 ... ♖e8∓.

b) 11 ... ♗g4 and now:

b1) 12 c3 ♗e7 13 ♕c2 h6 14 ♗e3 ♗d6= Alexander – Smyslov, Hastings 1954/55.

b2) 12 c4 h6 13 ♗h4 dxc4 14 ♗xc4 ♕xd1 15 ♖fxd1 g5 16 ♗g3 ♘e4= Hector – Wiedenkeller, Malmo 1986.

c) 11 ... 罝b8 12 ♘g3 ♗e7 13 b3 h6 14 ♗e3 c5 15 ♘f5 罝e8 16 ♘xe7+ 豐xe7 17 豐d2± Czerniak – Maderna, Mar del Plata 1955.

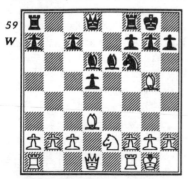

12 ♘d4

This move has a dual function: first, White would like to drop it into c6 and then capture on f6 to double Black's kingside pawns; and second, on d4 the knight is ideally placed to support a general build up of 罝e1, 豐f3 and ♗f5. Also worthy of consideration is long–established 12 f4 c5 (12 ... c6!?) 13 c4 dxc4 14 ♗e4 罝b8 15 ♗xf6 gxf6 16 ♘g3 f5 17 ♗xf5 ♗e7 18 豐g4++– Czerniak – Neikircti, Amsterdam 1954.

12 ... c5?

Black is unaware of the danger and takes immediate steps to oust the knight from its powerful outpost. His idea is based on the sequence 13 ♘c6 豐c7 14 ♗xf6 豐xc6 when White must retreat the bishop leaving Black with a strong central pawn mass. However, the best chance was 12 ... ♗d7 although Black remains worse.

13 ♘c6 豐c7
14 ♗xf6 gxf6 *(60)*

This unpleasant move is necessary here since Black's intended 14 ... 豐xc6 is refuted by 15 ♗xh7+! ♔xh7 16 豐h5+ ♔g8 17 豐g5 g6 18 豐h6 leading to mate. Now the shattered kingside is an open invitation for White to invade and destroy.

15 豐h5 f5
16 豐g5+ ♔h8
17 豐f6+ ♔g8
18 f4!

Even though the white knight is trapped, White leaves it undefended in order to bring his other pieces into the attack. Of course, the pawn cannot be taken 18 ... ♗xf4? 19 ♘e7++–.

18 ... 豐xc6
19 罝f3 罝fe8

The rook makes room for the king to seek sanctuary via f8.

20 豐h6 ♗xf4
21 罝xf4 ♗d7 *(61)*
22 罝g4+! 1-0

Black resigned due to 22 ... fxg4 23 ♗xh7+ ♔h8 24 ♗g6+ ♔g8 25 豐h7+ ♔f8 26 豐xf7 mate.

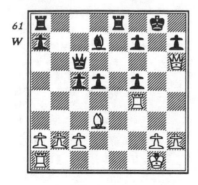

Instead of 11 ♘e2, White can also try 11 ♘b5. Although this idea used to be considered a drawing variation, Jakovic's surprising 14 ♕e1 breathes new life into White's chances, as we shall see.

Jakovic – Ernst
Gausdal 1991

1	e4	e5
2	♘f3	♘c6
3	d4	exd4
4	♘xd4	♘f6
5	♘c3	♗b4
6	♘xc6	bxc6
7	♗d3	d5
8	exd5	cxd5
9	0-0	0-0
10	♗g5	♗e6
11	♘b5	

This is probably the most dynamic possibility. It has a similar theme to 11 ♘e2 as in many cases White will bring the knight to d4. However, White can also go in for complications by a rapid expansion on his queenside.

11	...	c5
12	a3	

This has now become the regular move order in tournament practice. After 12 c3 ♗a5 White can practically force perpetual check but has nothing better:

a) 13 b4 and now:

a1) 13 ... cxb4 14 cxb4 ♗xb4 15 ♗xh7+ ♔xh7 16 ♕b1+ ♔g8 17 ♕xb4 ♖b8 gives Black the better game as the slightly exposed position of the black king is inadequate compensation for the passed pawn, Gabran – Bikov, USSR 1970.

a2) 13 ... a6 14 ♘d6 ♕xd6 16 ♗xf6 ♗c7-+ Janosevic – Nabtanovic, Yugoslavia Ch 1956.

b) 13 ♕a4! ♗b6 14 ♕h4 h6 15 ♗xh6 gxh6 16 ♕xh6 c4 (16 ... ♘e4? 17 ♗xe4 dxe4 18 ♖ae1+-) 17 ♕g5+ ♔h8 18 ♕h4+ ♔g7 ½-½ Ivkov – Gligoric, Buenos Aires 1960.

12	...	♗a5
13	b4	cxb4 *(62)*

The major alternative involves spurning the pawn offer by 13 ... ♗b6. A survey of this variation reveals:

a) 14 bxc5 ♗xc5 and now:

a1) 15 ♕f3 h6 16 ♗xf6 ♕xf6 17 ♕xf6 gxf6 18 c3 ♖fc8 19 ♖fc1 ♖ab8 20 ♔f1 ♗d7= Gheorghiu – Suba, Prague 1985.

a2) 15 c3 h6 16 ♗h4 ♖c8 17 ♘d4 ♗d6 18 ♖e1=.

b) 14 c3 h6 15 ♗h4 ♖b8 16 a4 a5 17 bxc5 ♗xc5 18 ♖e1 and

White has slightly the better game, Garcia - Panno, Mar del Plata 1959.

c) 14 ♕f3?! ♖c8 15 c3= Panno.

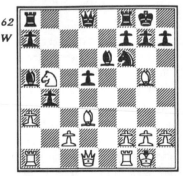

62
W

14 ♕e1!

A startling move which is based on a clever attacking idea. The a-pawn is discarded and can even be captured with a discovered attack. A more routine continuation is 14 axb4 ♗xb4 (14 ... ♘b6 15 ♖a6) and now White has:

a) 15 ♘xa7 h6 16 ♗h4 ♕b6 17 ♖a6 ♕b7 18 ♗xf6 ♖xa7= Barsky - A. Geller, USSR 1960.

b) 15 ♖xa7 ♖xa7 16 ♘xa7 h6 17 ♘c6 ♕d6 18 ♗xf6 ♕xc6 19 ♕f3 ♕c7 (19 ... gxf6? 20 ♕g3+ ♔h8 21 ♕h4 ♔g7 22 ♕xb4+-) 20 ♘d4 ♖c8 21 ♖b1= Salazar - Sanchez-Guisado, Vigo 1985.

14 ... bxa3

This is the critical test of White's idea but perhaps Black should adopt a more circumspect course of action: 14 ... ♘b6 15 axb4 h6 16 ♗h4 ♖e8 17 ♕d2 (17 ♕e5? a6 18 ♘d6 ♗c7 19 ♗xf6 gxf6 20 ♕g3+ ♔h8-+) 17 ... a6 (17 ... ♘e4 18 ♗xd8 ♘xd2

19 ♗xb6 axb6 20 ♘c7! ♖xa1 21 ♖xa1 ♖c8 22 ♖a8+-) 18 ♘c3 ♗c7 19 ♗g3 ♕xg3 20 hxg3 ♕d6 21 ♕f4±.

15 ♗xf6 gxf6

Black is obliged to loosen his kingside pawn barrier in view of 15 ... ♗xe1 (15 ... ♕xf6? 16 ♕xa5) 16 ♗xd8 picking up a piece.

16 ♕e3 ♗b6
17 ♕h6

White is understandably lured by visions of a mating attack but a more positional approach would have been more appropriate, exploiting Black's crippled pawns. For example: 17 ♘d4 ♗xd4 (17 ... ♖e8? 18 ♕h6 ♗xd4 19 ♗xh7+ ♔h8 20 ♖xa3+-) 18 ♕xd4±.

17 ... f5
18 ♖xa3

Now the rook is brought into the attack against Black's beleaguered king. Obviously White is not prepared to settle for a draw: 18 ♘d6 ♕xd6 19 ♗xf5 ♖fd8 20 ♗xh7+ ♔h8 21 ♗g6+ ♔g8 22 ♗h7+ with perpetual check.

18 ... ♔h8?! (63)

Ernst has suggested that Black could have put up much stiffer resistance here with 18 ... f6!?:

a) 19 ♖e1 ♕d7 20 ♗f1 (with the idea of 20 ... ♖xe8 21 ♖g3+ ♔h8 22 ♖xe6!+-) 20 ... ♖f7! when Black can struggle on.

b) 19 g4 ♔h8 29 gxf5 ♗f7 with an unclear position.

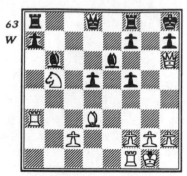

19 ♘d6!   ♗d4!

An essential move to ward off the attack. If instead 19 ... ♖g8? 20 ♗xf5 ♖g7 21 ♖g3! ♕g8 22 ♗xe6 fxe6 23 ♖xg7 ♕xg7 24 ♕xe6+– (White has won too many pawns). The other alternative 19 ... ♕xd6? fails to 20 ♗xf5 with mate looming on h7.

20 ♘xf5

White decides to keep his light-squared bishop in order to maintain attacking chances against the vulnerable h7-square. An advantage is also preserved after 20 ♗xf5 ♗xf5 21 ♘xf5 ♕f6 22 ♕h3 (not 22 ♕h5 ♗c3! 23 ♕f3 d4 with an unclear position) 22 ... ♖ac8 23 ♖d3 ♗b6±.

20 ...   ♕f6
21 ♕h5   ♗c5

Black reacts well to the crisis, avoiding the plausible 21 ... ♗b6 22 ♘h6 ♕g7 23 ♖a4 (intending ♖h4) 23 ... d4 24 ♖e1 with a clear advantage.

22 ♘e3!   h6
23 ♖a5   ♖ac8
24 ♘xd5   ♕g5
25 ♕xg5?!

The technical task in the endgame would have been somewhat easier after 25 ♘f6! ♕xh5 (25 ... ♕xf6 26 ♖xc5) 26 ♘xh5 when White remains a clear pawn up against a structure of three isolated pawns. Now, however, the connected black g- and f-pawns are potentially an asset rather than a hindrance.

25 ...   hxg5
26 ♘f6   ♗d4 *(64)*

27 ♘e4

The game has reached a critical juncture. White must try to consolidate his advantage and utilize the extra pawn. However, Black has good drawing chances due to his pair of bishops and the fragility of White's f2-pawn. Perhaps White should have preferred the more complicated variation: 27 ♘h7!? ♖g8 28 ♖xg5 (28 ♘xg5? ♗c3 29 ♖b5 a6∓) 28 ... ♖xg5 (28 ... f6 29 ♖h5 ♔g7 with a slight edge to White) 29 ♘xg5 a5 30 ♖e1 ♗d5 31 ♖d1 a4 32 ♗e4 ♗xe4 33 ♖xd4 ♖xc2 34 h3 a3?! (34 ... ♗c6 would leave

an unclear position) 35 ♖xe4 a2
36 ♖a4 f6 37 ♘e4 ♖c1+ 38 ♔h2
a1(♕) 39 ♖xa1 ♖xa1 40 ♘xf6 and
White is slightly better according to Ernst.

27	...	f6
28	♖d1	♗b6
29	♖a4	♖c6
30	h3	♗f5
31	♖b1	♗h7
32	♖b5	♖d8
33	g4	

White identifies the f6-pawn
as a possible target and uses
the g-pawn as a restraint.

33	...	♖e6
34	♔g2	♗xe4+
35	♗xe4	♖d2
36	♖f5	♔g7
37	♗d3?!	

It would have been more
accurate to play 37 ♖c4 to
prevent the note to move 38.
Although White still has good
practical chances, Black's
activity makes it difficult for
him and in the end Black manages to hold the draw. The
game concluded as follows:

| 37 | ... | ♖e5 |
| 38 | ♖f3 | ♖d1?! |

38 ... ♖e3!.

39	♖c4	♗c5
40	♖a4	♗b6
41	♖c4	♗c5
42	♖f5!	♖xf5
43	gxf5	♗b6
44	f4	gxf4
45	♖xf4	♖d2+
46	♔f3	♖f2+
47	♔e4	♖xf4+
48	♔xf4	a5
49	♗b5	♔h6
50	c4?	

50 ♔g4!.

50	...	♔h5
51	♔e4	♔h4!
52	♔d5	♔xh3
53	c5	♗c7
54	♔e6	♗e5

½–½

Another natural course for
Black in the main line of the
Scotch Four Knights is 10 ... c6.
In our next main game we look
at the new move 11 ♘a4, which
was introduced to grandmaster
practice by the young French
Grandmaster Joel Lautier.

Lautier – I. Sokolov
Correze (3) 1992

1	e4	e5
2	♘f3	♘c6
3	d4	exd4
4	♘xd4	♘f6
5	♘c3	♗b4
6	♘xc6	bxc6
7	♗d3	d5
8	exd5	cxd5 *(65)*

The standard and more
explored continuation. However, from time to time Black
dabbles with the relatively
neglected 8 ... ♕e7+. The unconventional 9 ♔f1?! cxd5 10
♗g5 c6 11 ♕f3 h6? 12 ♗b5! gave
White a tremendous attack in
Velimirovic – Lukic, Yugoslav
Ch 1962, but 11 ... 0–0 secures
equality. So White should
revert to the usual method of

blocking the check with 9 ♕e2. Play can then continue:

a) 9 ... ♕xe2+ 10 ♔xe2 and now:

a1) 10 ... ♘xc3 11 bxc3 cxd5 12 ♗a3 and White is slightly better according to Keres.

a2) 10 ... ♘xd5 11 ♘e4 f5 12 ♘g5 0–0 13 ♖d1 h6 14 ♘f3 ♗d6 15 ♔f1 ♗d7? 16 ♗c4 and White wins a pawn, Rossolimo – Gligoric, Amsterdam 1950.

a3) 10 ... cxd5 and:

a31) 11 ♘b5 and now:

a311) 11 ... ♔d8 12 ♖d1 c6 (12 ... ♖e8+ 13 ♔f1 c6 14 ♘d4 ♗d7 15 ♗g5± Cortlever – Pfeiffer, Amsterdam Ol 1954) 13 ♘d4 ♔c7 14 c4 ♗d6 15 h3 ♗d7 16 ♔f1 c5 17 ♘c2 d4 18 b4 cxb4 19 ♗b2 ♖ae8 20 ♗xd4 a5 21 ♖e1= Rodriguez – Mikhalchisin, Havana 1982.

a312) 11 ... ♗a5 12 ♗f4 ♔d8 (12 ... c5? 13 ♗c7 ♗xc7 14 ♘xc7+ ♔d8 15 ♘xa8 c4, van der Houette – C. Flear, Brussels 1988, and now 16 ♔d2! cxd3 17 cxd3 intending ♖c1, winning) 13 ♖hd1 ♗d7 14 c4 ♖b8 15 ♖ab1 ♖e8+ 16 ♔f1 a6 17 ♘d4 ♗b6± Chalfen – Muskinowitsch, Moscow 1979.

a32) 11 ♗b5+?! ♗d7 12 ♗xd7+ ♔xd7 13 ♖d1 ♖he8+ 14 ♔f1 ♗xc3 15 bxc3 ♔c6 16 ♗e3 ♘e4 17 ♖d3 ♘d6 18 ♗d4 f6 19 ♖g3 ♖e7 20 ♖e1 ♘e4 21 ♖g1 ♔d6 22 ♖ge3 c5 23 f3 cxd4 24 cxd4 f5 25 fxe4 fxe4 26 ♖a3 ♖c8 27 c3 ♖b7 28 ♔f2 ♖b2+ 29 ♖e2 e3+! 0–1 V. Knox – Wells, British Ch 1991.

b) 9 ... ♘xd5 10 ♕xe7+ ♔xe7 11 a3 and now:

b1) 11 ... ♗xc3+ 12 bxc3 ♖e8 13 ♗d2 ♘f5 14 0–0–0 ♗d3 15 cxd3 with a small edge for White, Braga – Weermals, Dubai 1986.

b2) 11 ... ♗a5 12 b4! and now:

b21) 11 ... ♘xc3+ 12 bxa5 ♘d5 14 0–0± Czerniak – Fenoglio, Argentine Ch 1949.

b22) 12 ... ♗xb4 (12 ... ♗b6 13 ♘e2±) 13 axb4 ♘xc3 14 ♗b2 ♘d5 15 ♗xg7 ♖d8 16 ♗d4 when the formidable pair of bishops gives White the advantage, Czerniak – Rellstab, Reggio Emilia 1951.

c) 9 ... cxd5 10 ♕xe7+ ♔xe7 11 ♗d2! (11 0–0 ♖d8 12 a3 ♗c5= Czerniak – Portisch, Amsterdam 1953) 11 ... c6 12 0–0–0 ♖d8 13 ♘a4 ♗d6 14 ♗e3 ♔f8 15 h3 h6 16 ♖he1± Radulov – Pinter, 1978.

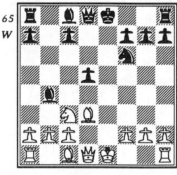

	9	0–0	0–0
	10	♗g5	c6
	11	♘a4	

This move has revitalised White's chances in the Scotch Four Knights. Most commentators do not even consider it because the knight routinely heads for d4 or f4 via e2 in this variation. White's plan is to restrict Black's queenside activity by fixing the c6- and d5-pawns, while at the same time building up his own forces on the kingside. Note that the knight on a4 also defends the vulnerable b2-pawn and nullifies ... ♖b8.

11 ... h6 *(66)*

It is natural for Black to deflect the pin but other continuations should also be considered:

a) 11 ... ♘e7 12 ♖e1 ♗e6 13 c3 ♕c7 14 ♕f3 ♖fe8 15 ♖e3 ♘g4 16 ♗f4 ♕d7 17 ♖e2 c5 18 b3 ♘f6 19 h3 ♗d6 20 ♖ae1 ♕c7 21 ♗g5 ♘d7 22 ♕h5 ♘f8 23 ♗d2 ♕d7 24 f4± Lautier – I. Sokolov, Correze (5) 1992.

b) 11 ... ♗d6 12 ♕f3 ♖e8 13 h3 ♕a5 14 ♗xf6 ♕xa4 15 b3 ♕f4 16 ♕xf4 ♗xf4 17 ♘d4 ♗d6 18 ♖fe1 ♖xe1+ 19 ♖xe1 ♗e6 20 c4 dxc4 21 ♘xc4 ♗xc4 22 bxc4 ♔f8 23 ♖d1 ♖d8 24 ♔f1 ♗e7 25 ♔e2 a6 26 ♖d3= Adams – Piket, Dortmund 1992.

A cautious response. Also possible are:

a) 12 ... ♘d6 13 ♖e1 ♗d7 14 c3 ♖e8 15 ♖xe8+ ♗xe8 16 ♕f3 c5 17 ♘c2 ♖b8 18 ♖e1 ♘xa4 19 ♘xa4 ♖xb2 20 ♕f5 g5 21 ♗xg5 hxg5 22 ♕xg5+ ♔f8 23 g3 ♗e7 24 ♕h6+ ♔g8 25 ♕g5+= Degraeve – Lane, Parthenay 1992.

b) 12 ... ♖e8 13 c4 ♗e6 14 ♖c1 ♖b8 15 cxd5 ♘xd5 16 ♘c4 ♗d6 17 b3 ♗e5 18 ♘xd5 cxd5 19 ♖c5 g5 20 ♗g3 ♕d6 21 ♕c2 ♖e6 22 ♖a5 ♘e4 23 ♖xa7 ♘xg3 24 hxg3 ♗d4 25 ♖a5 ♖be8 26 ♕d3 ♕e5 27 ♘c5 ♖6e7 28 ♕f3 ♕c7 29 b4 ♕c6 30 ♘b3 ♕c4 31 ♕d1 ♗b6 32 ♖xd5 ♖e2 33 ♕d3 ♕xb4? 34 ♖b5 1-0 Lautier – Campos-Moreno, Manila Ol 1992.

13 ♖e1 ♗e6
14 c3

A simple but correct move. The unorthodox knight on the edge of the board combines well with the text to cut short Black's ambitions of pushing the central pawns.

14 ... ♖e8
15 ♗c2 ♖b8
16 ♕d4 a5
17 ♖e3

White calmly increases the pressure by doubling rooks on the e-file, intending a future f4 to provoke concessions from Black.

17 ... ♕c7
18 ♖ae1 c5
19 ♕d3

Although Black has finally been able to mobilize his

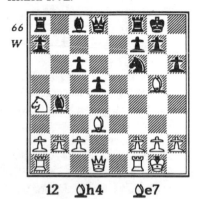

66
W

12 ♗h4 ♗e7

pawns, this merely allows Lautier to tighten his grip. Now Black is forced to take evasive action to prevent infiltration by 20 ♗xf6 ♗xf6 21 ♕h7+.

19 ... g5
20 ♗g3 ♗d6 *(67)*

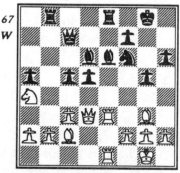

67
W

21 ♖xe6! 1-0

Black resigned in view of 21 ... ♖xe6 22 ♖xe6 fxe6 23 ♗xd6 ♕xd6 24 ♕g6+ ♔f8 25 ♕xf6++-.

Instead of 11 ♘a4, White can also try the more traditional 11 ♕f3 and 11 ♘e2, which are discussed in the following game.

Estevez – Rivera
Sagua la Grande 1988

1	e4	e5
2	♘f3	♘c6
3	d4	exd4
4	♘xd4	♘f6
5	♘c3	♗b4
6	♘xc6	bxc6
7	♗d3	d5
8	exd5	cxd5
9	0-0	0-0
10	♗g5	c6

Less common alternatives are:

a) 10 ... ♗e7 11 ♗xf6 ♗xf6 and now:

a1) 12 ♕h5 and:

a11) 12 ... h6?! 13 ♕xd5 ♕xd5 14 ♘xd5 ♗xb2 15 ♖ab1 ♗e5 16 ♖fe1 ♗d6 17 ♘e7+ and White is slightly better according to Keres.

a12) 12 ... g6 13 ♕xd5 and now:

a121) 13 ... ♕xd5 14 ♘xd5 ♗xb2 15 ♖ab1± Lutikov – Tarve, Parnu 1971.

a122) 13 ... ♗e6! 14 ♕a5 c6 15 ♕c5 ♕b6 16 ♘a4 ♕xc5 17 ♘xc5 ♗xb2= Hort – Short, Dubai Ol 1986.

a2) 12 ♘xd5 ♗xb2 13 ♖b1 and now:

a21) 13 ... ♗a3? 14 ♕f3 c6 15 ♘f4 ♕c7 16 ♗xh7+ ♔xh7 17 ♕xa3± Donner – Dunkelblum, Munich 1954.

a22) 13 ... ♗e5? 14 ♗xh7+ ♔xh7 15 ♕h5+ ♔g8 16 ♕xe5+-.

a23) 13 ... ♗f6! 14 ♕h5 h6 15 ♗e4 c6 16 ♘b4 ♗e6 17 ♘xc6 ♕c7±.

Instead of 11 ♗xf6, perhaps best is 11 ♕f3 which will transpose to the main lines after 11 ... c6 or 11 ... ♗e6.

b) The other option for Black is to eliminate the c3–knight but this has the drawback of leaving White with a pair of bishops on an open board, e.g. 10 ... ♗xc3 11 bxc3 h6 12 ♗h4 (12 ♗e3 ♘g4 13 ♗c5 ♖e8) 12 ... ♕d6 13 c4! (13 ♕f3 ♗g4 14 ♕g3 ♕xg3 15

♗xg3 ½-½ Hort – Vasyukov, Moscow 1962) and now:

b1) 13 ... dxc4 14 ♘xc4 ♕f4 15 ♗xf6 ♕xf616 ♖b1 ½-½ Trajkovic – Vasyukov, Belgrade 1961.

b2) 13 ... ♘a6 (13 ... d4 14 ♕f3!) 14 cxd5 ♘xd3 15 ♗xf6 ♕xd5 16 ♗xg7 ♔xg7 17 cxd3+– (the exposed black king is a handicap).

11 ♕f3 *(68)*

A major alternative is 11 ♘e2, which gives Black several alternatives:

a) 11 ... ♗g4 12 c3 ♗d6 13 ♕c2 h6 14 ♗h4 ♗d7 15 ♗h7+ ♔h8 16 ♗f5 ♗xf5 17 ♕xf5 ♕c8 18 ♕xc8 ♖axc8 19 ♗xf6 gxf6 20 ♘d4 ♖fe8 21 ♖fe1 ♖e5 22 ♔f1 a5 23 g3 a4 24 f4 ♖xe1+ 25 ♖xe1 h5 26 ♘f5± Christiansen – Gelfand, Munich 1992.

b) 11 ... h6 12 ♗h4 and now:

b1) 12 ... ♗d6 13 ♘d4 c5 14 ♘f5 ♗e5 (14 ... ♗xf5 15 ♗xf5 ♖b8= Lutz – Yusupov, Munich 1992) 15 c3 ♖e8 16 ♖e1 ♗xf5 17 ♗xf5 ♕d6 18 ♗g3 ♗xg3 19 hxg3 ♖xe1+ 20 ♕xe1 ♖e8 21 ♕d1 ½-½ Ljubojevic – Nikolic, Wijk aan Zee 1988.

b2) 12 ... c5 13 c3 ♗a5 14 ♖e1 ♖b8 15 ♖b1 ♗b7 16 ♘g3! g5 17 ♘f5 gxh4 18 ♕d2 ♗c8 19 ♕xh6 ♗xf5 20 ♗xf5 d4 21 ♕g5+ ♔h8 22 ♕xh4+ ♔g7 23 ♕g5+ ♔h8 24 ♖e4! 1-0 Afek – Jacobs, Southampton 1986.

11 ... ♗e7

The bishop normally retreats at this stage to lend support to the c- and d-pawns. An inde-

pendent line is 11 ... h6!? 12 ♗xf6 ♕xf6 13 ♕xf6 gxf6 14 ♘e2 ♗d6 and now:

a) 15 ♘d4 c5 16 ♘b5 ♗e5 17 f4 ♗xb2 18 ♖ab1 a6 19 ♘c7 ♖b8 20 ♘xd5 ♗e6 21 c4 ♗xf5 22 cxd5 ♖b5= Parsonage – Harks, Adelaide 1986/87.

b) 15 ♘g3 ♗e5 16 c3 ♖b8 17 f4 ♗c7 18 b3 ♖e8 19 ♖ae1 ♖xe1 20 ♖xe1 ♔f8 21 ♘h5 ♗d8 22 ♔f2 a5= Sveshnikov – Yusadin, USSR 1986.

12 h3 *(69)*

This is slightly unusual; previously 12 ♖ae1 was more often seen:

a) 12 ... h6!? 13 ♗xh6 gxh6 14 ♕e3 and now:

a1) 14 ... ♗d6? 15 ♕xh6 ♗d7 16 f4 ♗c5+ 17 ♔h1 ♖e8 18 ♖xe8+ ♗xe8 19 ♖f3 ♘g4 20 ♖g3 f6 21 ♖xg4+ ♔f7 22 ♖g7+ ♔e6 23 f5+ ♔e5 24 g3 1-0 van Houtte – El Haddahoui, Brussels 1988.

a2) 14 ... ♗e6 15 ♕xh6 ♗d6 16 ♕g5+ ♔h8 17 f4 ♖e8 18 ♖f3 ♘g8 19 ♕h5+ ♔g7 20 ♖g3+ ♔f8 21 ♖xg8+ ♔xg8 22 ♕h7+ ♔f8 23 ♕h6+ ♔g8 24 ♗h7+ ♔h8 25 ♗f5+ ♔g8 26 ♕h7+ ♔f8 27 ♕h8+

♔e7 28 ♖xe6+! Rublevsky – Novik, Sochi 1990.

a3) 14 ... ♖e8 15 ♕xh6 ♕c7 16 ♖e3 ♗g4 17 h3 d4 18 ♖g3 ♕e5 19 f4+– Miyasaka – Tarazi, Siegen Ol 1970.

a4) 14 ... d4! 15 ♕xh6 ♕d6 16 ♕g5+ (16 f4? ♘e4!) 16 ... ♔h8 17 ♖xe7 ♕xe7 18 ♘e4?! (18 ♕h6+=) 18 ... ♘g8! (the correct defence, suggested by Euwe) 19 ♕h5+ ♔g7 20 ♘f6! (20 f4? f5! 21 ♖f3 ♘h6 22 ♖h3 ♘g4–+) 20 ... ♔xf6 21 ♕h4+ ♔e6 22 ♖e1+ ♔d7 23 ♖xe7+ ♘xe7 24 ♕xd4+=.

b) 12 ... ♖e8 13 ♘e2 ♘g4? (13 ... h6!?) 14 ♗f4 ♗f6 15 ♘g3 ♗d7 16 h3 ♘e5 17 ♗xe5 ♗xe5 18 ♗xh7++– Condie – Thomas, Oakham 1986.

c) 12 ... ♗e6 13 ♘e2 c5 14 ♗f5 ♕d7 15 ♗xe6 fxe6 16 ♘f4 ♘e4= Bikov – Lilienthal, USSR 1962.

d) 12 ... ♖b8 13 ♘d1 (13 b3?! ♗b4) 13 ... ♖e8 14 h3 h6 15 ♗h4 ♗e6 16 b3 ♖b4= Singer – Samisch, Rogaska Slatina 1929.

12 ... ♗e6!?
A more cautious continuation is 12 ... ♖e8 13 ♖fe1 ♗e6 14 ♘e2± Radulov – M. Kovacs,

Decin 1976.

13 ♘e2
White continues in accepted fashion by preparing ♘d4 and ♖fe1 to undermine the bishop on e6.

13 ... ♘d7
14 ♗xe7 ♕xe7
Black tries to ease the tension with an exchange of pieces.

15 ♖fe1
Another option is 15 ♘f4 ♖ab8 16 ♖fe1 ♕f6 17 b3 ♖b4 18 ♘xe6 fxe6 19 ♕e3 e5 20 ♕xa7 ♖f7 21 f3 ♖f4 22 ♕e3 ♕g5 23 ♔h2 ♕h5 24 ♕e2 ♕h6 25 ♖f1 ♕d6 26 ♔h1 with an unclear position, Popov – Orlov, Leningrad 1991.

15 ... ♘c5
16 ♘d4 ♕d6
17 ♗f5!
White snatches the chance to increase the pressure on e6. If the bishop is taken then a knight on f5 will be more useful in an attack focused on g7.

17 ... g6 (70)

18 b4!

At a stroke Black's game collapses. The threat to the bishop on f5 is ignored in favour of a counterstroke against the black knight.

18 ...   ♘e4

This is the best chance for Black; White can look forward to a straightforward victory after 18 ... ♗xf5 (18 ... gxf5 19 bxc5 ♕xc5 20 ♕g3+ ♔h8 21 ♕e5+ ♔g8 22 ♖e3+−) 19 ♘xf5 gxf5 20 bxc5 ♕xc5 21 ♕g3+ ♔h8 22 ♕e5+ f6 (22 ... ♔g8 23 ♖e3+−) 23 ♕xf5 intending 24 ♖e6 and 25 ♖ae1+−.

19 ♗xe4   dxe4
20 ♕f6

The most accurate continuation, prohibiting any chance of counterplay as in the variation 20 ♕xe4 ♗d5!, when Black's control of the a8-h1 diagonal offers some compensation for the pawn.

20 ...   ♕d5
21 c4!   ♕d7

This is abject retreat but if 21 ... ♕xc4? 22 ♖ec1 ♕d3 23 ♘xc6 ♖fe8 24 ♘e7+ ♔f8 25 ♖c7 and mate on h8 is inevitable.

22 ♖xe4   ♖ac8
23 ♖ae1   a5
24 a3   axb4
25 axb4   ♖b8

Black puts up a stubborn

resistance despite the pawn deficit and the dominating central presence of the white pieces.

26 b5   cxb5
27 cxb5   ♕d8
28 ♖xe6!   fxe6
29 ♕xe6+   ♔h8
30 ♘c6   ♕b6
31 ♕e5+

It is also perfectly acceptable to enter an ending a clear two pawns up since 31 ♘xb8! ♕xf2+ 32 ♔h1 ♖xb8 33 ♕e5+ wins.

31 ...   ♔g8
32 ♘e7+   ♔f7
33 ♘d5   ♕d8
34 ♘c7   ♖b6
35 ♘e6   ♕f6
36 ♕xf6+   1-0

Conclusion

Recent evidence suggests that the Scotch Four Knights is more than a drawing weapon; it can also be used as a good practical means of forcing Black to play accurate positional moves in order to achieve roughly equal chances. In particular, the new ideas of Salov's and Lautier's prove that even at the highest level White can win with the Scotch Four Knights.

8 Mieses Variation: 8 ... ♘b6

Although the Scotch Four Knights is clearly nothing like as innocuous as its reputation, modern grandmaster practice has in fact concentrated on an alternative variation for White, 5 ♘xc6 bxc6 6 e5. This was successfully introduced to top-level practice by Mieses, who played it at the 1895 Hastings tournament and elsewhere, although Botterill and Harding doubt whether it was actually his 'invention'.

With 6 e5 White aims to establish a space advantage and rapid mobilization of his pieces. Black's problem piece is his queen's bishop, which is often blocked out of the game on a6 by a white pawn on c4. It is difficult for Black to organize the freeing move ... d5, so usually his counterchances rest on the vulnerability of the advanced white e-pawn. If this pawn is supported by f4 this leaves numerous holes behind the extended pawn which Black may well be able to exploit.

The main line of the Mieses Variation runs 6 ... ♕e7 7 ♕e2 ♘d5 8 c4 when Black has a choice between two main continuations, 8 ... ♘b6 and 8 ... ♗a6. In this chapter we shall discuss the former of these which appears to offer White good chances of an advantage, as evidenced by two wins by the World Champion.

Kasparov – Karpov
World Championship
Lyon (16) 1990

1	e4	e5
2	♘f3	♘c6
3	d4	exd4
4	♘xd4	♘f6
5	♘xc6	bxc6
6	e5 *(71)*	

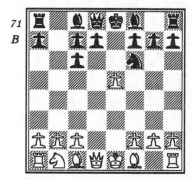

This is the characteristic move of the Mieses Variation.

6	...	♕e7

7	♕e2	♘d5
8	c4	♘b6
9	♘d2	♕e6

Black's alternatives at this juncture are analysed in the illustrative game Shirov – Agdestein.

10 b3 a5 *(72)*

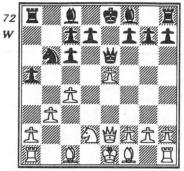

72
W

A natural response, planning to establish a bishop on b4 and reserving the right to undermine White's queenside with ... a4. However, in itself this move does nothing to assist Black's retarded piece development. The alternatives, 10 ... ♗b4 and 10 ... ♗e7, are analysed in the illustrative game Kasparov – Piket.

11 ♗b2 ♗b4

This is rather slow: a more consistent approach is 11 ... a4 although White still has the better game. Play might continue 12 ♕e3 ♗b4 13 ♗d3 and now:

a) 13 axb3 14 axb3 ♖xa1+ 15 ♗xa1 0-0 16 0-0 and White's space advantage can be consolidated after ♘f3.

b) 13 ... d6 14 0-0-0 dxe5 15 ♕xe5 when the ending is good for White.

c) 13 ... d5 14 0-0 (with the idea of ♘f3) 14 ... ♗xd2 15 ♕xd2 dxc4 16 bxc4 ♘xc4 17 ♗xc4 ♕xc4 18 ♗a3 when the black king is stuck in the middle of the board.

12 a3 ♗xd2+
13 ♕xd2 d5?!

Black's original intention was to relieve the pressure immediately by trading off one of White's bishops. However, in that case White is able to undertake a dangerous attack: 13 ... a4 14 c5 ♘d5 15 b4 ♗a6 (15 ... f5 16 ♗c4! ♗a6 17 ♗a2±; 15 ... 0-0!?) 16 ♗xa6 ♖xa6 17 0-0 intending f4. However, the game continuation is unsatisfactory for Black; he should have tried 13 ... 0-0!? 14 0-0-0 when the position would still be double-edged.

14 cxd5 cxd5
15 ♖c1 0-0

Black takes the best practical course, hoping to exploit White's undeveloped kingside in return for a pawn. The alternatives were no better:

a) 15 ... c6 16 ♗d3 ♗b7 (16 ... 0-0 17 ♕c2) 17 0-0 when the prospect of f4 presents grave difficulties for Black.

b) 15 ... a4? 16 ♖xc7 axb3 17 ♗b5+ ♗d7 18 ♕b4+–.

c) 15 ... ♖a7 16 a4±.

16 ♖xc7 ♕g6

A more provocative try was 16 ... d4?!, but Kasparov casts

doubt on this idea in his analysis: 17 ♕xd4 ♕xb3 18 ♗e2 ♗a6 (18 ... ♗e6 19 ♗d1±) 19 e6! f6 20 ♕g4 g6 21 ♕h4 h5 22 ♗xf6+−. White's rook on the seventh is too powerful an influence for Black to ignore.

17 f3   ♗f5 *(73)*

73
W

18 g4!

A bold way to contest Black's command of the b1-h7 diagonal, which would otherwise enable Black to infiltrate with ... ♖c2 after an exchange of rooks on c8. Although the advance on the kingside weakens the pawn structure, White must break up the co-ordination of Black's pieces. Of course not 18 ... ♗xg4? 19 ♖g1 ♕b1+ 20 ♖c1+−.

18 ...   ♗b1
19 ♗b5   ♖ac8
20 ♖xc8   ♖xc8
21 0-0   h5
22 h3?!

The opening phase has been successful for White and he now enjoys a clear advantage, based on his extra pawn, two active bishops and the probab-

ility of creating a passed pawn on the queenside. The test is a calm approach with the long-term plan of concentrating his pieces on a kingside attack. However, Kasparov himself pointed out a quicker way of ending the game: 22 ♕d4! hxg4 23 ♕xg4 ♗f5 (23 ... ♕xg4+ 24 fxg4 ♗e4 25 ♖c1+−) 24 ♕xg6 fxg6 25 ♖c1 with a clear advantage.

22 ...   hxg4
23 hxg4   ♗c2

Black cannot make any impression even with an invasion of the second rank: 23 ... ♖c2?! 24 ♕d4 ♕h6 25 ♖f2 ♕h3 (25 ... ♕h4 26 ♔g2+−) 26 ♘f1! ♕g3+ 27 ♘g2+−.

24 ♕d4   ♕e6

Out of the question is 24 ... ♗xb3? 25 e6!+−.

25 ♖f2   ♖c7

The pawn is poisoned: 25 ... ♗xb3? 26 ♗d3 g6 27 ♕f4 ♘c4 (27 ... ♗c4 28 ♖h2 ♗xd3 29 ♕h6+−) 28 ♗d4 intending ♖h2+.

26 ♖h2   ♘d7!
27 b4

At last White mobilizes his extra pawn but Black is well placed to block it. Another enterprising idea is 27 a4!? leaving a3 free for the bishop and supporting the other bishop on b5. For example: 27 ... ♘f8 (27 ... ♗xb3? 28 ♕d3+−; 27 ... ♕b6? 28 ♗xd7 ♕xd4+ 29 ♗xd4 ♖xd7 30 ♖xc2+−) 28 ♗a3 ♗xb3 (28 ... ♘g6 29 ♗d6 ♖c8 30 ♗a6 ♖c6 31 ♕a7+−) 29 ♗xf8

♖c1+ 30 ♔g2 ♖c2+ 31 ♔g3 ♖xh2 32 ♗xg7+–.

27	...	**axb4**
28	**axb4**	**♘f8**
29	**♗f1?!**	

In a period of mutual time-trouble White plays a slight inaccuracy. The f-pawn could have been advanced after 29 ♗e2.

29	...	**♗b3**
30	**♗d3**	**♗c4**
31	**♗f5**	**♕e7**
32	**♕d2**	**♖c6!**

This clever defensive ploy cuts out White's ambitions of a mate on the h-file. An immediate attempt to make use of the open a-file would be a mistake: 32 ... ♖a7? 33 ♖h3 ♖a2 34 ♕h2 ♕a7+ 35 ♔h1 ♖a1+ 36 ♗xa1 ♕xa1+ 37 ♕g1+–.

33 ♗d4

Now that Black's rook can switch to h6 the plan of doubling on the h-file is ineffective as Black can counter-attack with his queen: 33 ♖h3?! ♕a7+ 34 ♕f2 ♕a2 35 ♗d4 ♕a3 which is unclear according to Kasparov.

33	...	**♖a6**
34	**♗b1**	**♖a3**
35	**♖h3**	**♖b3**
36	**♗c2**	**♕xb4**

Black has little choice but to give up the exchange since if the rook captures on b4 Black suffers a complete disaster: 36 ... ♖xb4? 37 ♕h2 ♘g6 38 ♖h8+! ♘xh8 39 ♕h7+ ♔f8 40 ♕xh8 mate.

37	**♕f2**	**♘g6**
38	**e6?**	

A more sober choice was the simple 38 ♗xb3 ♕xb3 39 ♕e3 preventing Black's counterplay after the text:

38	...	**♖b1+**
39	**♗xb1**	**♕xb1+**
40	**♔h2**	**fxe6** (74)

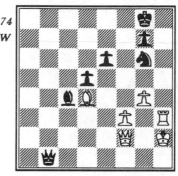

74
W

41 ♕b2!

Kasparov forces a queen swap due to the threat against g7. The technical part of the game is very difficult for White as he is unable to create a passed pawn.

41	...	**♕xb2+**
42	**♗xb2**	**♘f4**
43	**♖h4**	**♘d3**
44	**♗c3**	**e5**

This is necessary since White would otherwise have greater freedom of movement after ♔g3 and f4.

45	**♔g3**	**d4**
46	**♗d2**	**♗d5**
47	**♖h5**	**♔f7**
48	**♗a5**	**♔e6**
49	**♖h8**	

It is less accurate to attack the e5-pawn: 49 ♗c7?! ♔f6 50

♖f5+ ♚e6 51 ♖f8 ♚d7 and White has made no progress. The rest of the game shows White accumulating small advantages by restricting the mobility of the black pieces. It concluded as follows: 49 ... ♞b2 50 ♖e8+ ♚d6 51 ♗b4+ ♚c6 52 ♖c8+ ♚d7 (52 ... ♚b5 53 ♗d6+-) 53 ♖c5 ♚e6 54 ♖c7 g6 55 ♖e7+ ♚f6 56 ♖d7 ♗a2 57 ♖a7 ♗c4 58 ♗a5 ♗d3 59 f4 exf4+ (59 ... e4? 60 ♗b6+-) 60 ♚xf4 ♗c2 61 ♖a6+ ♚f7 62 ♚e5 ♞d3+ 63 ♚xd4 ♞f2 64 g5 ♗f5 65 ♗d2 ♚e7 66 ♚d5 ♞e4 67 ♖a7+ ♚e8 68 ♗e3 ♞c3+ 69 ♚e5 ♚d8 70 ♗b6+ ♚e8 71 ♖c7 ♞e4 72 ♗e3 ♞g3 73 ♗f4 ♞h5 74 ♖a7 ♚f8 75 ♚h2 ♞g7 76 ♗g1 ♞h5 77 ♗c5+ ♚g8 78 ♚d6 ♚f8! 79 ♗d4 ♗g4 80 ♗e5 ♗f5 81 ♖h7 ♚g8 82 ♖c7 ♚f8 83 ♚c6 ♚g8 84 ♖e7 ♚f8 85 ♗d6 ♚g8 86 ♖e8+ ♚f7 87 ♖e7+ ♚g8 88 ♗e5 ♚f8 89 ♖a7 ♗g4 90 ♚d6 ♗h3 91 ♖a3 ♗g4 92 ♖e3 ♗f5 93 ♚c7 ♚f7 94 ♚d8 ♗g4 95 ♗b2 ♗e6 96 ♗c3 ♗f5 97 ♖e7+ ♚f8 98 ♗e5 ♗d3 99 ♖a7 ♗e4 100 ♖c7 ♗b1 101 ♗d6+ ♚g8 102 ♚e7 1-0.

In the next game, Kasparov faced 10 ... ♗b4. The ensuing ending is a good example of how to exploit the doubled c-pawns.

Kasparov – Piket
Dortmund 1992

1	e4	e5
2	♞f3	♞c6
3	d4	exd4
4	♞xd4	♞f6
5	♞xc6	bxc6
6	e5	♕e7
7	♕e2	♞d5
8	c4	♞b6
9	♞d2	

White's other moves are not dangerous for Black:

a) 9 ♞c3 and:

a1) 9 ... ♕e6!? and:

a11) 10 b3 ♗b4 11 ♗b2 0-0 12 0-0-0 ♖e8 13 ♕c2 ♕xe5 14 ♞d5 (14 ♗d3!?) ♗a3! 15 ♗xa3 cxd5 16 c5 ♕a1+ 17 ♚d2 ♕d4+ 18 ♚c1 ♕a1+ ½-½ Botterill – Corden, Birmingham 1975.

a12) 10 ♕e4 ♗b4 (10 ... ♗a6!? 11 b3 ♗b4 12 ♗d2 ♗xc3 13 ♗xc3 d5 14 ♕h4 dxc4 15 ♗e2 0-0 16 0-0 ♞d5 17 ♗xc4 ♗xc4 18 ♕xc4 with an edge) 11 ♗d2 0-0 12 ♗d3 f5 13 exf6 ♖xf6 14 0-0-0 ♕xe4 15 ♞xe4 ♗xd2+ 16 ♖xd2± Oll – Rozhdestvensky, Parnu 1982.

a2) 9 ... ♗a6 10 b3 0-0-0 11 ♗b2 g6 12 0-0-0 ♗g7 13 f4 ♖he8 14 ♕f2 ♗b7 15 c5± A. Osborne – Wilcox, Paignton 1987.

b) After 9 b3 g6 (9 ... a5! is met by 10 ♗a3 rather than 10 a4 ♕b4+! 11 ♞d2 ♕c3 12 ♖b1 ♗b4) White has played:

b1) 10 ♗b2 ♗g7 11 ♞d2 0-0 12 0-0-0 d5 with an unclear position, Zhuravlev – Christiansen, Corr 1983.

b2) 10 a4 a5 11 ♗a3 c5 12 ♞c3 ♗g7 13 f4 f6? 14 ♗xc5!± ♕xc5 15 exf6+ ♚f7 16 fxg7 ♚xg7 17 0-0-0 ♗b7 18 ♕e5+ ♕xe5 19 fxe5 ♖ad8 20 ♞b5 ♖he8 21 ♗d3

♖xe5 22 ♖he1 ♖de8 23 ♖xe5 ♖xe5 24 g3 c5 25 ♔d2 ½–½ van der Wiel – Piket, Dutch Ch 1992.

c) 9 ♗f4?! ♕b4+! 10 ♔d1 (10 ♘c3 ♗a6; 10 ♕d2 ♘xc4 wins a pawn) 10 ... ♗a6 11 b3 0-0-0 and White is in great difficulties, Jouser – Kiprov, Corr 1983.

9 ... ♕e6
10 b3 ♗b4 *(75)*

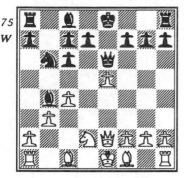

This modern method is regarded as the most positive for Black. However, the older system 10 ... ♗e7 11 ♗b2 0-0 preparing ... d5 is also sound:

a) 12 ♕e4 d5 13 exd6 cxd6 14 ♗d3 d5 (better is 14 ... a5! 15 0-0 ♕xe4 16 ♗xe4 d5 17 cxd5 cxd5 18 ♗d3 a4 with equal chances according to Gligoric) 15 cxd5 cxd5 16 ♕xe6 fxe6 17 0-0 ½–½ Bednarsky – Gligoric, Havana 1967.

b) 12 ♕e3!? d5 13 ♗d3 (13 ♗e2!? ♗b4 14 ♗c3!?) 13 ... ♗b4 14 0-0! ♗xd2 15 ♕xd2 dxc4 16 ♗c2 ♗a6 17 ♖fd1 cxb3 18 axb3 with an unclear position according to Hjartarson, Steingrimsson – Sigfusson, Icelandic Ch 1991.

c) 12 0-0-0 d5! 13 exd6 cxd6

14 ♕f3 (14 ♕xe6 ♗xe6 15 ♘d3=) 14 ... d5 15 ♘d3 ♕h6 16 ♔b1 ♗g5 17 ♘c3 ♖b8 18 ♔a1 f5 19 ♖he1 ♘f6 20 ♘c2 f4 21 ♘e5 ♗xe5+ 22 ♖xe5 ♕f6 23 ♕h5 h6 24 ♔b1 ♗g4!-+ Thorhallsson – Hjartarson, Icelandic Ch 1991.

11 ♗b2 0-0
12 0-0-0

White must concentrate on rapid development before he undertakes anything himself. Black met the sluggish 12 a3?! in an energetic manner in Nijboer – Winants, Wijk aan Zee 1992: 12 ... ♗xd2+ 13 ♕xd2 f6! 14 c5 ♘d5 15 0-0-0 fxe5 16 ♗c4 d6 17 g3 ♖f3 18 cxd6 cxd6 19 ♕a5 ♗b7 20 ♖d2 ♔h8 21 ♗b1 a6 22 ♖c1 ♖af8 23 ♔a1 h6 24 h4 ♕g6 25 h5 ♕f6 26 ♗xd5 cxd5 27 ♕b6 ♗a8 28 ♖c7 d4 29 ♖d7 ♕g5 30 ♗c1 ♖xf2! 31 ♕xd6 ♖f1 32 ♔a2 ♖c8 33 ♖d1 ♖xd1 0-1.

12 ... d5
13 exd6 ♕xd6
14 ♘f3

White does not allow ... ♘f5 after which his king would begin to look vulnerable.

14 ... ♕h6+
15 ♕e3 ♕xe3+
16 fxe3 ♖e8 *(76)*

A dynamic endgame (or middlegame without queens!) has arisen. The e-pawn is an obvious target and ... a5-a4 to open the a-file would also be desirable for Black. However, White has the long-term plan of attacking the weak c-pawns, and in the meantime can use his space advantage to restrict the opponent's pieces.

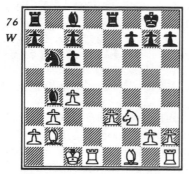

17 e4! ♘d7

The weakness of the back rank makes the pawn taboo.

18 e5 a5
19 ♗d3 ♘c5
20 ♗c2 a4
21 ♘d4

In the space of five moves Kasparov has secured a powerful initiative. The e-pawn has been transformed from a potential weakness to a strength and pressure is already being applied to the c-pawns.

21 ... axb3
22 axb3 ♖a6
23 h3

A sly move to prevent the manoeuvre ... ♗g4–h5–g6 which would allow Black to exchange his most ineffectual piece. However, Piket prefers 21 ♖hf1 ♗g4 22 ♘f3±.

23 ... ♘e6
24 ♖hf1 ♘xd4
25 ♖xd4 g6

Black is understandably frustrated by the problems associated with his back rank and aims to rectify the situation. However, the pair of bishops on b2 and c2 ensure that the black king does not find a safe haven.

26 ♗e4 ♗e6
27 ♔c2 ♗e7 (77)

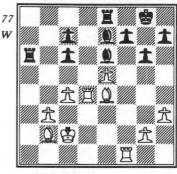

28 ♖a1

A systematic campaign is being waged against the doubled c-pawns. Now that their main defender is taken away, the other rook is obliged to take up a passive role since ... c5 would not alleviate Black's problems.

28 ... ♖xa1
29 ♗xa1 ♖a8
30 ♗b2 ♖a2
31 c5

A far-sighted idea to firmly blockade the black c-pawns, since 31 ... ♗xc5 would allow White to create a passed a-pawn after 32 ♖a4, e.g. 32 ... ♖xa4 33 bxa4 ♗d5 34 ♗f3 ♗b6 35 ♗c3 ♗xf3 36 gxf3 c5 37 a5 ♗a7 38 ♔d3 followed by 39 ♔c4 and ♘d2–e3, winning for White.

31 ... ♖a5

32	b4	♖a6
33	♗c3	f6
34	♖d1	fxe5
35	♖a1	♖xa1
36	♗xa1	♘f6

Not very enticing is 36 ... ♗d7 37 ♗xe5 ♘d8 38 ♔b3 intending a decisive invasion via a4-a5-a6-b7. However, in time-trouble, Black fails to spot a chance to equalize: 36 ... ♘f5! 37 ♗xf5 gxf5 38 ♗xe5 ♘d8=.

37	♗xc6	♘f5+
38	♔b3	♔f7
39	b5	♔e7
40	♔c4	♘e6+
	1-0	

Black lost on time, but after 41 ♘d5 his position would be hopeless in any case.

In the Mieses Variation there is still great scope for innovation. In the following game White meets 9 ... a5!? (instead of 9 ... ♕e6) by the remarkable 10 h4.

Shirov – Agdestein
Oslo 1992

1	e4	e5
2	♘f3	♘c6
3	d4	exd4
4	♘xd4	♘f6
5	♘xc6	bxc6
6	e5	♕e7
7	♕e2	♘d5
8	c4	

Even at this early stage White can try 8 h4!? although this looks premature after 8 ...

f6!:

a) 8 ... d6 9 c4 ♘b6 10 exd6 cxd6 (van der Wiel – van der Sterren, Budel 1987) 11 ♘e3±.

b) 8 ... a5 9 c4 ♘b6 10 ♘c3 ♕e6 11 ♗d2 a4 12 ♕e4 ♗a6 13 b3 d5 14 exd6 cxd6 15 ♘e3= van der Wiel – Wedberg, Stockholm 1987.

c) 8 ... f6! 9 c4 ♗a6 10 ♖h3 fxe5 11 ♖a3 ♘b4 12 ♘c3 ♕xh4 13 g3 ♕d4 14 ♖xa6 ♘xa6 15 ♗f4 (van der Wiel – Timman, Netherlands 1987) 15 ... ♕c5!∓.

8	...	♘b6
9	♘d2	a5

Black immediately advances his a-pawn to meet White's intended 10 b3 with ... a4, disrupting his pawn structure. Also worthy of consideration is the fianchetto: 9 ... ♗b7 10 b3 0-0-0 11 ♗b2 c5 (11 ... ♕e6 12 0-0-0 ♗e7 13 f4 ♖he8 14 ♘f3± Padevski – Holmov, Dresden 1956) 12 0-0-0 d6 13 exd6 ♕xd6 14 ♕g4+?! (14 g3!? ♗xh1 15 ♗h3+ ♔b8 16 ♖xh1 and White is slightly better according to Keene) 14 ... ♔b8 15 ♗e2 h5 16 ♕f5 ♕h6! 17 ♘f3 ♗c8 18 ♕e4? (18 ♕e5!? or 18 ♕c2) 18 ... f5 19 ♕e3 g5! 20 ♕e5 (20 ♗xh8 ♕xh8 when the dark squares around the white king are too vulnerable) 20 ... ♗d6 21 ♕f6 g4 22 ♗e2 (22 ♕xh6 ♖xh6 23 ♗e2 ♗f4 and Black is better) 22 ... ♕f4 23 f3 ♖he8 24 ♗d3 ♕e3 25 ♗c2 ♘f4 26 ♕c3 ♕f2 27 g3 ♗e5 28 ♕xe5 ♖xe5 29 ♗xe5 gxf3 30 ♖hf1 ♕e2 31 ♘f4 0-1 Chandler –

Adams, Hastings 1991/92.

10 h4?! *(78)*

The idea behind White's unconventional moves is to build up a pawn chain with f4 and g3 without having to to worry about the counter-blow ... g5. White reasons that Black's cramped situation will prevent him from being able to undermine the pawns. However, White can also try 10 ♕e4 (10 g3 ♗a6 11 ♗g2 0-0-0 12 b3 f6 13 ♗b2 fxe5 14 0-0! is unclear according to Shirov) 10 ... g6 11 ♗d3 ♘a4 12 ♘b3! (12 0-0?! ♘c5 13 ♕e2 ♗g7 14 ♘f3 ♘e6 15 h4 0-0 16 h5 d6 17 hxg6 hxg6 18 exd6 ♕xd6 19 ♖d1 ♘f4 20 ♗xf4 ♕xf4 21 ♕e4 ♕xe4 22 ♗xe4 ♖b8= Lau - Emms, Copenhagen 1992) 12 ... ♗g7 13 0-0 0-0 14 ♖e1 ♗b7 15 ♖b1 f5 16 exf6 ♕xf6 17 ♗e3 ♖ae8 18 ♕g4 c5 19 ♘xa5 ♗a8 20 ♖e2 d6 21 h4 and Black had insufficient compensation for the pawn: Lau - Emms, Copenhagen rapid play 1992.

10 ... a4!

The normal support of c4 by

b3 is now ruled out.

11 g3 ♖a5!

A novel way to activate the rook, adding pressure against e5. Normally, this rook is largely redundant on a8, so this is an interesting venture.

12 f4 ♗a6

13 ♖h2!

As Black has given up the right to castle queenside, White is confident that the rook move will not place the white king in any danger, since Black cannot afford to open up the kingside whilst his own monarch is in the centre. Of course, White can always castle queenside later if necessary.

13 ... f6? *(79)*

An incautious move, played is the mistaken belief that Black can force the dismantling of White's pawn structure. Agdestein himself suggests 13 ... ♔d8! intending 14 ... f6 as an improvement: 14 ♔d1 f6 15 exf6 ♕xe2+ (15 ... ♕xf6 16 ♘e4 ♕e7 17 ♕c2 with an unclear position; or 15 ... gxf6 16 ♕d3 ♕b4 17 a3 ♕d6 18 ♕c3 ♖c5 19 ♔c2 ♕e6∓)

16 ♖xe2 gxf6 17 ♖e3 ♗c5 18 ♖f3 with chances for both sides.

14 exf6 gxf6
15 b4!

The latent power of the rook on h2 will be revealed after the queen exchange but in the meantime White tries to trap the loose rook on a5.

15 ... axb3

The ending is rather bleak after ... ♖h5 since White controls all the key squares and Black's pawn structure is very weak.

16 ♘xb3 ♖a4
17 ♘c5 ♕xe2+

A whole piece is lost after 17 ... ♖a5 18 ♘xa6 ♖xa6 19 c5, with the threat of 20 ♕xe7+ releasing the bishop to take on a6.

18 ♖xe2+ ♔f7
19 ♘xa4 ♘xa4
20 ♖c2

White is the exchange up and should be able to convert it to victory. The pawn on c4 is a slight handicap, but as soon as one of the rooks infiltrates Black's situation will become desperate. Shirov is now prepared to meet 20 ... ♖g8 by 21 ♔f2 ♘c5 22 ♔f3 f5 23 ♗d2 ♘e4 24 ♗e1, when Black's counterplay has dissolved.

20 ... ♗c5
21 ♖b1 ♖e8+
22 ♗e2 ♘b6
23 ♔d1 ♖e4
24 ♗d3 ♖d4
25 ♔e2 *(80)*

The only way to continue the struggle is to capture the c-pawn; otherwise White will continue with 26 ♘b3 and quickly consolidate his material advantage. However, Shirov suggests that the other capture would have been better: 25 ... ♗xc4! 26 ♗xc4+ ♘xc4 27 ♖b8 when White still has some technical difficulties to overcome.

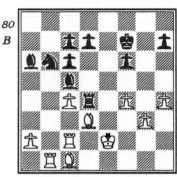

25 ... ♘xc4
26 ♖b8! ♖xd3
27 ♔xd3 ♘e3+
28 ♔c3 d5?!

White should be able to win after 28 ... ♘xc2!? due to the passed a-pawn: 29 ♔xc2 h5 30 f5 ♗e2 31 a4 ♗g4 32 a5 ♗xf5+ 33 ♔c3 ♗e4 34 ♖b7! ♗f2 35 a6 c5 36 ♖xc7 ♔e6 37 a7 and White has a won position according to Tisdall.

29 ♗xe3 ♗xe3
30 ♔b4 ♔e7
31 ♖xc6 ♗e2
32 ♖xc7+ ♔d6
33 ♖c3 ♗d2
34 ♖d8+ 1-0

An inventive game by both players.

Conclusion

It is clearly too early to make a definite assessment of the 8 ... ♘b6 variation. However, practical results have been in White's favour and it would appear that Black has more problems to solve in this line than White.

9 Mieses Variation: 8 ... ♗a6 9 b3

Although 8 ... ♘b6 has been seen in many recent grand-master games, it is still not as popular as 8 ... ♗a6, pinning the white c-pawn and preparing to castle queenside. Of course, this move has the drawback that Black can no longer create early counterplay with ... a5-a4, but it does mean that Black can consider placing his d5-knight on another square. Although 9 ♘d2 has been the traditional response to 8 ... ♗a6, Kasparov has recently popularized 9 b3, which was seen to devastating effect in his crushing victory over Anatoly Karpov at Tilburg in 1991.

Kasparov – Karpov
Tilburg 1991

1	e4	e5
2	♘f3	♘c6
3	d4	exd4
4	♘xd4	♘f6
5	♘xc6	bxc6
6	e5	♕e7
7	♕e2	♘d5
8	c4	♗a6
9	b3	*(81)*

This is the move that has

revitalized the Mieses Variation in recent times, largely due to Gary Kasparov's influence.

9	...	g6

Karpov chooses to steer clear of 9 ... 0-0-0, which is examined in the next illustrative game, and 9 ... ♕h4, which is featured in Sax - van der Wiel. If White responds routinely to Black's fianchetto he can easily find himself in difficulties, e.g. 10 ♗b2 ♗g7 11 ♘d2 (11 g3!?) 11 ... ♘b4 (here we see the black knight taking up a more active out post than b6) 12 ♘f3 c5 13 g3 0-0 14 ♗g2 and now:

a) 14 ... ♖ae8 15 0-0 d6 16 ♘e1 ♕d7 17 ♕d2 ♗xe5 18 ♗xe5 ♖xe5 19 a3 ♘c6 20 ♘d3 ♖e7 21 ♘f4 (Hjartarson - Portisch, Reykjavik 1991) 21 ... ♘b7 22 b4 ♘d4 23 ♗xb7 c6∓.

b) 14 ... d5 15 0-0 dxc4 16 bxc4 ♖ad8 17 ♖fd1 ♕e6 18 ♘f1 ♗b7 19 ♘g5 ♕f5 20 f4 (20 h4!?) 20 ... h6 21 ♘f3 g5∓ Sveshnikov - Kharitonov, St. Petersburg 1991.

10 f4!

Kasparov is well prepared and immediately reveals his novelty. This supports the e5-pawn and can itself be supported by g3.

10 ... f6

An instant attempt to undermine the advanced pawn. In a later game Karpov chose a more sedate path: 10 ... ♕b4+ 11 ♗d2 ♕b6 12 ♘c3 ♗b4 13 ♕f3 ♘xc3 14 ♗xc3 ♗b7 15 0-0-0 c5 16 ♕e3 ♗xc3 17 ♕xc3 0-0-0 18 h4 ♖he8 19 ♖h3 d6 20 ♖hd3 dxe5 21 ♕xe5 ♕c6 22 ♖xd8+ ♖xd8 23 ♖xd8+ ♔xd8 24 ♔d2 ½-½ Gelfand - Karpov, Linares 1992.

11 ♗a3! ♕f7!

The alternatives leave Black in an awkward situation.

a) 11 ... c5!? and now:

a1) 12 ♗b2 ♘xf4 (12 ... ♗g7!?) 13 ♕e4+-.

a2) 12 g3 fxe5 13 ♗g2 and now:

a21) 13 ... c6 14 fxe5 ♗g7 15 ♗b2 0-0 16 ♘d2 intending ♘f3, when Kasparov considers the position to be slightly better for White.

a22) 13 ... e4 14 ♗b2 (14 ♕xe4 ♕xe4+ 15 ♗xe4 ♗g7 with an

unclear position) 14 ... ♗g7 15 ♗xg7 ♕xg7 16 ♕xe4+ ♔f8 17 ♕xd5 ♖e8+ 18 ♔f2 ♕xa1-+.

b) 11 ... ♘b4 12 ♗b2 fxe5 13 a3 ♘d5 14 ♕xe5 ♘f6 15 ♗e2 ♗g7 16 ♘d2 d6 17 ♕xe7+ ♔xe7 18 ♘f3±.

12 ♕d2

In his analysis of the game (upon which these notes are based), Kasparov demonstrates that forcing Black to forfeit the right to castle is not good enough for an advantage: 12 exf6+ ♔d8 13 ♕d2 ♕xf6 14 ♗b2 ♕e6+ 15 ♗e2 ♗b4 16 ♘c3 ♖e8 17 0-0-0 ♗xc3 18 ♗xc3 ♕xe2 (18 ... ♘xc3 19 ♕xc3 ♕xe2 20 ♖he1 ♕g4 21 ♕f6++-) 19 cxd5=.

12 ... ♘b6

The forcing 12 ... ♗xa3 13 cxd5 ♗xf1 14 ♘xa3 ♗a6 (14 ... ♕e7 15 ♘c2) favours White:

a) 15 dxc6 dxc6 16 0-0-0±.

b) 15 ♕a5! and:

b1) 15 ... ♕xd5 16 ♕xa6 ♕e4+ 17 ♔d1 ♕d4+ 18 ♔c2 ♕f2+ 19 ♔c3+-.

b2) 15 ... ♗b7 16 ♕xc7 ♕xd5 17 ♕xb7 ♕e4+ 18 ♔d1 ♕d4+ 19 ♔c2 ♕f2+ (19 ... ♕e4+ 20 ♔b2 ♕d4+ 21 ♔b1) 20 ♔c3 ♕e3+ 21 ♔b2 ♕d4+ 22 ♔b1 and White is winning according to Speelman.

13 c5 ♗xf1
14 cxb6 axb6? (82)

Even at this early stage Black has to play extremely accurately to survive. Karpov was obviously relying on the variation 15 ♗xf8 ♗xg2! 16 ♕xg2 ♖xf8 17 ♘c3 fxe5 18 fxe5 ♕f4 with an unclear position. How-

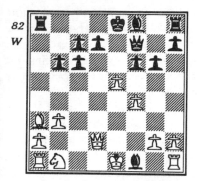

ever, he had two alternatives, one good and one bad:

a) 14 ... ♗a6! 15 bxc7 fxe5! 16 ♕a5 ♕xf4! 17 ♕xa6 ♕h4+ 18 ♔d1 (18 g3 ♕e4+ 19 ♔f2? ♗xa3∓) 18 ... ♕d4+ 19 ♔c2 (19 ♘d2 ♗xa3 20 c8(♕)+ ♖xc8 21 ♕xc8+ ♔e7 22 ♕xh8 ♕xa1+ 23 ♔e2 ♕xh1 24 ♕xe5+ ♔f7 25 ♕f4+ which is equal according to Kasparov) 19 ... ♕e4+ and now:

a1) 20 ♔c3 ♕d4+ 21 ♔c2 ♕e4+=.

a2) 20 ♔b2 ♕xg2+∓.

a3) 20 ♔c1 and:

a31) 20 ... ♗h6+? ♕e3+! 21 ♘d2 and now:

a311) 21 ... ♗xd2+ 22 ♔xd2 ♕f4+ 23 ♔e1 ♕h4+ (23 ... ♕e3+ 24 ♕e2 ♕c3+ 25 ♔f2) 24 g3 ♕e4+ 25 ♔d2+−.

a312) 21 ... ♕d4 22 ♔b1! ♗xd2 23 c8(♕)+ (23 ♖f1 ♗f4) 23 ... ♖xc8 24 ♕xc8+ ♔f7 25 ♕a6 ♕e4+ 26 ♔b2 ♕d4+ 27 ♔c2 ♕c3+ 28 ♔b1+−.

a32) 20 ... ♕e3+! 21 ♘d2? ♗xa3+ 22 ♕xa3 ♕c3+!−+.

a4) 20 ♕d3 ♕xg2+ 21 ♘d2 ♗xa3 22 ♖he1 0-0 23 ♕xd7 (23 ♖xe5 d6) 23 ... ♕d5 24 ♕xd5+

(24 ♕g4 ♗d6) 24 ... cxd5 25 ♖xe5 ♖ac8 26 ♖xd5 ♖xc7+ 27 ♘c4 ♗b4 and Black is slightly better according to Speelman.

b) 14 ... ♗xa3? 15 b7 ♖b8 16 ♘xa3 ♗a6 17 0-0-0! ♗xb7! (17 ... ♖xb7? 18 e6!) 18 ♖he1 0-0 19 ♕xd7 and Kasparov considers the position to be clearly better for White.

15 e6!!

A powerful intermezzo which places the black position on the brink of collapse. Obviously after 15 ... ♕xe6+ 16 ♔f1 ♗xa3 17 ♘xa3 ♖xa3 18 ♖e1 the black queen leaves the board.

15 ... dxe6
16 ♗xf8 ♖d8
17 ♕b2 ♗xg2

Black could also retain the bishop in order to highlight the exposed position of the white king after an eventual ... g5:

a) 17 ... ♗d3! 18 ♗a3 g5! 19 ♘d2 gxf4 20 0-0-0 c5 21 ♕c3±.

b) 17 ... ♗a6 18 ♗b4! c5 19 ♗c3 0-0 20 ♘d2 intending 0-0-0, when White is again slightly better according to Kasparov.

18 ♕xg2 ♔xf8

The difference between Karpov's intended variation after 15 ♗xf8 and the game position is now clear. Since the c6-pawn is unprotected Black will only have two pawns for the piece and the white king in the centre is not a problem since the black pieces are restricted by their own pawns.

19 ♕xc6 ♖d6

20	♕c3	♔g7
21	♘d2	♖hd8
22	0-0-0	♕e8?

Black threatens to win the queen with 23 ... ♖c6, but a much better move was 22 ... ♖d5! with the same idea. Instead, after 22 ... ♕d7 23 ♕c2 ♖c6 24 ♘c4 ♕c8 25 a4 or 23 ... b5 25 ♘e4 White would have few problems.

23 ♕xc7+! ♖8d7

Stealing the c-pawn seems risky as it opens up the c-file but White has it all under control. The point is that 23 ... ♔g8 fails to 24 ♘c4 exchanging rooks.

24	♕c2	♕b8
25	♘c4	♖d5 *(83)*

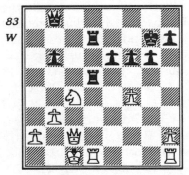

There is no way out either after 25 ... ♖xd1+ 26 ♖xd1 ♕xf4+ 27 ♔b1 ♖xd1+ 28 ♕xd1 ♕xh2 29 ♕d7+ ♔h6 30 a4!+− (Kasparov).

26 ♕f2!

Although White has a material plus there is still some way to go before this can be converted into a victory. First he must restrict Black's counterplay, before advancing his queenside pawns or marching in with his king. The knight on c4 has a vital role as it safeguards White's king, freeing his other pieces for more active duties.

26	...	♕c7
27	♕xb6	♕xf4+
28	♕e3	♕g4

Obviously Black cannot afford to exchange queens as White could then simply advance his queenside pawns.

29	♖dg1	♕h4
30	♖g3	e5
31	♖h3	♕g4
32	♖g1	

White has marshalled his forces with great care. The only way Black can make progress is to advance his passed pawns but then White would be ideally placed to exploit the exposed position of the king.

32	...	♖d1+
33	♖xd1	♕xd1+
34	♔b2	h5
35	♖g3	♕h1
36	♕f2	h4
37	♕g2	♕xg2+
38	♖xg2	g5
39	a4	♔g6
40	a5	e4
41	b4	h3
42	♖g3	♖h7
43	a6	f5
44	♖a3	1-0

Prior to the Tilburg encounter Kasparov and Karpov had already contested this variation in the fourteenth game of their 1990 World Championship match. On that occasion Karpov choose 9 ... 0-0-0 and, after a fascinating struggle, the game was drawn.

Kasparov – Karpov
World Championship
Lyon (14) 1990

1	e4	e5
2	♘f3	♘c6
3	d4	exd4
4	♘xd4	♘f6
5	♘xc6	bxc6
6	e5	♕e7
7	♕e2	♘d5
8	c4	♗a6
9	b3	0-0-0 *(84)*

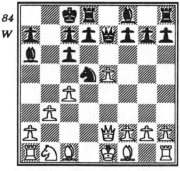

10 g3

This is Kasparov's innovation, a gambit idea which has breathed new life into the Mieses Variation. Breaking the pin immediately with 10 ♕b2!? promises little; Ljubojevic – Seirawan, Wijk aan Zee 1988, continued 10 ... ♘b6 11 ♗e2 ♖e8 12 ♗f4 g5 13 ♗g3 ♗g7 14 ♘c3 f5 15 f4 gxf4 16 ♗xf4 ♗xe5 17 ♗xe5 ♕xe5 18 0-0∓. Also harmless is

10 ♗b2 f6!=.

10	...	♖e8

Not so good is 10 ... g5?! 11 ♗a3 when White is better.

11	♗b2	f6
12	♗g2	fxe5 *(85)*

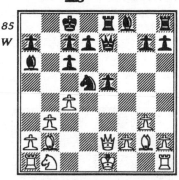

13	0-0	

White's compensation for the pawn lies in the weaknesses in Black's pawn structure and the sorry-looking black bishop on a6. One of Kasparov's team of analysts, Azmaiparashvilli, has suggested that White can improve at this point with 13 ♘d2!?, a move which has been successfully tested: 13 ... g6 14 0-0-0 ♗h6!? (14 ... ♗g7 15 ♘e4, intending ♕d2-a5±) 15 ♔b1 ♖hf8 16 ♘e4 ♔b8?! 17 ♕e1! ♘f6 18 ♘xf6 ♖xf6 19 f4 ♖f7 20 ♕a5 ♗b7 21 ♗xe5± Thorhallsson – Stefansson, Iceland 1991.

13	...	h5!

Not content with a passive stance, Black goes on the offensive.

14	♕d2	

The right response; on 14 ♘d2? h4 15 ♖fe1 hxg3 16 hxg3 ♕g5 17 ♘f3 ♕h5 Black has the brighter prospects due to his pressure on the h-file.

14 ...   ♘f6
15 ♕a5

A powerful riposte. Now the pawn is regained and White begins to make inroads into the black king position.

15 ...   ♗b7 *(86)*

If 15 ... ♔b7 16 ♗a3 ♕e6 17 ♘c3, intending ♗xf8 and ♘a4, leaves Black in dire straits.

16 ♗a3!

A necessary precautionary measure as after 16 ♕xa7?! ♕c5! 17 ♕a4 (17 ♕xc5 ♗xc5 with the idea of ... h4∓) 17 ... ♕b6 and ... ♗c5 Black has excellent chances.

16 ...   ♕e6
17 ♗xf8   ♖hxf8

White can consider a rapid queenside pawn storm after 17 ... ♖exf8? 18 ♕xa7 h4 19 a4! hxg3 20 a5 ♖xh2 21 a6+–.

18 ♕xa7   ♕g4!

A marvellous move to counter White's fearsome but rather slow attack. Left to his own devices Kasparov can play a4-a5-a6 or ♘a3-c2-b4-a6, so

Black must play actively. The text simultaneously prepares ... ♕d4 to exchange queens and supports the advance of the h-pawn to h3, where it smothers the white kingside.

19 ♘a3   h4

The offer to trade queens is wisely delayed, since the white knight would become too powerful after 19 ... ♕d4 20 c5 ♕b4 (otherwise ♘c4-a5 is too strong) 21 ♘c4 ♕b5 22 ♖fe1, when the e5-pawn is under fire and White can follow up with ♗f1. After 19 ... h4, however, 20 c5 hxg3 21 hxg3 ♕h5 leaves Black in the ascendancy.

20 ♘c2   h3
21 ♗h1   ♘e4
22 a4!

The attempt to win the piece meets with an amusing finale: 22 f3? ♘xg3 23 fxg4 ♘e2 mate. In this incredibly complicated position Kasparov finds the only move to deny Black an advantage:

a) 22 ♘e3 ♕g6∓.

b) 22 ♘b4 ♘c3 23 ♖ae1 ♕d4∓.

c) 22 ♕e3 ♘g5∓.

22 ...   ♘c3
23 ♖ae1?!

Kasparov should have given his king an escape square, but not with 23 f3? ♘e2+ (23 ... c5? 24 ♕xb7+!) 24 ♔f2 ♕g6∓. Of course, a stronger continuation is 23 ♖fe1! ♘e2+ 24 ♔f1 ♘d4 25 ♘xd4 ♕xd4 26 ♕xd4 exd4 27 ♖xe8+ ♖xe8 28 ♖e1 ♖f8 29 f4!

g5 30 ♔f2! gxf4 31 g4 f3 32 c5
when White is slightly better
according to Azmaiparashvilli,
but Kasparov was probably
worried about the vulnerability
of his f2-square.

23	...	♘e2+
24	♖xe2	♕xe2
25	♘b4	d5!?

A risky attempt to open up
the position. Black was not
content with the forcing variation 25 ... ♖f3 26 ♘a6 ♔d8 27
♕b8+ ♔e7 28 ♕xb7 ♖xf2 29
♕b4+ d6 30 ♖xf2 ♕d1+ with a
draw by perpetual check. Less
enticing is 25 ... e4? 26 ♘a6 ♔d8
27 ♕xb7 ♖xf2 28 ♕xc7+ ♔e7 29
♕e5+ ♔d8 30 ♕a5+ ♔e7 31 ♕g5+
♔e6 32 ♘c7++−.

| 26 | cxd5 | cxd5 |
| 27 | ♗xd5 | |

The other capture leads
nowhere: 27 ♘xd5?! ♕a6 28 ♕c5
♕d6 and White's attack peters
out. A more searching test is 27
♖c1! ♕d2 (27 ... ♖d8? 28 ♗xd5
♖xd5 29 ♘xd5 ♖f7 30 ♘b6++−)
28 ♕c5 ♖e7 (28 ... ♖f7!?)± , e.g.
29 ♘xd5 ♗xd5 30 ♗xd5 ♖xf2 31
♗e6+ ♔d8 32 ♗xh3 ♖xh2 33 ♖c2
♕xc2 34 ♕d5+ and mate follows.

27	...	♗xd5
28	♘xd5	♕c2
29	♕a6+	♔d7
30	♘e3	♕e4
31	♖c1?!	

White is on the point of
consolidating his position. At
the moment he has a pawn for
the sacrificed exchange, and

has targets at c7, e5 and h3.
However, a more accurate
choice was 31 ♖d1+ ♔e7 32 ♕f1
♖d8 33 ♖e1± ♖d3 34 ♘c4?? (34
♘g4!) 34 ... ♖xg3+ 35 hxg3 h2+
36 ♔xh2 ♖h8+ 37 ♔g1 ♖h1 mate.

31	...	♖b8!
32	♕f1	♖xb3
33	♕xh3+	♔d8
34	♕h5	♔c8
35	♕d1	(87)

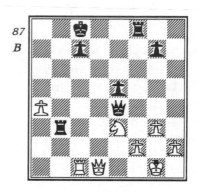

87
B

| 35 | ... | ♖xe3 |

In mutual time-trouble,
Karpov settles for a draw.
Hopeless is 35 ... ♖b2? 36 ♘c4
and the dual threat against the
rook and the brutal check on
d6 wins.

36	fxe3	♕xe3+
37	♔h1	♕e4+
38	♔g1	♕e3+
39	♔h1	♕e4+
40	♔g1	♖d8
41	♕c2	½–½

One of the most enterprising
lines against Kasparov's 9 b3 is
9 ... ♕h4. This early queen
sortie leads to great complications.

Sax – van der Wiel
Wijk aan Zee 1992

1	e4	e5
2	♘f3	♘c6
3	d4	exd4
4	♘xd4	♘f6
5	♘xc6	bxc6
6	e5	♕e7
7	♕e2	♘d5
8	c4	♗a6
9	b3	♕h4

A tricky reply for White to meet as Black threatens both 10 ... ♗b4+ and ... ♕d4. Although rarely seen in tournament play, White needs to be properly prepared to meet this move, as it will no doubt become very fashionable if the evidence of the stem game is anything to go by.

10 a3

This is considered by van der Wiel to be the only feasible move, but 10 ♗b2 has also been played:

a) 10 ... ♗b4+ and now:

a1) 11 ♔d1 ♘f4 12 ♕e3 ♘e6 13 g3 ♕g4+ 14 ♗e2 ♕h3∓ Gufeld – Vistanetskis, USSR 1956.

a2) 11 ♘d2 0-0 12 ♕f3!? (12 g3!?) 12 ... ♗xd2+ 13 ♔xd2 ♕g5+ 14 ♔d1 ♘b6 15 ♗d3 ♖ad8 16 ♕h3 g6 17 ♔c2 d5 18 exd6 ♗c8 (A. Osborne – C. M. Brown, Torquay 1987) 19 ♕g3! ♕xg3 20 hxg3 cxd6 21 ♖xh7! ♔xh7 22 ♖h1+ ♔g8 23 ♖h8 mate.

b) 10 ...♗c5 11 g3 ♕g5 12 ♘d2 ♘b6 13 ♗g2 0-0 14 0-0 ♖fe8 15 ♘e4 ♕e7 16 ♕g4 ♔h8 17 e6 f6 18 ♘xc5 ♕xc5 19 exd7 ♖e7 20 ♖ad1 ♖d8 21 ♖fe1 ♘b7 22 ♘d4 ♕b4 23 ♗c3 ♖xe1+ 24 ♖xe1 ♕f8 25 ♘b4 ♕g8 26 ♖e7 1-0 S. Arkell – Chukhrova, Cappelle la Grande 1992.

10 ... ♗c5 (88)

A sharp line which leads to incredible complications. The relatively tame 10 ... ♘f4 should not cause White any problems after 11 ♕e4 ♘g6 12 ♕e3 c5 and now:

a) 13 ♘c3 ♕d4 14 ♕xd4 cxd4 15 ♘b5 ♗xb5 16 cxb5 ♘xe5 17 ♗b3 0-0-0 18 ♗xd4 ♖e8 19 ♔d2 ♔b8 20 f4 ♘g6 21 g3 ♘e7 22 ♖e1 f6 24 b4± Karasev – Nasibullin, Novosibirsk 1989.

b) 13 g3 ♕d4 14 ♕xd4 cxd4 15 f4 ♗b7 16 ♖g1 d6 17 exd6 ♗xd6 18 ♗d3 a5 19 ♔f2 0-0 20 ♖e1 ♖fd8 21 ♘d2 ♘f8 22 ♖b1 ♘e6 23 b4 axb4 24 axb4 ♖a2 25 c5 ♗f8 26 ♗c4 ♖c2 27 ♘b3 ♖c8 28 ♘e4 ♗xe4 29 ♖xe4 d3 30 ♗d2 ♖c2 31 ♔e1 ♘d4 32 ♖xd4 ♖xd4 33 ♗xc3 dxc2 34 ♖c1+- Karasev – Aleksandrov, Podolsk 1990.

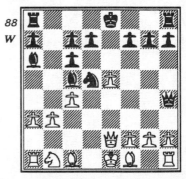

88
W

11 ♗b2

If White attempts to chase

the queen away with 11 g3 then Black has a spectacular sacrifice, 11 ... ♘xf2+, and now:

a) 12 ♔xf2?! ♕d4+ 13 ♔f3 ♕xa1 14 ♕c2 (14 ♕e4 ♖b8!?) 14 ... ♕xe5 15 cxd5 ♕xd5+ 16 ♕e4+ ♕xe4+ 17 ♔xe4 ♗xf1 18 ♖xf1 0-0∓.

b) 12 ♕xf2 ♕e4+ 13 ♔d1! (13 ♔d2 ♕xh1 14 ♗g2 ♕xh2 15 cxd5 cxd5 16 ♘c3 c6 [16 ... d4!? intending 17 ♘d5 ♗b7] 17 ♗b2 ♕h6+ 18 ♕f4 with an unclear position) 13 ... ♕xh1 14 ♘d2 ♘c3+ (14 ... 0-0 15 ♔c2! f6 16 e6 dxe6 17 ♗b2 intending 18 cxd5) 15 ♔c2 ♘e4 16 ♘xe4 ♕xe4+ 17 ♗d3 ♕g4 (17 ... ♕xe5 18 ♗b2 ♕g5 19 h4 ♕h6 20 ♖e1+ ♔f8 21 ♖f1) 18 ♗f5 ♕h5 19 h4! f6 20 exf6 gxf6 21 ♕e1+! which Gutman indicates as clearly better for White.

Another interesting idea is 11 ♕f3 ♗d4 12 ♖a2 ♘b6 13 ♗d3 0-0-0 14 ♖e2∞ Thorhallsson - Jonsson, Hafnarfirdi 1992.

11 ...   ♘f4

In his analysis to the game - (upon which these notes are based) van der Wiel shows that the ambitious 11 ... ♘e3!? does nothing to resolve the complications after 12 g3! ♕e4 13 fxe3 ♕xh1 14 ♘c3 (intending 15 0-0-0 or 15 ♔d2) 14 ... ♖b8 15 b4 ♕g1 (15 ... ♗xe3?! 16 ♕xe3 ♗xc4 17 0-0-0 ♗xf1 18 ♕f2±; 15 ... ♗xc4!? 16 ♕xc4 ♗xe3 17 ♕e2 ♕g1 with an unclear position) 16 bxc5 ♗xc4 17 ♕xc4 ♖xb2 18 0-0-0 ♖xh2∞.

12   ♕f3!?

It might be more accurate to cover e4 from another angle: 12 ♕c2 (12 ♕d2? ♘h3! 13 gxh3 ♕e4+) 12 ... ♕g4 13 f3 ♕g6 14 ♕d2 ♕h6 15 ♗c1 (15 g3?! ♘e3! 16 ♕a5 ♘e6 17 ♕xa6 ♗c1 with an unclear position) 15 ... g5 16 ♘c3, which is unclear according to van der Wiel.

12 ...   ♘e6

13 g3 *(89)*

White had been waiting to play this for the last five moves and takes the first opportunity to do so. Also worth considering is the risky 13 ♗d3 ♘d4 14 ♕d1 ♘xb3 15 ♕xb3 ♕xf2+ 16 ♔d1 with an unclear position.

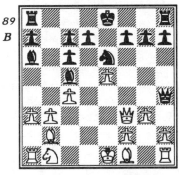

89
B

13 ...   ♕h6!

This maintains the momentum by keeping active in order to exploit White's lack of development. Black also has two other interesting possibilities:

a) 13 ... ♘g5 14 ♕g2 ♕e4+ 15 ♕xe4 ♘xe4 16 f4! ♘f2 17 b4 ♗e3 18 ♔e2 ♗b6 19 ♔e1 ♗e3 (19 ... ♘xh1 20 c5) 20 ♔e2=.

b) 13 ... ♕e7 14 ♘d2 0-0-0!?

15 b4 ♘d4 16 ♘xd4? ♘xd4 17
♕e4 ♘c2+-+ A. Gomez - L.
Valdes, Cuba 1991

| 14 | ♘d2 | ♜b8 |
| 15 | ♕d3? | |

A more precise continuation
is the immediate 15 b4! ♘d4?!
(15 ... 0-0!) 16 ♗xd4 ♘xd4 17
♕d3 c5 18 ♗g2±.

15	...	0-0
16	♗g2	♜fd8
17	b4	d6

The drawback of White's
fifteenth move, voluntarily
placing his queen on the d-file,
is now apparent. Black gains a
tempo due to the discovered
attack, as White must sidestep
with his queen. For example: 18
♗xc6? dxe5 19 ♕e2 (19 ♕c2
♗xf2+-+) 19 ... ♘d4-+.

| 18 | ♕c2 | ♘d4? |

This gives White a chance to
get back into the game. It is
better to play 18 ... ♗d4 when
White is forced to enter a
series of exchanges which are
in Black's favour: 19 exd6 (19
♗xc6 dxe5∓) 19 ... ♜xd6 20 ♘e4
♗xb2 21 ♕xb2 ♜d4 22 0-0 (22
♘c5 ♕f6!) 22 ... ♗xc4∓.

| 19 | ♗xd4! | |

White sensibly gives up a
pawn rather than face the
Black attack which would
follow after 19 ♕c3 ♕h5! 20
♘f3 (20 ♔f1 ♕e2+ 21 ♔g1
♘b5!-+) 20 ... dxe5 21 bxc5 ♜b3
winning.

19	...	♗xd4
20	♜d1	dxe5
21	♘b3	♜d6 *(90)*

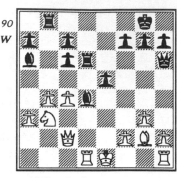

| 22 | 0-0 | |

White is counting on the
weakness of the double c-
pawns and the immobility of
Black's light-squared bishop to
provide compensation for the
pawn.

| 22 | ... | ♜bd8 |
| 23 | ♜fe1 | ♕f6 |

An accurate move which
highlights the weakness of the
pawn on f2. If 23 ... ♗xc4 24
♘xd4! (24 ♕xc4 ♗xf2+ 25 ♔xf2
♜xd1 26 ♜xd1 ♜xd1 27 ♕xc6
♕xc6 28 ♗xc6 ♜d3∓) 24 ...
♜xd4 25 ♜xd4 ♜xd4 26 ♜xe5
and White emerges with an
equal game.

24	♜d2	g6
25	c5	♜e6
26	♜ed1	♔g7
27	a4	h5
28	h4	♗c8
29	♘xd4?!	

White misses a golden
opportunity to restore the
balance: 29 ♘h3! ♜e7 30 ♗xc8
♜xc8 31 ♘xd4 exd4 32 ♜xd4=.

29	...	♜xd4
30	♜xd4	exd4
31	♕c4	♜e5?!

In mutual time-trouble both players begin to make errors. Black could have preserved an edge after 31 ... ♖e8 intending 32 ... ♖d8.

32 ♕xd4?

Now White overlooks a way of safeguarding the f-pawn and winning the black d-pawn: 32 f4! ♖e3 33 ♔h2 and 34 ♖xd4.

32	**...**	**♖e1+**
33	**♔h2**	**♖xd1**
34	**♕xd1**	**♕b2**

Amazingly, Black fails to notice that the f2-pawn can be captured. After 34 ... ♕xf2 35 ♕a1+! ♔h7 (35 ... ♕f6 36 ♕d1; 35

... f6?! 36 ♕d1 with the initiative) 36 ♕e5 ♗e6 37 ♔h1 Black retains an advantage.

| **35** | **♕e1** | **♗d7** |
| ½–½ | | |

Conclusion

Kasparov's 9 b3 in the main line of the Mieses Variation has proved to be a very dangerous weapon. Clearly Black has problems to solve after both 9 ... g6 and 9 ... 0-0-0, but the counter-attacking 9 ... ♕h4 leads to highly complex positions.

10 Mieses Variation:
8 ... ♗a6 9 ♘d2

The variation with 9 ♘d2 is a flexible choice that for a long time was considered the main line, but has been rather eclipsed in recent years by Kasparov's devotion to 9 b3. However, it is not necessarily inferior; Grandmasters Timman and Sveshnikov have both experimented with it and practical results have been very encouraging.

Harding – Zhividov
Corr 1976

1	e4	e5
2	♘f3	♘c6
3	d4	exd4
4	♘xd4	♘f6
5	♘xc6	bxc6
6	e5	♕e7
7	♕e2	♘d5
8	c4	♗a6
9	♘d2	

We now arrive at a critical juncture; Black has several playable alternatives but it is not firmly established which is most promising. White's task is made easier by the similarity of each variation, but he must always be on the look-out for a sudden tactical opportunity.

| 9 | ... | ♘b6 *(91)* |

91
W

The main alternatives are 9 ... g6, considered in Sveshnikov – Schüssler, 9 ... 0-0-0 in Timman – Karpov, and 9 ... ♘b4 in Oll – Kalinin, though Black has also tried:

a) 9 ... f6 and now:

a1) 10 exf6! ♘xf6 11 b3 c5?! (11 ... ♕xe2+!?) 12 ♗b2 ♗b7 13 f3 ♔f7 14 0-0-0 ♕xe2 15 ♗xe2 ♗d6 16 g3 ♖ae8 17 ♖he1 ♖e7 (17 ... ♖e3?! 18 ♘e4 ♗xe4 19 fxe4 ♖xe4 20 ♗h5+ ♔f8 21 ♖xe4 ♘xe4 22 ♖f1+ ♘f6 23 ♗xf6 gxf6 24 ♖xf6+ ♔e7 25 ♖f7+±) 18 ♗d3 ♖he8 19 ♖xe7+ ♗xe7 20 ♖e1 g6 21 ♔d1 gives White a small edge, Sveshnikov – Tarjan, Hastings 1977/78.

a2) 10 ♘f3!? ♕b4+ 11 ♔d1

♗e7? 12 ♕c2! ♘b6 13 a3 ♕a5 14 ♗d2 ♕c5 15 ♗b4 1–0 Asaturin – Marczell, Corr 1978.

b) 9 ... ♘f4 10 ♕e4 ♘g6 11 f4 0–0–0 and now:

b1) 12 g3 d5?! (12 ... f6!?) 13 cxd5 ♗xf1 14 d6! ♕d7 15 dxc7 ♔xc7 16 ♔xf1 ♕h3+ 17 ♔e2 ♖d5 18 ♘b3 ♕g4+ 19 ♕f3 ♘xe5 20 fxe5 ♕c4+ 21 ♔f2 ♗c5+ 22 ♘xc5 ♕xc5+ 23 ♔g2+– Alburt – Radashkovich, USSR 1970.

b2) 12 b3 f6 (12 ... ♗b7!? 13 ♗b2 c5 14 ♕e3 ♕h4+ 15 g3 ♕h6 16 ♖g1 d6 17 exd6 ♗xd6 18 0–0–0 ♕xh2 with an unclear position Tompa – Mestrovic, Corr 1980) 13 ♗b2 ♖e8 (or 13 ... fxe5 14 fxe5 ♕g5 15 0–0–0 ♖e8 16 h4 ♕f4 17 ♕xf4 ♘xf4 18 g3 ♘h5 19 ♘e4± Chumak – Gostkhorzhevich, Yurmala 1976) 14 0–0–0 fxe5 15 f5 ♘f4 16 ♘f3 d6 17 c5! ♗b7 18 ♕a4 ♔b8 19 g3 ♘d5 20 ♖xd5 cxd5 21 c6 ♗c8 22 ♗a6 ♔a8 23 ♘d4!+– Kozlov – Suleimanov, Erevan 1969.

10 b3 g6

The aggressive-looking 10 ... d5?! merely leads to a favourable ending for White: 11 exd6 cxd6 12 ♗b2 f6 13 0–0–0 ♕xe2 14 ♗xe2 ♔f7 15 ♖he1 d5 16 cxd5 ♗xe2 17 ♖xe2 cxd5 18 ♘f3 ♗b4 19 ♘d4 ♖he8 20 ♖c2± Schmidt – Radovici, Tel Aviv Ol 1964.

11 ♗b2 ♗g7
12 0–0–0 0–0–0
13 f4 *(92)*
13 ... d5!?

A suggestion of Evans's, this aims to exploit White's relative

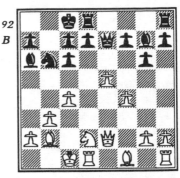

92
B

lack of development by opening up the position. The major alternative, 13 ... ♖he8, is rather slow and leaves Black with a dour defensive task. After 14 ♕f2 Black may continue:

a) 14 ... d6 15 c5! ♗xf1 16 ♕xf1 dxc5 17 ♕a6+ ♔b8 18 ♘c4 ♘xc4 19 bxc4♕e6 20 ♗c3 ♔a8 21 ♗a5 ♖b8 22 ♖d2 ♖b7 23 ♖b2 ♖xb2 24 ♔xb2 f6 (24 ... ♖b8+ 25 ♔a3 ♕d7 26 ♖c1 ♕c8 27 ♕xc8 ♖xc8 28 ♖d1+–) 25 ♔a3 fxe5 26 ♖d1! exf4 (26 ... ♖b8 27 ♗xc7 ♕c8 28 ♕xc6+ ♕b7 29 ♖b1 ♕xc6 30 ♖xb8 mate) 27 ♗xc7 ♕e3+ 28 ♔a4 ♕e4 29 ♖d3 ♕xg2 30 a3 ♖b8 31 ♖b3 ♖b4+ 32 ♖xb4 1–0 Pinkas – Pioch, Polish Ch 1973.

b) 14 ... ♗b7 (a suggestion of Keres's) 15 c5 ♘d5 16 ♘e4 f6? (16 ... ♔b8 17 ♗c4±) 17 ♘d6+ cxd6 18 cxd6 ♕e6 19 ♕xa7 ♘b4 20 ♖d4 ♘xa2+ 21 ♕xa2 ♔b8 22 ♕a5 ♕xb3 23 ♖b4 ♕e3+ 24 ♔b1+– Botterill – Holmes, Corr 1989.

14 ♕e3! dxc4
15 ♗xc4 ♗xc4

If 15 ... ♘xc4? then 16 ♕xa7 wins immediately.

16	♘xc4	♘xc4
17	bxc4	♗b7
18	♕b3+	

White continues a vigorous prosecution of the offensive against the black king. By attacking the a7-pawn he is able to tie down the black pieces and deploy his rooks on the abandoned d-file. Much less appropriate was 18 ♖xd8+ ♖xd8 19 ♖d1, aiming to exploit the doubled c-pawns in the endgame.

18	...	♔a8
19	♗d4	♖b8
20	♕a4	♖b7
21	♖d3	(93)

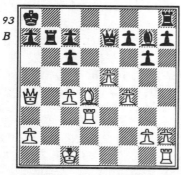

93
B

21	...	♕e6

Harding gives the following variations to illustrate the difficulty of Black's situation:

a) 21 ... ♖hb8 22 ♖a3 c5 (22 ... ♖b1+ 23 ♔c2) 23 ♕c6 cxd4 24 ♖xa7+! ♔xa7 25 ♕a4+ ♔b6 26 ♕b5+ ♔a7 27 ♕a5 mate.

b) 21 ... ♕b4 22 ♕xc6 ♕b1+ 23 ♔d2 ♕xa2+ (23 ... ♕xh1 24 ♖b3 ♖hb8 25 ♖a3 and 26 ♖xa7+) 24 ♔e3 ♔b8 (24 ... ♕a5 25 ♖a1 ♕b4 26 ♖da3 ♔b8 27 ♗xa7+) 25 ♖a1

♕c2 26 ♗xa7+ ♖xa7 (26 ... ♔a8 27 ♗b6+ ♔b8 28 ♗xc7+!) 27 ♖xa7 ♕c1+ 28 ♔e2 ♗xa7 29 ♕xc7++-.

22	♖hd1	♖c8

A passive response but Black really has to way out:

a) 22 ... ♖hb8 23 ♖a3 ♖b1+ 24 ♔c2 ♖8b7 (24 ... ♕f5+ 25 ♔c3 ♖8b7 26 ♗xa7) 25 ♗xa7 ♖7b2+ (25 ... ♖1b2+ 26 ♔c3 ♕xe5+ 27 ♗d4+ ♔b8 28 ♕a8+) 26 ♔c3 ♔b7 27 ♕a6++- (Harding).

b) 22 ... ♘h6 23 g3 ♕h3 24 ♗xa7 ♖xa7 25 ♕xc6+ ♖b7 26 ♖d8+ ♖xd8 27 ♖xd8+ ♔a7 28 ♕a4+ ♔b6 29 ♕b5+ ♔a7 30 ♕a5 mate (Harding).

23	♖b3	♖cb8
24	♗xa7!	1-0

Black resigned in view of the continuation:

a) 24 ... ♖xb3 25 ♖b6+ ♔b7 26 ♕a7+ ♔c8 27 ♕xc7 mate.

b) 24 ... ♖xa7 25 ♖xb8+ ♔xb8 26 ♖d8+ ♔b7 27 ♕b4+ ♔a6 28 ♖d3 and 29 ♖a3+.

Instead of 9 ... ♘b6 10 b3 g6, Black can also play the immediate 9 ... g6, deferring a decision on where to place the d5-knight. However, even then his task is not easy, as the next game shows.

Sveshnikov – Schüssler
Palma 1989

1	e4	e5
2	♘f3	♘c6
3	d4	exd4

4	♘xd4	♘f6
5	♘xc6	bxc6
6	e5	♕e7
7	♕e2	♘d5
8	c4	♗a6
9	♘d2	g6 *(94)*

This traditional move used to be considered the main line but Black has struggled with it recently.

10 b3

After the more sedate 10 ♘f3, the game Barczay - Pogacs, Hungarian Ch 1964, continued 10 ... ♗g7 11 ♗g5 f6?! (11 ... ♕b4+ 12 ♕d2 ♕xd2+ 13 ♔xd2 ♘b6 14 b3=) 12 exf6 ♕xe2+ 13 ♗xe2 ♘xf6 14 0-0-0 0-0-0 15 ♘d4 c5 16 ♘b3 ♗b7 17 f3 ♖de8 18 ♗d3 d6 19 ♖de1 ♘d7 20 ♘a5 ♘e5 21 ♗c2 ♗a8 22 ♗d2 ♖hf8 23 h4!± Barczay - Pogacs, Hungarian Ch 1964

10 ...   ♗g7
11 ♗b2   0-0-0!? *(95)*

The point of Black's play is to reach a position similar to the previous game but with the black knight still on d5. This makes it harder for White to support the pawn on e5 as the

f4-advance now requires preparation. With the same idea, also possible is 11 ... 0-0 12 0-0-0 when Black can continue:

a) 12 ... c5?! 13 ♘e4 ♘b4 (13 ... ♘f4 14 ♕e3 ♗xe5 15 ♘xc5 ♗xb2+ 16 ♔xb2 ♕f6+ 17 ♕c3 and White is slightly better according to Jovcic) 14 ♘f6+ ♔h8 15 h4 ♕e6 16 h5 g5 17 ♘xd7 ♕f5 (17 ... ♖fd8 18 h6! ♗xh6 19 ♖xh6 ♕xh6 20 e6+-) 18 ♗c3 h6 19 ♘xc5 ♖ae8 20 ♗xb4 ♖xe5 21 ♕f3 ♖xc5 22 ♕xf5 ♖xf5 23 ♗xf8 ♗xf8 24 f3 ♔g7 25 ♗d3 1-0 Zhuravlev - Shaposnic, Corr 1970.

b) 12 ... ♖ab8 13 ♕e4 ♘b6 14 f4 ♖fe8 15 ♕c2 d5 16 h4! (16 c5? ♗xf1 17 cxb6 ♗xg2 18 bxa7 ♖a8 19 ♖hg1 ♗h3∓ Hennings - Savon, Harrachov 1967) 16 ... ♗c8 17 h5 ♗g4 18 hxg6 fxg6 19 ♖e1 a5 20 ♗d3 ♖f8 with an unclear position, Zverev - Lisenkov, Corr 1974.

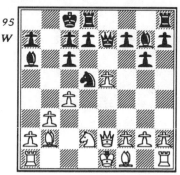

12 0-0-0   ♖he8

Black now embarks on a straightforward-looking plan of undermining e5 by ... f6. However, in this instance White is able to utilize his space advantage to launch a crushing attack.

13   g3

A necessary measure to support f4.

13   ...   ♘b6
14   f4   f6

The extra tempo would have been better expended by safeguarding against tactics on the queenside. One possible idea is 14 ... ♔b8 and then 15 ... ♗b7.

15   ♕f2   fxe5?

A crisis point has now been reached; Black's best choice was 15 ... ♗b7 though after 16 c5 ♘d5 17 ♘e4 White remains in top.

16   c5!   (96)

A typical tactical idea to blast open the queenside.

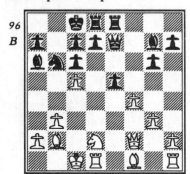

96
B

16   ...   ♗xf1
17   cxb6   ♗d3
18   bxc7   ♔xc7
19   ♕xa7+

White is now a clear pawn up and Black's king position has been shattered.

19   ...   ♔c8
20   ♘f3   e4

21   ♘e5   ♗b5
22   a4   ♗e2
23   ♖d2   d6
24   ♕a8+   ♔c7
25   ♕xc6+   ♔b8
26   ♕b6+   ♔a8
27   ♘c6   ♖c8
28   ♖xe2   1-0

In the next game we discuss the immediate 9 ... 0-0-0. However, before this the two players embark on the charade 9 ♕e4 ♘f6 10 ♕e2 ♘d5 repeating moves, so this move is actually 11 ... 0-0-0.

Timman – Karpov
Amsterdam 1985

1   e4   e5
2   ♘f3   ♘c6
3   d4   exd4
4   ♘xd4   ♘f6
5   ♘xc6   bxc6
6   e5   ♕e7
7   ♕e2   ♘d5
8   c4   ♗a6
9   ♕e4   ♘f6

An independent variation is 9 ... ♘b6, which is examined in the next chapter.

10   ♕e2   ♘d5
11   ♘d2

Obviously White does not 'offer' Black a draw by 11 ♕e4, but elects to enter the variation under discussion in this chapter.

11   ...   0-0-0
12   ♕e4   (97)

White aggressively takes up

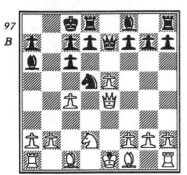

the gauntlet. A more cautious approach is 12 ♘f3 ♖e8 13 ♕c2 ♘f6 14 h3 d6 15 c5! ♗b7 16 cxd6 cxd6 17 ♗a6 ♕c7 18 ♗xb7+ ♔xb7 19 ♗e3± Estrin – Liberzon, Moscow Ch 1958.

12 ... ♘b6
13 a4?! *(98)*

Timman has also tried 13 c5 in this position (see the next chapter), which is probably also too ambitious. Practice has also seen:

a) 13 b3 f6 14 ♗b2 fxe5 15 0-0-0 ♔b8 16 ♕xe5 ♕xe5 17 ♗xe5 ♗a3+ 18 ♔c2 ♖hf8 19 f3 ♖f7 (W. Schmid – R. O'Reilly, Jersey 1973) 20 c5! ♗xf1 21 cxb6 d6 22 ♘xf1+-.

b) 13 ♗e2?! ♖e8 14 f4 f6 15

♘f3 fxe5 16 fxe5 d5! 17 cxd5 ♕b4+ 18 ♕xb4 ♗xb4+ 19 ♘d2 ♗xd2+ 20 ♔xd2 ♗e2 21 ♔xe2 cxd5 22 ♔d3 ♘c4∓ Greenfeld – Lev, Tel Aviv 1992.

13 ... d5!

A classical response to White's flank attack, counter-attacking in the centre. This is a marked improvement on Handoko – Kovacevic, Zagreb 1985, which continued: 13 ... ♗b7?! 14 a5 ♘c8 15 b4 ♔b8 16 ♗e2 f6 17 f4 fxe5 18 fxe5 ♖e8 19 ♘f3 ♕e6 20 c5 ♗xe2 21 ♕xe2 d6 22 ♖b1 dxe5 23 ♕a6 ♕g6 24 ♖b2 ♗e7 25 0-0 intending 26 ♗e3 and 27 b5+-.

14 cxd5 ♗xf1
15 d6 ♖xd6

Instead 15 ... cxd6 16 ♕xc6+ ♕c7 17 ♕xc7+ ♔xc7 18 exd6+ ♗xd6 19 ♔xf1 ♗b4 20 ♘f3 ♖d1+ 21 ♔e2 ♖xh1 22 ♗f4+ ♔b7 23 ♖xh1 ♖e8+ 24 ♗e3 ♘xa4 leaves an equal game according to Timman. Karpov prefers to keep the rook active in order to put pressure on e5.

16 ♘xf1!

Obviously bad is 16 exd6 ♕xe4+ 17 ♘xe4 ♗xg2-+. Not much better is 16 ♔xf1 ♖d5 or 16 ♖xf1 ♖d5 when Black is ready to play ... f6 and catch the white king in the centre.

16 ... ♖e6!

Karpov finds the most exact way of undermining the e-pawn. Other moves would allow White to create counter-play:

a) 16 ... f6 17 ♘e3! ♕xe5 18 ♕c2 intending to castle and continue the queenside attack.

b) 16 ... ♖d5 17 f4 ♕d7 (17 ... g5 18 ♘e3!) 18 ♗e3 f5 (18 ... a5!?) 19 exf6 gxf6 20 a5! f5 21 ♕c2 ♗b4+ 22 ♔f2 ♖xa5? (22 ... ♘a8±; 22 ... ♗xa5? 23 ♖xa5 ♖xa5 24 ♕c3+−) 23 ♖xa5 ♗xa5 24 b4! ♗xb4 25 ♕b2+−.

17 f4 g5
18 g3

The only effective way to reinforce f4:

a) 18 ♘g3 gxf4 19 ♗xf4 ♕b4+ 20 ♕xb4 ♗xb4+ 21 ♔f2 ♘d5 22 ♔f3 ♘xf4 23 ♔xf4 ♖he8−+.

b) 18 ♘d2 gxf4 19 0-0 ♕c5+ 20 ♔h1 ♕xe5∓.

18 ... ♕b4+

Black decides that the best chance of exploiting White's loose pawn formation lies in the endgame. With the queens on, White can create some complications: 18 ... gxf4 19 gxf4 f6 (19 ... ♕h4+ 20 ♘g3 ♘d5 21 ♗d2 ♗h6 22 0-0 ♖g8 23 ♖a3) 20 ♘g3 fxe5 21 f5 with the initiative according to Karpov.

19 ♕xb4 ♗xb4+ *(99)*

20 ♗d2

White reluctantly parts with his bishop, recognising that now the f4-pawn will be harder to defend. However, the alternative was also unattractive: 20 ♔f2 f6! 21 fxg5 fxg5 22 ♗xg5 ♖xe5 23 ♗f4 ♖f8±.

20 ... ♗xd2+
21 ♘xd2 gxf4
22 gxf4 ♘d5
23 0-0

Also worthy of consideration is 23 ♖f1 to keep the white king away from the marauding rooks.

23 ... ♖g8+
24 ♔h1 ♖g4
25 ♘b3?!

A stiffer defence was 25 ♘c4 when Black must be very accurate to maintain his advantage:

a) 25 ... ♘xf4 26 ♘e3 ♖h4 27 ♘f5 ♖g4 28 ♘e3=.

b) 25 ... ♖xf4 26 ♖xf4 ♘xf4 27 ♖f1 ♘d3 28 ♖xf7=.

c) 25 ... f6! 26 f5 ♖e8 27 b3 fxe5 28 f6 e4 29 f7 ♖f8 30 ♘e5 ♖g5 31 ♘xc6 ♔d7∓.

25 ... ♘xf4

The task for Black is much harder after 25 ... ♖xf4 26 ♖xf4 ♘xf4 27 ♘d4! (27 ♖f1 ♘d3 28 ♖xf7 ♖xe5∓) 27 ... ♖xe5 28 ♘xc6 and 29 ♘xa7+.

26 ♖ae1 ♖eg6
27 ♖f3 h5
28 ♘d4 ♘d5

If the h-pawn is advanced then White's knight comes into the game with devastating effect: 28 ... h4? 29 Nf5! with the unpleasant threats of 29 Ne7+ and 29 Ne3.

29	Rd1	Re4
30	Nb3	Re2
31	Rg1	

White is careful not to allow the rooks to double on the second rank with 31 ... Rgg2.

31	...	Rxe5

Timman had prepared a clever defence in case of the immediate rook exchange: 31 ... Rxg1+ 32 Kxg1 Rxb2 33 Nc5 Rc2! 34 e6 f6 35 Ne4 Re2 36 Nxf6 Rxe6 (36 ... h4 37 Nd7! Rxe6 38 Nc5) 37 Nxh5.

32	Rxf7	Rxg1+
33	Kxg1	Nb4
34	Rh7	Nd3
35	Nd4	Kb7
36	b3	a5
37	Rh6	Nb4
38	Kf2	Re4?!

In time-trouble Black begins to go astray; instead he should play 38 ... c5 39 Nb5 c4! 40 bxc4 c6 41 Nd6+ Kb6 with excellent chances.

39	Ne6	Kb6
40	Kf3	Re1
41	h4!	

Now White has good chances of holding the game due to his potential passed h-pawn. The game concluded:

41	...	Nd5
42	Nd4	Re3+
43	Kf2	Rc3
44	Rxh5	Rd3
45	Nf3	Rxb3
46	Rf5	Rb4?!

46 ... Kc5!.

47	h5	Kc5
48	h6	Rb8
49	Rh5	Rh8
50	h7	Kb4
51	Rh6	Nf6!

51 ... Kxa4? 52 Ng5 and 53 Nf7+-.

52	Rxf6	Rxh7
53	Rf4+	Ka3
54	Ke2	Rd7
55	Nd2	Rd8

55 ... c5? 56 Nc4+ Kxa4 57 Nb6++-; 56 ... Kb4 57 Ne5+ Rd4 58 Nc6++-.

56	Rc4	Rb8
57	Rc1	Rb4

½-½

In this chapter we have so far examined systems for Black with 9 ... Nb6, 9 ... g6 and 9 ... 0-0-0, or a combination of these moves. However, Black also has the interesting 9 ... Nd4, intending to redeploy the knight via c6 to d4. It is to this system that we now turn our attention.

Oll – Kalinin
USSR 1986

1	e4	e5
2	Nf3	Nc6
3	d4	exd4
4	Nxd4	Nf6
5	Nxc6	bxc6
6	e5	Qe7
7	Qe2	Nd5
8	c4	Ba6
9	Nd2	Nb4!?

This is arguably Black's toughest line of resistance, exploiting the vulnerability of the c2-square to gain time to bring the knight to c6.

10   ♘f3 *(100)*

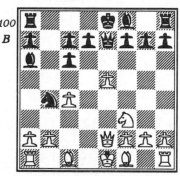

10   ...   c5

The tempting 10 ... d5?! only leaves the black pieces in a tangle if White finds the correct response:

a) 11 b3? dxc4 12 bxc4 0-0-0 13 ♕e4 ♕d7 14 ♗e2? (14 ♗d2!?) 14 ... f5! 15 ♕b1 ♗xc4 16 ♗g5 ♘d3+ 17 ♔f1 ♗e7 18 ♗xe7 ♕xe7 19 ♘e1 ♕xe5 20 ♘xd3 ♗xd3 21 ♗xd3 ♖xd3 22 g3 ♕e4 23 ♖g1 ♖hd8 24 ♕c2 ♕f3 25 ♖e1 ♖d2 26 ♕c5 ♖d1 0-1 Saeed - Thipsay, Dubai 1985.

b) 11 a3! ♗xc4 12 ♕d1 ♗xf1 13 ♔xf1 ♘a6 14 ♕a4 ♘b8 15 ♗g5 and now:

b1) 15 ... ♕e6 16 ♖c1 h6 17 ♗h4 g5 18 ♗g3 ♗e7 19 h4 g4 20 ♘d4 ♕d7 21 ♕b3+- Kopayev - Zhukovitsky, Kiev 1945.

b2) 15 ... ♕d7 16 e6! fxe6 17 ♘e5 ♕d6 18 ♕f4+-.

b3) 15 ... ♕c5 16 ♘d4 ♕b6 17 ♖c1 ♗c5 18 ♘f5 ♖g8 19 ♕g4

♘a6 20 b4 ♗xf2 21 ♖c2 h5 22 ♕f4 f6 23 ♖xf2 fxg5 24 ♘d6+ cxd6 25 ♕f7+ 1-0 Zaidel - Rapoport, Riga 1966.

11   a3

The unusual 11 ♕e4 prevents Black from castling queenside but presents a target for the bishop when it comes to b7. The game Gobet - Carlhammer, St. Martin 1991, turned out better for Black after: 11 ... ♖b8 12 b3 ♗b7 13 ♕e2 f6 14 ♗b2 ♗xf3 15 gxf3 fxe5 16 ♗h3 ♘c6 17 0-0-0 ♕g5+ 18 ♔b1 ♗d6 19 ♖hg1 ♕h6 20 ♗f5 ♕f6 21 ♗e4 ♘d4 22 ♕d3 g6 23 ♗c1 a5 24 ♗g5 ♕g7 25 ♖d2 a4 26 ♖b2 axb3 27 axb3 ♗e7 28 ♗c1 ♖f8 29 ♖g3.

A rarely-seen idea is 11 ♘f4 ♕e6 12 ♕e4 ♕c6 13 ♕xc6 ♘xc6 14 0-0-0 h6 15 h4± Cuartas - Zuidema, Skopje 1972.

11   ...   ♘c6
12   ♗d2   0-0-0 *(101)*

An innovation which turns out well for Black. After the older 12 ... ♕e6 13 ♗c3 White has good chances of an advantage:

a) 13 ... h6?! 14 0-0-0 0-0-0 15 h4 g6 16 g3 ♗b7 17 ♕d3 ♗g7 18 ♗h3 ♕e7 19 ♖he1 ♔b8 20 ♕e3 ♖hg8 21 ♖d5 ♗f8 22 ♕d3± Makropoulou - Litinskaya, Malaysia 1990.

b) 13 ... ♗e7 14 0-0-0 f6 15 exf6 ♕xe2 16 f7+ ♔xf7 17 ♗xe2 and now:

b1) 17 ... ♖hd8 18 ♖d5 (18 h4!) 18 ... ♗b7 19 ♖e1 ♘d4 20 ♖h5 ♘xe2+ 21 ♖xe2 ♗xf3 22 ♖f5+

♘f6 23 ♖xf3± Barczay - Forintos, Hungarian Ch 1964.

b2) 17 ... d6 18 ♘d3 ♖he8 19 ♘e4 ♗b7 20 ♕d5+ ♔f8 21 h4 ♘d8 22 ♖he1 ♗xd5 23 cxd5 ♘f6 24 ♖xe8+ ♔xe8 25 ♗xf6 gxf6 26 ♘d2 ♔f7 27 ♘c4 ♘b7 (Jovanovic - Eretova, Skopje Ol 1972) 28 ♖d3! intending ♖b3±.

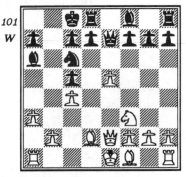

13   ♗c3

Kalinin considers 13 0-0-0 h6 14 ♗c3 ♕e6 15 h4 g6 to be unclear.

13   ...   d5!
14   exd6   ♖xd6!
15   ♕xe7   ♗xe7

In compensation for the doubled c-pawns, Black has active pieces. However, if White can develop his forces harmoniously, then the superior pawn structure will ensure his advantage in the long run.

16   ♗e2

If 16 ♗xg7 the king in the middle of the board becomes a liability: 16 ... ♖e8 17 ♗e2 ♖e6!-+. However, White could have chosen the simple 16 ♖d1 ♖e6+ 17 ♔d2 ♖d8+ (17 ... ♗f6!?) 18 ♔c1 ♖xd1+ 19 ♔xd1 ♗f6=.

16   ...   ♖e6
17   b3   ♖e8
18   ♖a2

A clever way of lending support to e2. White has not yet solved all his problems since his king's rook does not have any scope.

18   ...   ♗f6
19   ♗xf6   gxf6
20   ♔d1   ♘a5
21   ♗d3   ♖b6
22   ♗xh7?!

There is no need to snatch the h-pawn as White can afford to give up a pawn and still draw due to Black's crippled pawns, e.g. 22 ♘d2! ♘xb3 23 ♘xb3 ♖xb3 24 ♔c2 ♖b6 25 ♔c3 h6 26 ♖e2=.

22   ...   ♘xb3

Kalinin suggests 22 ... ♖xb3 as an alternative but it does not promise Black an advantage: 23 ♘d2 ♖c3 24 h4 ♘xc4 25 ♘xc4 ♗xc4 26 ♔d2 ♖b3 27 ♗c2 ♖e2+ 28 ♔d1 ♖xf2 29 ♔e1 (29 h5 ♖c3 30 h6 ♗xa2 31 h7 ♖cxc2 32 h8♕+ ♔b7-+) 29 ... ♖e2+ 30 ♔d1=.

23   ♗d3   ♘a5
24   ♘d2   ♘xc4
25   ♔c2

The double capture on c4 fails to ... ♖b1+.

25   ...   ♘d6 (102)
26   h4

This advance is the only way to divert Black's forces from the attack against the white king. Less clear is 26 ♗xa6+ ♖xa6 27 h4 ♘b5 28 h5 ♘d4+.

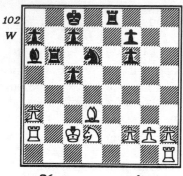

26	...	c4
27	♗f1	♘f5
28	h5	

White must be consistent; anything else allows Black to create insurmountable problems:

a) 28 ♘xc4? ♖c6 29 ♔b3 ♖e1-+.

b) 28 ♗xc4? ♗xc4 29 ♘xc4 ♖e2+-+.

| 28 | ... | ♘d4+ |

In time-trouble Black understandably settles for a perpetual check. However, 28 ... ♖e1 would have caused White a few more difficulties in making the draw: 29 ♘f3 (29 h6? ♘d4+ 30 ♔c3 ♘e2+-+) 29 ... ♖eb1 30 h6 ♗b7 31 h7 (31 ♘d2 ♘d4+ 32 ♔c3 ♘e2+ 33 ♔xc4 ♗a6+ 34 ♔d5 ♗d3!-+; or 33 ♗xe2 ♖xh1 34 ♗g4+ f5 35 ♗xf5+ ♔d8 36 h7 ♗xg2-+) 31 ... ♗e4+ 32 ♔c3 (32 ♔d2!?) 32 ... ♖c1+ 33 ♔d2 c3+ 34 ♔e2 ♖b2+ 35 ♖xb2 cxb2 36 h8♕+ ♔b7 37 ♘d2 ♖c2 38 ♔d1! ♖c1+ 39 ♔e2 ♖c2= (Kalinin).

29	♔c3	♘b5+
30	♔c2	♘d4+
31	♔c3	♘b5+
32	♔c2	½-½

Conclusion

The older 9 ♘d2 is still a dangerous threat to Black, especially against the set-up that Black employed in Harding – Zhividov. Probably 9 ... ♘b4 offers the safest path to equality.

11 Mieses Variation:
8 ... ♗a6 9 ♕e4

Although 9 b3 and 9 ♘d2 are viable methods of playing for an advantage with the white pieces in the Mieses Variation, 9 ♕e4 has rather gone out of fashion. Primarily this has been because Black can force a repetition of moves after 9 ... ♘f6 10 ♕c2 ♘d5 although it is far from clear that White can achieve any advantage after 9 ... ♘b6 either.

Timman – Karpov
London 1984

1	e4	e5
2	♘f3	♘c6
3	d4	exd4
4	♘xd4	♘f6
5	♘xc6	bxc6
6	e5	♕e7
7	♕e2	♘d5
8	c4	♗a6
9	♕e4	

White wastes no time in breaking the pin. A less well analysed idea is also possible: 9 g3!? g6 (9 ... f6 10 e6! dxe6 11 ♘h3 with an unclear position) 10 ♗g2 ♗g7 11 0-0 0-0 12 ♖e1 ♖ae8 13 ♘a3 f6 (not 13 ... ♗xe5?! 14 ♗xd5! cxd5 15 ♘h6 winning

material; but 13 ... ♘b6 14 ♕c2! ♕c5 15 ♗f4 ♗xe5 16 ♘h6 ♗g7 17 ♗xg7 ♔xg7 18 ♕c3+ ♔g8 19 b4 is unclear according to van der Wiel) 14 ♕c2! ♘b6?! (14 ... ♘b4 15 ♕b3 fxe5 16 ♗d2 ♖b8 17 ♘b5 ♘d5! 18 cxd5 ♖xb5 19 ♕a4 ♗b7 with an equal position according to Nikolic) 15 e6 c5 16 ♘b5 dxe6 17 ♘xa7 ♗xc4 18 ♗e3 ♖f7 19 ♖ad1 and White has the better chances, van der Wiel – Nikolic, Tilburg 1992.

9	...	♘b6

Black can also choose to repeat moves here with 9 ... ♘f6 10 ♕e2 ♘d5, as we saw in the game Timman – Karpov, Amsterdam 1985, in chapter 10.

10	♘d2	

Other continuations lead to an equal game:

a) 10 ♗d3 ♗xc4! 11 ♗xc4 d5= ECO.

b) 10 ♘c3 and now:

b1) 10 ... 0-0-0 11 c5 ♗xf1 12 cxb6 ♗a6 13 bxc7 intending ♗f4± Randvir – Raisa, USSR 1961.

b) 10 ... f5 11 ♕xf5 ♗xc4 12 ♗xc4 ♘xc4 13 0-0 g6 14 ♕e4 ♕e6 is unclear, Sveshnikov – Zaitsev, USSR 1975.

10 ... 0-0-0 *(103)*

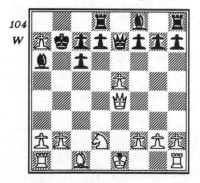

A standard manoeuvre in such positions. The king is fairly safe on the queenside and Black can eventually unravel his pieces after ... d5 and ... f6.

11 c5

The text move signals an all-out assault on the king. White's alternatives at this point were examined (by transposition) in the previous chapter (see Timman - Karpov, Amsterdam 1985). It is important that the reader keeps a close eye out for such transpositions in his or her own games.

11 ... ♗xf1
12 cxb6 ♗a6
13 bxa7 ♔b7 *(104)*

Following the series of exchanges Black has few problems; he can use the a7-pawn as shelter for his own king and delay capturing it until the endgame, whilst White's monarch is trapped in the centre of the board.

14 ♘b3 f6!

Black immediately takes steps to open up the position.

15 f4

If White sacrifices the e-pawn he is left with an unsatisfactory ending due to Black's powerful central pawn mass: 15 ♗d2 ♕xe5 16 ♕xe5 fxe5 17 0-0-0 d5 18 ♘a5+ ♔b6 19 b4 ♗b5!∓.

15 ... fxe5
16 fxe5 ♖e8
17 ♗f4 ♕h4+

It is ironic that after all of White's early aggression it is Black who now creates a strong attack against the white king. It is less precise for Black to enter the endgame: 17 ... ♕b4+ 18 ♕xb4+ ♗xb4+ 19 ♔d1 ♖hf8 and Black is only slightly better.

18 g3 ♕h5
19 ♖c1 ♔a8
20 h4 d5!

Karpov displays commendable energy in conducting his offensive. This is much more difficult to meet than the greedy: 20 ... ♗d6?! 21 ♖c5 ♗xe5 22 ♗xe5 (22 ♖xe5 ♖xe5 23 ♗xe5 ♖e8) 22 ... d5 23 g4 ♖xe5 24 gxh5 ♖xe4+ 25 ♔d1∓.

21 ♕e3

White tries to keep e5 well protected or else he would run into an exchange sacrifice: 21 ♕c2 ♖xe5+ (21 ... c5!?) 22 ♘xe5 ♕xe5+ 23 ♔f2 (23 ♔d1 ♕h5+!) 23 ... ♗d6∓.

21 ... g5
22 ♘xg5 ♗b4+
23 ♔f2 ♖hf8+
24 ♔g2 *(105)*

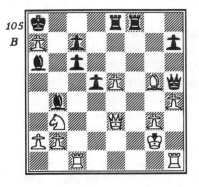

105
B

24 ... ♖xe5!

A fitting coup de grâce to Black's impressively managed attack, smashing a hole in White's fortress.

25 ♕xe5 ♕f3+
26 ♔h2 ♕f2+
0–1

White resigned in view of 27 ♔h3 ♗c8+ 28 g4 ♖f3+ 29 ♕g3 ♕xg3 mate.

Conclusion

It would appear that 9 ♕e4 is not sufficient to promise White anything from the opening. Since White has interesting possibilities after both 9 b3 and 9 ♘d2 these variations are the ones to which White should turn.

12 Mieses Variation: Other Lines

One of the main advantages of the Mieses Variation is that after 4 ... ♘f6 Black has very few means of avoiding the main line with 8 ... ♗a6 or 8 ... ♘b6. This chapter deals with these few deviations, which are rarely seen in tournament play, and not without good reason.

Smagin – Murey
Vienna 1991

1	e4	e5
2	♘f3	♘c6
3	d4	exd4
4	♘xd4	♘f6
5	♘xc6	bxc6
6	e5	♕e7
7	♕e2	♘d5
8	c4	♕b4+

With this check Black avoids the fashionable and heavily analysed variations after 8 ... ♗a6 or 8 ... ♘b6. However, the queen soon becomes a target on b4 and White is able to quickly mobilize his pieces.

9	♘d2	♘f4
10	♕e3	(106)

Prior to this game, White invariably played 10 ♕e4 here. After 10 ... ♘e6 11 ♗e2 Black

can choose between:

a) 11 ... a5 12 0-0 a4 13 ♘f3 ♗e7 14 ♖b1 0-0 15 ♘d4 ♘xd4 16 ♕xd4= Botterill – Rumens, Birmingham 1975.

b) 11 ... ♗b7 and now:

b1) 12 0-0 c5 13 ♕e3 ♘d4 14 ♗d3 ♗e7 15 ♘e4± Estrin – Levenfish, USSR 1950.

b2) 12 a3 ♕b6 13 0-0 c5 14 ♕e3 ♗e7 15 f4 ♘d4 16 ♗d3± Estrin – Sinser, Moscow 1968.

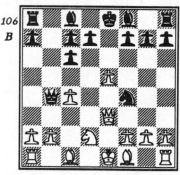

10	...	♘e6
11	♗d3	♕b6
12	♕g3	

The centralization of the knight by 12 ♘e4 fails to achieve anything after 12 ... ♗b4+! 13 ♗d2 ♕xe3+ 14 fxe3=.

| 12 | ... | d5?! |

This works out badly for Black so he should have tried

either 12 ... ♘e7 or 12 ... d6.

13 0-0 a5
14 ♔h1!

A preliminary measure to allow the f-pawn to advance.

14 ... h5
15 h4 g6
16 ♘f3!

The plan of f4-f5 is abandoned as Black is now ready to meet f4-f5. However, in doing so he made serious concessions and it is now the dark-square weaknesses around the king that come under scrutiny.

16 ... ♘c5

An attempt to establish a blockade on the f5-square would backfire: 16 ... ♘g7? 17 ♗xg6! fxg6 18 ♕xg6+ ♔d8 19 ♗g5++-. Now, however, 17 ♗xg6 is well met by 17 ... ♖g8.

17 ♗e3 ♕b4

If 17 ... ♕xb2 18 ♗d4 ♕b4 19 e6 ♖g8 20 exf7+ ♔xf7 21 ♘e5+ and Black is left in a miserable position.

18 a3 ♕b3 *(107)*

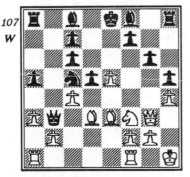

19 ♗xg6!

This tremendous shot allows White to rip a hole in Black's flimsy defences.

19 ... ♖g8

It is hopeless to capture the bishop: 19 ... fxg6 20 ♕xg6+ ♔d8 21 ♕f6++-.

20 ♗xf7+ ♔xf7
21 e6+!

The tactical point of White's play is revealed. The king has to defend g8 so more open lines are created.

21 ... ♗xe6

Forced, in view of 21 ... ♘xe6 22 ♘e5+ ♔e7 23 ♕xg8+-. However, the development of the bishop comes too late to save Black; too much time has been spent on moving the queen and knight backwards and forwards and on weakening pawn moves.

22 ♕xc7+ ♔g6

Other possibilities bring no joy to Black:

a) 22 ... ♘d7 23 ♘e5+ ♔e8 24 ♘xd7 ♗xd7 25 ♖fe1+-.

b) 22 ... ♔e8 23 ♕xc6++-.

c) 22 ... ♗e7 23 ♗xc5+-.

23 ♘e5+ ♔f5

If 23 ... ♔f6 24 ♗d4! is decisive.

24 ♘xc6 ♖g4

The best chance; preparing to meet 25 ♘d4+ with 25 ... ♖xd4 removing a key attacking piece. Obviously bad is 24 ... ♕xc4 25 ♕e5+ ♔g6 26 ♕g5+ ♔h7 (26 ... ♔f7 27 ♘e5+) 27 ♕xh5+ ♔g7 28 ♗d4++-.

25 ♗xc5 ♖xh4+
26 ♔g1 ♔g6
27 ♘e5+ ♔f6
28 ♘f3?! *(108)*

A more precise method is 28 ♗xf8 ♖xf8 29 ♘f3 ♕xf3 30 gxf3 ♖g8+ 31 ♔g3+−.

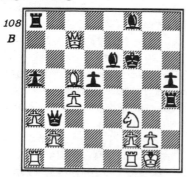

108
B

28 ... ♕xf3!

This remarkable move must have come as something of a shock to White. Black hopes to exploit the open lines which would appear around the white king after 29 gxf3 ♗xc5 30 ♖fe1 (30 ♕xc5?? ♖g8+) 30 ... ♖g8+ 31 ♔f1 ♗h3+ 32 ♔e2 ♖e8+ 33 ♔d2 ♖d4+ 34 ♔c3 ♖xc4+ 35 ♔b3±.

29 ♗xf8! ♖g4

After 29 ... ♖xf8 30 gxf3! transposes to the note to White's 28th move.

30 ♕e7+ ♔f5
31 ♕h7+! ♔e5

There is no way out now: 31 ... ♖g6 32 ♕xg6+! ♔xg6 33 gxf3+−; or 31 ... ♔f6 32 ♗e7++−.

32 ♖fe1+ ♔d4
33 ♖ad1+ 1−0

Black resigned in view of the classic king hunt: 33 ... ♔xc4 34 ♖c1+ ♔b5 35 ♕b7+ ♔a4 36 ♕c6+ ♔b3 37 ♖c3+ ♔xb2 38 ♖c2+ ♔b3 39 ♖b1 mate. The most remarkable feature of this game is that Black's king avoided

checkmate for as long as it did!

In the next game we examine alternatives to 6 ... ♕e7. As we have seen, after 7 ♕e2 both sides have difficulties in developing their kingside pieces, but, as the following game shows, neither 6 ... ♘d5 nor 6 ... ♘e4 promise Black an equal game so he should go in for 6 ... ♕e7 regardless.

Stanisevski – Gordienko
Corr 1987

1	e4	e5
2	♘f3	♘c6
3	d4	exd4
4	♘xd4	♘f6
5	♘xc6	bxc6
6	e5	♘d5

The omission of 6 ... ♕e7 7 ♕e2 makes it easier for White to develop his king's bishop. Neither does 6 ... ♘e4 promise Black an equal game:

a) 7 ♕f3 and now:

a1) 7 ... ♘c5 8 ♗c4 ♘e6 9 0-0 ♕h4 10 ♘d2± Wade – Balanel, Bucharest 1954.

a2) 7 ... ♘g5 8 ♕g3 ♘e6 9 ♗d3 d5 10 0-0 g6 11 ♘d2 f5 12 ♘b3± Bednarski – Prameshuber, Kecskemet 1964.

a3) 7 ... ♕h4 8 g3 (8 ♗e2!?) 8 ... ♘g5 9 ♕e2 (9 ♕e3?! ♕d4 10 ♗g2 ♘e6= Troianescu – Radulescu, Romania 1955) 9 ... ♕e4 10 ♗xg5 ♕xh1 11 ♘c3 h6 (11 ... ♗b4 12 0-0-0 ♗xc3 13 bxc3 ♕xh2 14 ♕f3!± Hünerkopf – Klundt,

West Germany 1983/84; 11 ... a5? 12 0-0-0 ♘a6 13 ♕g4! 1-0 Richter - Kosmata, Czechoslovakia 1977) 12 ♗f4 ♕xh2 13 ♘e4 ♗e7 14 0-0-0 0-0 15 ♕f3± Gusamov - Efimov, USSR 1959.

b) 7 ♗e3 d5 8 exd6 cxd6 9 ♗d3 ♘f6 10 0-0 ♗e7 11 c4 0-0 12 ♘c3 ♗e6 13 ♖e1 d5 14 cxd5 ♘xd5 15 ♘xd5 ♗xd5 16 ♕c2± Timman - Korchnoi, Sarajevo 1984.

7   h4!? *(109)*

An experimental idea which takes the game into relatively uncharted territory. We have already come across a similar idea in chapter eight (Shirov - Agdestein) where both 6 ... ♕e7 7 ♕e2 ♘d5 8 h4!? and 8 c4 ♘b6 9 ♘d2 a5 10 h4 are discussed. White's idea is to prevent Black from playing ... ♕h4 and to support ♗g5. White also has chances of an advantage after the more standard alternatives:

a) 7 ♗d3 d6 8 exd6 cxd6 9 0-0 ♗e7 10 ♗e4 ♕c7 11 ♗xd5 cxd5 12 ♘c3± Arseniev - Veselov, USSR 1960.

b) 7 c4 ♘b6 and now:

b1) 8 ♘c3 ♕e7 9 ♕e2 ♘a6 10 ♕e4 ♕e6 11 b3 ♗b4 12 ♗d2 ♗xc3 13 ♗xc3 d5 14 ♕f3 dxc4 15 ♗e2 0-0 16 0-0 ♖ad8 17 ♖fe1 ♖fe8 18 ♖ac1 c5 19 ♗f1 ♘d5 20 bxc4 (20 ♗xc4 ♗xc4 21 bxc4 ♘b4 intending ♘c6-d4=) 20 ... ♘b4 21 ♗xb4 cxb4 22 ♕e3 ½-½ Ljubojevic - Spassky, Montreal 1979.

b2) 8 ♗d3! ♘a6 9 0-0 (9 ♕e2 ♗e7 10 0-0 0-0 11 ♘c3 ♖e8 12 ♕g4 and White is slightly better according to Keres) 9 ... ♗xc4 10 ♗xc4 ♘xc4 11 ♕g4 ♘b6 12 ♘c3 ♘d5 13 ♘xd5 cxd5 14 ♗g5 ♕b8 15 ♖ad1 ♕b5 16 ♖fe1± Padevski - Witkowski, Laibach 1955.

7   ...   d6
In his analysis of the game (upon which these notes are based) Velickovic suggests 7 ... ♕e7 which transposes to the variation 6 ... ♕e7 7 ♕e2 ♘d5 8 h4 after 8 ♕e2. Indeed, the analysis given in the notes to Shirov - Agdestein in chapter eight would indicate that this is Black's best chance here.

8   c4   ♘b6
After 8 ... ♘e7 9 exd6 cxd6 10 ♘c3 White can concentrate his forces on the weak pawn at d6.

9   c5
A spectacular idea hoping to open lines against the black king. A more natural course was the solid 9 exd6 ♗xd6 (9 ... cxd6 10 ♕f3!±) 10 ♗g5 f6 11 ♗e3±.

9   ...   ♘d5

The prospect of triple c-pawns in an ending has little appeal: 9 ... dxc5 10 ♕xd8+ ♔xd8 11 ♘c3±.

10 ♗b5

It is also possible to make use of the h-pawn with 10 ♗g5:

a) 10 ... ♕d7 11 exd6 cxd6 12 ♗c4! ♕e6+ (12 ... dxc5 13 0-0±) 13 ♔d2 ♔d7 14 ♖e1 ♕f5 15 ♕e2±.

b) 10 ... f6 11 exf6 ♘xf6±.

c) 10 ... ♗e7 11 ♕a4 ♗d7 (11 ... ♕d7 12 ♗xe7 ♘xe7 13 ♘c3 dxe5 14 ♖d1 ♕g4 15 ♕a5!±) 12 exd6 cxd6 (12 ... ♗xg5 13 hxg5 ♕xg5 14 ♘d2!±) 13 cxd6 ♗xg5 14 hxg5 ♕xg5 15 ♘d2! 0-0 16 0-0-0! intending ♕h4±.

10 ... ♗d7

Almost an automatic reaction to White's threat; the alternatives are no better:

a) 10 ... cxb5 11 ♕xd5 ♗e6 12 ♕c6+ ♗d7 13 ♕e4 dxc5 (13 ... dxe5 14 ♗e3!±) 14 ♗g5 intending ♘c3 and 0-0-0.

b) 10 ... ♘e7 11 ♕f3 ♗d7 (11 ... d5 12 ♗a4 ♖b8 13 a3!) 12 ♗a4 dxe5 13 ♘c3 with the idea of ♗e3 and 0-0-0±.

11 e6 ♕e7?!

Here Black should take up the gauntlet by accepting the pawn sacrifice: 11 ... fxe6 12 ♗d3 ♗e7 (12 ... ♘f6 13 g4!) 13 ♕h5+ ♔f8 with an unclear position.

12 ♕xd5!! *(110)*

A scintillating sacrifice, audaciously giving up the queen with only one other piece developed. However, White is soon able to box in the black queen.

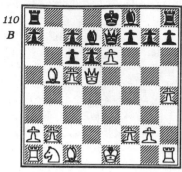

12 ... cxd5

Of course, 12 ... fxe6 13 ♕f3! wins due to the potentially loose rook on a8.

13 ♗xd7+ ♔d8
14 ♗g5 f6
15 ♘c3 c6

There is no easy way out: 15 ... fxg5 16 ♘xd5 gxh4 17 ♘xe7 ♗xe7 18 ♖h3!±.

16 ♗f4 dxc5

Other means of obtaining an escape square for the queen are flawed:

a) 16 ... g6 17 cxd6 ♕g7 18 ♗xc6 ♖c8 19 ♗xd5+-.

b) 16 ... g5 17 ♗xd6! ♕g7 18 ♗xc6 ♖c8 19 ♗xd5 ♖xc5 (19 ... ♗e7 20 ♗b3+-) 20 ♗xc5 ♗xc5 21 0-0-0±.

17 ♘e4! *(111)*

17 ... dxe4?!

Black finally buckles under the strain. The only way to prolong the struggle was 17 ... a5!? to free the rook. Other defences are also unsatisfactory:

a) 17 ... g5? 18 ♘xg5? (18 hxg5!) 18 ... ♕g7 19 ♘f7+ ♕xf7

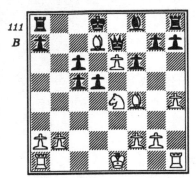

111
B

(19 ... ♔e7 20 ♗d6 mate) 20 exf7 ♔xd7-+.

b) 17 ... c4 18 ♘d6 ♕xd6 19 ♗xd6 ♗xd6 20 ♗xc6±.

18	0-0-0	c4
19	♗xc6+	♔c8
20	♖d7	♕xe6
21	♖c7+	♔d8
22	♖d1+	

The dormant rook joins in the attack with devastating consequences.

22	...	♗d6
23	♖xd6+	♕xd6
24	♗xd6	♖c8
25	♖d7+	♔e8
26	♗a4	1-0

Conclusion

The main merit of deviations in this chapter is to avoid the main lines. After 8 ... ♕b4+ White is quickly able to mobilize his forces, as Smagin showed, whilst 6 ... ♘d5 and 6 ... ♘e4 allow White good chances of advantage. The speculative line 6 ... ♘d5 7 h4!? leads to very complicated play; 7 c4 ♘b6 8 ♗d3 is a safe alternative which guarantees a slight advantage.

13 Neo-Mieses Variation

Apart from the Mieses Variation, White has several other possibilities after 4 ... ♘f6 5 ♘xc6 bxc6 which are considered in this chapter. However, neither 6 ♕d4, 6 ♗d3 nor 6 ♘d2 are sufficiently testing to force an advantage, although they are suitable for those who wish to avoid a theoretical battle in one of the main lines.

Papp – Csapo
Hungary 1981

1	e4	e5
2	♘f3	♘c6
3	d4	exd4
4	♘xd4	♘f6
5	♘xc6	bxc6
6	♕d4	*(112)*

An unusual line which might be successful if used as a surprise weapon. The queen supports e4 and White intends to discourage the freeing ... d5 in view of the formation ♘c3, ♗g5 followed by 0-0-0. Black should, however, be able to equalize without too much difficulty.

The other alternatives to 6 e5 lead the game in a different direction:

a) 6 ♗d3 and now:

a1) 6 ... d6 7 0-0 ♗e7 8 ♘c3 0-0 9 h3 ♘d7 10 ♗e3 ♘f6 11 ♕d2 ♖e8 12 ♖ad1± Hoen – Vasquez, Skopje 1972.

a2) 6 ... ♗c5 7 e5! ♘d5 8 0-0 0-0 9 ♘d2! ♘f4 10 ♘e4 ♘xd3 11 ♕xd3 ♗e7 12 ♗f4±.

a3) 6 ... d5! 7 ♘d2 (7 ♘c3 ♗b4 transposes to the Scotch Four Knights but White can also consider 7 exd5!?) 7 ... ♗d6 8 h3 0-0 9 0-0 ♖e8 10 ♖e1 ♗b7 11 ♔f1 ♗f4 12 exd5 cxd5 13 ♘f3 ♗xc1 14 ♖xe8+ ♕xe8 15 ♕xc1 ♕a4 16 b3 ♕b4 17 ♕d2 ♕d6 18 ♖e1 a5 19 a4 c5 20 ♔g1 ♔f8 21 ♕g5 h6 22 ♕e5 ♖d8 23 ♕xd6+ ♖xd6 24 ♘d2 ♖e6 25 ♔f1= Gunnarsson – Ernst, Reykjavik 1990.

b) 6 ♘d2 and now:

b1) 6 ... d6 7 ♗d3 (7 ♗e2!? g6 8 0-0 ♗g7 9 f4 0-0 10 ♗f3±) 7 ... g6 8 0-0 ♗g7 9 ♘f3 0-0 10 ♗g5 h6= Bilek – Szabo, Budapest 1954.

b2) 6 ... d5 7 exd5 cxd5 8 ♗b5+ ♗d7 9 ♗xd7+ ♕xd7 10 0-0 ♗e7 11 ♘f3 0-0 12 ♗g5 ♖fe8 (12 ... h6!?) 13 ♖e1 c6 (Tartakower – Wolf, Germany 1922) 14 ♘e5 ♕b7 15 ♕f3 gives White a small edge.

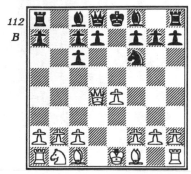

6 ... d6!?

This is rather passive; Black prepares to develop his kingside and then to strike out with ... c5. The alternatives are worth investigating.

a) 6 ... d5 7 ♘c3 and now:

a1) 7 ... ♗e6 8 ♗g5 ♗e7 9 exd5 cxd5 10 ♗b5+ ♗d7 11 ♗xf6 ♗xf6 12 ♕e3+ ♗e7 13 0-0-0 c6 14 ♖he1 a6 15 ♗xc6! ♗xc6 16 ♘xd5 ♗xd5 17 ♖xd5 ♕c7 18 ♖e5 ♖a7 19 ♖xe7+ ♕xe7 20 ♕d2 1-0 Thomas - Arrantes, Corr 1987.

a2) 7 ... ♗e7 8 exd5 0-0 9 ♗f4 cxd5 10 0-0-0 c5 11 ♕e5 ♗e6= Sax - Byrne, Amsterdam 1970.

b) 6 ... ♕e7 7 ♘c3 ♕b4 8 ♕e5+ ♗e7 9 ♗d3 0-0 10 0-0 ♕d6 11 ♕f5 ♕e6 12 ♕a5! d5 13 ♖e1 d4 14 ♘e2 c5 15 e5! ♘d5 16 ♘g3 ♖e8 17 ♗d2 ♗b7 18 c4! dxc3 19 bxc3 ♕b6 20 ♕a4 ♕e6 21 f4 ♕c8 22 f5 ♘b6 23 ♕g4 ♔h8 24 ♘h5 ♖g8 25 e6 ♕e8 26 ♘f4 (intending 27 exf7 and 28 ♘g6+!) 26 ... ♖f8 27 f6 ♗xf6 28 ♕f5 1-0 Thomas - Crusi, Corr 1987.

c) 6 ... c5 7 ♕e3 intending ♘c3, ♗d2 and 0-0-0±.

7 ♘c3 ♗e7
8 h3

White introduces a safeguard against ... ♘g4 in order to develop the bishop on e3.

8 ... 0-0
9 ♗e3 c5

Now that the king has moved to safety, Black chases the queen from its central outpost and prepares to counter-attack against the e4-pawn.

10 ♕a4 ♗d7
11 ♕a5!

The queen looks out of play here but it can no longer be attacked and fixes the black queenside pawns. If White can advance with e5 the black c5-pawn will now be lost.

11 ... ♗c6 *(113)*

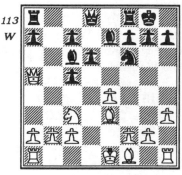

12 0-0-0

White must mobilize his forces quickly or Black will be able to take advantage of his king's central position. The threats of 13 e5 and 13 ♗xc5 force Black to act forcefully.

12 ... ♘xe4
13 ♘xe4 ♗xe4

14 ♗xc5

Although Black has managed to dispense with one of his doubled pawns, White still enjoys the better chances and his queen now looks very well placed on a5.

14 ... ♕e8?!

An instinctive response to break the pin and create some counterplay. Black intends 15 ... ♕c6 with a double attack against c2 and g2. However, he should have preferred 14 ... ♗f6.

15 ♗d4 c5

Black is obliged to change track as the white bishop's influence on g7 allows a tactical trick after 15 ... ♕c6 16 ♗d3! ♗xg2? 17 ♖hg1 f6 18 ♕h5 h6 (18 ... f5 19 f3+-; 18 ... ♗e4 19 ♗xe4 ♕xe4 20 ♖ge1+-) 19 ♕g6+-.

16 ♗b5! ♕c8

If 16 ... ♗c6 White can increase the pressure by 17 ♗xc6 ♕xc6 18 ♕c3!.

17 ♖he1 ♕f5
18 g4 ♗g5+
19 ♗e3 ♕xf2
20 ♕d2!

The ending offers White excellent prospects after he wins back the pawn with a finesse.

20 ... ♗xe3
21 ♖xe3 *(114)*
21 ... ♕f4?

Black is understandably reluctant to enter the ending after 21 ... ♕xd2+ 22 ♖xd2 d5 23 ♗c6 ♖ad8 24 c4!±; but this was

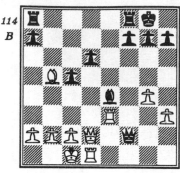

114
B

his best chance.

22 ♖f1 ♕e5
23 ♗c6 ♖ab8
24 ♖xe4

White captures the piece, having accurately calculated that Black's series of checks lead nowhere.

24 ... ♕xb2+
25 ♔d1 ♕a3
26 ♕d3 ♕xa2
27 ♗d5

Naturally, White takes steps to restrict the black forces in order to release the pressure on his own king. He identifies f7 as Black's Achilles' Heel and rapidly consolidates his position.

27 ... ♕a5
28 ♔e2! ♔h8
29 ♖xf7 ♕a1
30 ♕f3 ♖fe8
31 ♖ee7

By a neat twist, defence has been turned into attack.

31 ... ♖g8
32 ♖xa7 ♕e5+
33 ♕e4 ♖ge8
34 ♖ae7 ♖xe7
35 ♖xe7 ♕h2+

36	♕g2	♕f4
37	♕f3	♕h2+
38	♔d3	♕g1
39	♕e3	♕d1+
40	♕d2	♕f1+
41	♕e2	1-0

Conclusion

White's early divergencies are not dangerous if Black responds actively with 6 ... d5. However, if Black reacts carelessly White may be able to establish his superiority early on.

14 Steinitz Variation: 4 ... ♛h4

By far the most aggressive Black defence against the Scotch is Steinitz's 4 ... ♛h4. Black immediately counterattacks against the white e-pawn but in doing so goes against a basic principle of opening play: do not bring your queen out too early. Despite this, Black's move is surprisingly difficult to refute, as the following games show. However, White can hope for a clear advantage if he is well prepared.

Azmaiparashvili – Hector
San Sebastian 1991

1	e4	e5
2	♘f3	♘c6
3	d4	exd4
4	♘xd4	♛h4
5	♘c3!	(115)

This is the move which causes Black the most problems; White aims for rapid development and is not afraid of sacrificing the e4-pawn. The main alternative is 5 ♘b5 which is examined in the next illustrative game, but other moves have also been tested:

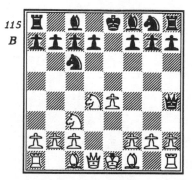

115
B

a) 5 ♘xc6?! ♛xe4+ 6 ♗e2 dxc6 7 0-0 ♗e6 8 ♘c3 (Radulov – Zuckerman, Vrsac 1973) 8 ... ♛h4! 9 ♖e1 ♗c5 10 g3 ♛d4∓.

b) 5 ♘f3?! ♛xe4+ 6 ♗e2 ♛e7! 7 ♘c3 ♘f6 8 ♗g5 ♛d8! 9 ♘d5 ♗e7 and Black is slightly better according to Evans.

c) 5 ♛d3?! ♘f6 and now:

c1) 6 ♘c3 ♗b4 7 ♘xc6 dxc6 transposes to c43.

c2) 6 ♘b5 ♔d8 7 ♘d2 ♗c5 g3 ♛h5 9 ♗e2 ♛g6 10 f3 d6 11 ♘b3? ♘b4 12 ♛d1 ♘xe4-+.

c3) 6 ♘d2?! ♘g4! 7 g3 ♛f6 8 ♘2f3 (8 ♘4f3 ♘ce5 9 ♛e2 ♗c5 and Black is winning according to Winter) 8 ... ♘ce5 9 ♛c3 (9 ♛b3 c5) 9 ... ♗b4 0-1 Prugel – Dyckhoff, 1930.

c4) 6 ♘xc6 dxc6 and now:

c41) 7 e5? ♘g4 8 g3 ♛h5 9 f4

♗c5∓.

c42) 7 ♘d2 ♗c5 8 g3 ♛h5 9 f3 ♗e6 10 ♗g2 ♖d8 11 ♛e2 0-0 12 c3 ♖fe8 13 b4 ♗b6 14 ♗b2 ♘d5!-+ Milovic - Muir, Corr 1968.

c43) 7 ♘c3 ♗b4 8 ♗d2 ♗xc3 (8 ... 0-0!?) 9 ♗xc3 ♘xe4 10 ♛d4 ♛e7 11 0-0-0 ♛g5+? (11 ... ♘xc3 12 ♛xg7 ♘xa2+ 13 ♔b1 ♖f8 14 ♔xa2 with an unclear position) 12 f4! ♛xf4+ 13 ♗d2 ♛g4 14 ♛d8+! ♔xd8 15 ♗g5+ ♔e8 16 ♖d8 mate Maczuski - Kolisch, Paris 1864.

d) 5 ♗e3 ♛xe4 6 ♘d2 (for 6 ♘b5 see note to move 5 in the next main game) and now:

d1) 6 ... ♛g6?! 7 ♘b5 ♘b4 8 ♛f3 ♘xc2+ 9 ♔d1 ♘xa1 10 ♗d3! ♛c6 (10 ... ♛xd3? 11 ♘xc7+ ♔d8 12 ♗g5+-) 11 ♛xc6 bxc6 12 ♘xc7+ ♔d8 13 ♘xa8+- Roth - Schleiffer, Corr 1984.

d2) 6 ... ♛e7 7 ♗e2 (7 ♘b5 d5!∓) 7 ... ♘xd4? (7 ... d5!) 8 ♗xd4 ♘f6 9 0-0 ♛d8 10 ♖e1 ♗e7 11 ♗d3 0-0 12 ♛e2 and the bishops are a potent attacking force, Krutikhin - Ishmbaev, Kirgistan Ch 1957.

e) 5 ♘f5?! ♛xe4+ 6 ♘e3 ♘f6 7 ♗d3 ♛h4 (7 ... ♛e5!?) 8 0-0 d5 9 ♗f5 ♗e6 10 ♖e1 0-0-0∓ Delmar - Steinitz, New York 1894.

5 ...   ♗b4
6 ♗e2

White has no sensible means of defending the e-pawn so elects to sacrifice it for active play. Also possible is 6 ♘b5 ♛xe4+ 7 ♗e2 transposing to the main line, but not worth serious consideration is 6 ♘f3?! ♛xe4+ 7 ♗e2 ♘f6 8 0-0 ♗xc3 9 bxc3 0-0 10 ♘g5 ♛e5 11 ♛d3 d6 12 f4 ♛a5 13 f5 ♗d7∓ Hadjitofi - Levy, Siegen Ol 1970.

6 ...   ♛xe4

It hardly makes sense for Black not to take the pawn immediately:

a) 6 ... ♘f6?! 7 0-0 ♗xc3 8 ♘f5! (8 bxc3 ♘xe4 9 ♗d3 ♘xd4 10 cxd4 d5 11 ♗a3 ♗e6 12 c4 ½-½ Thorhallsson - Mitkov, Cappelle la Grande 1993) 8 ... ♛xe4 9 ♗d3 ♛g4 10 f3 ♛a4 11 bxc3 0-0 12 ♘xg7! ♔xg7 13 ♗h6+ ♔h8 (13 ... ♔xh6 14 ♛d2+ ♔g7 15 ♛g5+ ♔h8 16 ♛xf6+ ♔g8 17 ♛g5+ ♔h8 18 ♛h6+-) 14 ♗xf8 d6 15 ♛d2 ♛h4 16 ♗h6 ♘g8 17 ♗g5 ♛a4 18 c4 ♛a5 19 ♛f4 ♘e5 20 ♗f6+ ♘xf6 21 ♛xf6+ ♔g8 22 ♛g5+ 1-0 Vukovic - Mozetic, Yugoslav Ch 1992.

b) 6 ... ♘ge7 7 0-0 ♗xc3 8 bxc3 ♘xd4 9 ♛xd4 d6 10 f4 0-0 11 ♖b1 ♘c6 12 ♛d3 ♖b8 13 ♖b5 ♛e7 14 ♖g5 f6 15 ♖h5 f5 16 ♗f3 ♛f6 17 h3 h6 18 g4 fxg4 19 hxg4 ♛g6 20 g5 hxg5 21 ♖xg5 ♛h6 22 ♖h5 ♛g6+ 23 ♖g5 ♛h6 24 ♖f2 ♗e6 25 ♖fg2 ♖f7 26 ♖h2 ♛f6 27 e5! ♘xe5 28 ♛h7+ ♔f8 29 ♖xe5 dxe5 30 ♛h8+ ♔e7 31 ♗a3+ c5 32 ♗xc5+ ♔d7 33 ♛xb8+- H. Olafsson - Hector, Copenhagen 1992.

7 ♘b5   ♘f6

Until recently, attention has focused on 7 ... ♗xc3+ 8 ♘xc3 ♛d4 (8 ... ♛e7!? with the idea of

9 ♘b5 ♛d8) 9 ♘d3 ♘b4 10 0–0!
♘xd3 11 ♘b5 ♛c4 12 ♛xd3 ♛xd3
13 cxd3 ♚d8 14 ♗f4 d6 15 ♖ac1
♗d7 16 ♘xc7 ♖c8 when the
position is equal according to
Harding and Botterill, but it is
more logical for White to
deprive his opponent of castling
rights with 8 bxc3! ♚d8 9 0–0
♘ge7 10 ♗d3 (10 ♗f3!?) 10 ...
♛h4 11 ♖e1 f5 12 ♗a3 ♛f6 13 ♛d2
a6 14 ♘d4± De Greef – Lane,
Wijk aan Zee 1992. Black's
innovation offers the queen's
rook in return for an attack.

8 0–0!

White sensibly declines the
proferred material and concen-
trates on his development.
Instead, 8 ♘xc7+ ♚d8 9 ♘xa8
♛xg2 (9 ... ♘d4 10 0–0 ♗xc3 11
♗d3+–) 10 ♗f3 ♖e8+ 11 ♗e3 ♛h3
12 ♗xc6 bxc6 (12 ... ♖xe3+? 13
fxe3 ♛xe3+ 14 ♛e2 ♗xc3+ 15
bxc3 ♛xc3+ 16 ♚f2±) 13 ♛e2
♘d5 14 0–0–0 ♘xe3 15 fxe3
♛xe3+ 16 ♛xe3 ♖xe3 leaves an
unclear position according to
Azmaiparashvilli.

8 ... ♗xc3
9 bxc3

Normally White would avoid
saddling himself with doubled
pawns in this fashion, but here
they give White attacking
options on the b–file while the
important d4–square is con-
trolled. If instead the pawn
structure is kept intact, White's
momentum would peter out: 9
♘xc3!? ♛d4! 10 ♘b5 ♛xd1 11
♖xd1 ♚d8 12 ♗f4 d6 with an

unclear position.

9 ... ♚d8
10 ♗e3 ♖e8 *(116)*

The best chance for Black
was to activate the queenside
rook by 10 ... d6, ... ♗e6, ... ♚d7
and ... ♖ae8, although he must
always be wary of a disruptive
sacrifice on d6. If Black tries to
dislodge the powerful knight
from b5 then he runs into
trouble: 10 ... a6 11 ♘f3 (11 ♘d6?!
♛e6 12 ♘xc8 ♚xc8 with a very
slight edge to White) 11 ... ♛e5
12 ♘d4 ♘xd4 13 ♗xd4 and
White is better according to
Azmaiparashvilli.

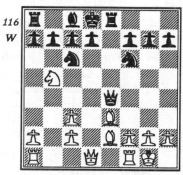

11 ♖e1 ♛d5
12 ♛c1

It is essential for White to
avoid an exchange of queens in
order to maintain his attacking
chances.

12 ... ♛f5
13 ♛a3 d6
14 ♖ad1

White has successfully
managed to activate the whole
of his army whilst Black's
forces remain largely dormant.
A sacrifice on d6 is now firmly

on the horizon.

| 14 | ... | ♖e7 |
| 15 | c4 | |

White now begins to batter Black's defensive bastions; the immediate threat is 16 c5.

| 15 | ... | ♗e6 |
| 16 | ♘f3! | |

Black had prepared 16 c5 d5 17 c4 ♖d7 with a firm defensive barrier but White does not allow him this. Clearly Black cannot accept the pawn sacrifice: 16 ... ♗xc4 17 ♘xd6 cxd6 18 ♗xc6 bxc6 (18 ... d5 19 ♗b6+!) 19 ♕xd6+ ♘d7 (19 ... ♕d7 20 ♗b6+ axb6 21 ♕xe7++-; 19 ... ♖d7 20 ♕f8+ ♔c7 21 ♕xa8+-) 20 ♗b6+ axb6 21 ♖xe7 ♗e6 (21 ... ♘d5 22 c4) 22 ♖xd7+ ♗xd7 23 ♕f8+ ♔c7 24 ♕xa8+-.

16	...	♖d7
17	♗xc6	bxc6
18	♘d4	♕h5 *(117)*

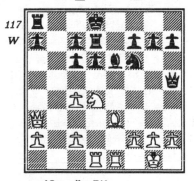

| 19 | ♗g5!! | |

A brilliant stroke which places Black in grave difficulties. If now 19 ... ♕xg5 20 ♖xe6 ♕c5 21 ♕a6 ♕xd4 22 ♖xd4 fxe6 23 ♕xc6 ♖b8 24 h3 wins for White. Black could have

wriggled on after the less forcing 19 ♘xc6+ ♔e8 20 ♘d4 ♖e7±.

19	...	c5
20	♗xf6+	gxf6
21	♘c6+	♔e8
22	♕b2	

White is ready to penetrate via b7 or f6.

22	...	♕h4
23	♕b7	♖ad8
24	♖d3!	1-0

In this hopeless position Black resigned. One possible finish is 24 ... ♕xc4 25 ♖g3 ♔f8 26 ♘xd8 ♖xd8 27 ♕xc7 ♖d7 28 ♕b8+ ♔e7 29 ♖g8 f5 30 ♕f8+ ♔f6 31 ♕g7+ ♔e7 32 ♕g5+ f6 33 ♕g7 mate.

Instead of 5 ♘c3 White often tries 5 ♘b5, but Black has more defensive resources in this instance, as the next game shows.

Milu – Dumitrache
Romania 1991

1	e4	e5
2	♘f3	♘c6
3	d4	exd4
4	♘xd4	♕h4
5	♘b5	♗c5 *(118)*

Black has two main alternatives:

a) 5 ... ♕xe4+?! and now:

a1) 6 ♗e2 ♔d8 7 0-0 a6 8 ♘1c3 ♕e5 9 ♘d5! ♘f6 (9 ... axb5 10 ♗f4 ♕xb2 11 ♗xc7+ ♔e8 12 ♘b6 ♕a3 13 ♖e1 ♗e7 14 ♗xb5 ♔f8 15 ♘xa8 ♕xa8 16 ♗d6! ♕a5

17 ♘xc6 bxc6 18 ♘xe7+ ♘xe7 19
♕d6 ♕g5 20 ♕c7+−) 10 ♘bxc7
♘d4 11 ♗f3 ♘xd5 12 ♘xd5 ♘e6
13 ♖e1 ♕d4 14 ♕e2 ♗d6 15 ♗e3
♕xb2 16 ♖ab1 ♕xa2 17 ♘c3 ♕a3
18 ♖b3 ♗xh2+ 19 ♔xh2 ♕d6+ 20
♔g1 1-0 Herbert − Biyiasis,
Canadian Ch 1978.

a2) 6 ... ♗e3 and now:

a21) 6 ... ♗b4+? 7 ♘d2 ♗xd2+
8 ♕xd2 ♔d8 9 0-0-0 ♕e6 10
♗f4 d6 11 ♗xd6! cxd6 12 ♘xd6
♕xa2 13 ♘b5+ ♔e8 14 ♘c7+ ♔f8
15 ♕d6+ ♘ge7 16 ♕d8+ ♘xd8 17
♖xd8 mate, Grimshaw − Steinitz, London 1890.

a22) 6 ... ♕e5! 7 ♘d2 d5 8
♘f3 ♕e7 9 ♕xd5 ♗e6 10 ♕e4?!
(10 ♕d2!?) 10 ... ♘f6 11 ♕h4 a6 12
♘c3 ♘b4 13 ♖c1 0-0-0∓
O'Hanlon − Mikenas, Buenos
Aires 1939.

b) 5 ... ♗b4+ 6 ♗d2 and now:

b1) 6 ... ♕xe4+ 7 ♗e2 ♕xg2?
(7 ... ♔d8!?) 8 ♗f3 ♗xd2+ 9
♘xd2 ♕h3 10 ♗xc6 bxc6 11
♘xc7+ ♔d8 12 ♘xa8+− Gal-
lagher − Costa, Berne 1991.

b2) 6 ... ♗c5! 7 ♕e2 d6 8 g3
when Black has:

b21) 8 ... ♕d8 9 ♗e3 ♗xe3 10
♕xe3 ♘f6 11 ♘1c3 0-0 12 0-0-0
♖e8 13 ♗g2 ♗d7 14 h3 a6 15 ♘d4
♘xd4 16 ♕xd4 ♗c6 ½-½ Bar-
bero − Wells, Graz 1991.

b22) 8 ... ♕e7 9 ♘1c3 ♘f6 10
♘d5 ♘xd5 11 exd5 ♘e5 12 h3 a6
13 ♘xc7+ ♕xc7 14 f4 0-0 15
fxe5 ♖e8 16 ♗c3 ♗b4! 17 ♗xb4
♖xe5 18 0-0-0 ♖xe2 19 ♗xe2
♕b6 20 ♗c3 ♕e3+ 21 ♖d2 ♗f5 22
g4 ♗xc2 23 ♖f1 ♗g6 24 h4 ♖c8

25 ♗f3 b5 26 ♔d1 b4 27 ♘d4
♗c2+ 28 ♖xc2 ♕d3+ 29 ♖d2
♕xf1 mate 0-1 Wiede − Wells,
London 1989.

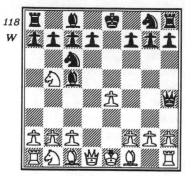

118
W

6   ♕e2

White can also prevent the
mate by 6 ♕f3 when Black has:

a) 6 ... ♘f6?! 7 ♘xc7+ ♔d8 8
♘xa8 ♖e8! 9 ♗d3 ♘xe4 10 ♗xe4
♖xe4+ 11 ♔f1 ♘d4 12 ♕d3 ♘b3
13 ♗e3 ♗xe3 14 fxe3 ♘xa1 15
♘d2 ♖a4 16 ♔e2+−.

b) 6 ... ♘d4 and now:

b1) 7 ♘xc7+ ♔d8 8 ♕f4
♘xc2+ 9 ♔d1 ♕xf4 10 ♗xf4
♘xa1 (10 ... d6 11 ♔xc2 ♗xc7 12
♘c3 ♗e6 13 ♖c1 ♘e7 14 ♔b1 ♘c6
with an unclear position) 11
♘xa8 d6 12 ♗c4 ♗e6 13 ♗xe6
fxe6 14 ♘c3 ♔d7 15 f3 ♘e7 16
♔d2 ♘b3+ 17 axb3 ♖xa8 when
Black is slightly better according to Novoselski.

b2) 7 ♘xd4 ♗xd4 8 c3 ♗b6 9
♘d2 (9 ♗e3!?) 9 ... d6 10 h3 a6 11
♘c4 ♗a7 12 ♗e3 ♗xe3 13 ♕xe3
♘f6 14 ♗d3 0-0 15 0-0 ♗e6 16
♘d2 ♖ae8 17 f4 ♘d7 18 ♖ae1=.

6   ...   ♘f6

Black aims for a rapid de-
ployment of his kingside pieces,

hoping to exploit the position of the white queen by ... ♖e8. Also possible is 6 ... ♞d4 7 ♞xd4 ♝xd4 8 c3 ♝b6 9 g3 ♛e7 10 ♝g2=.

7   ♝e3!   ♝b4+
8   ♞d2   ♝a5

With the manoeuvre 7 ... ♝b4+ 8 ♞d2 ♝a5 Black has avoided having to displace his king with ... ♚d8, but at the cost of several tempi.

9   0-0-0   a6
10   e5   ♞d5
11   ♞f3   ♛e4 (119)

Black should prefer 11 ... ♛a4 as the text move loses time, for example:

a) 12 ♖xd5 ♛xa2! (12 ... axb5 is given in most sources) 13 ♞xc7+ (13 ♞c3 ♝xc3) 13 ... ♝xc7-+.

b) 12 ♞a3! ♞xe3 (12 ... ♞db4 13 ♛c4) 13 ♛xe3 0-0 (13 ... ♝b4 14 ♛b3) 14 ♝c4±.

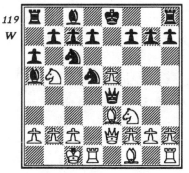

119
W

12   ♞g5!   ♛a4
13   ♛f3

Black's careless eleventh move has allowed White his own attack.

13   ...   0-0

14   ♛xd5   axb5
15   ♝xb5   ♛g4
16   h3

Now the black queen is being chased all over the board as White gains time.

16   ...   ♛h5
17   g4   ♛h4 (120)

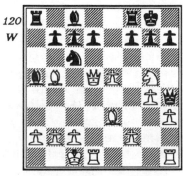

120
W

18   ♝c4   ♞d8
19   ♞f3   ♛e7
20   ♝c5

Black's position collapses.

20   ...   d6
21   exd6   ♛f6
22   d7   ♝xd7
23   ♛xd7   ♛f4+
24   ♚b1   ♛xc4
25   ♝xf8   ♚xf8
26   ♞e5   ♛a6
27   ♛f5   ♝d2
28   a3   g6
29   ♞d7+   ♚g8
30   ♛e4   1-0

Conclusion

Whilst the Steinitz Variation can be dangerous for White if he reacts carelessly, accurate play should enable him to claim an advantage with 5 ♞c3!.

15 Other Black Defences

This section deals with rare fourth moves for Black. The early queen sortie 4 ... ♛f6 is inferior to the Steinitz Variation as Black does not create any pressure against the e-pawn, while 4 ... g6, planning a kingside fianchetto, is too slow if White reacts energetically with queenside castling and a kingside attack.

Narodizky – Kempter
Moscow 1990

1	e4	e5
2	♘f3	♘c6
3	d4	exd4
4	♘xd4	♛f6!? *(121)*

With this move order Black hopes to transpose to the 4 ♗c5 5 ♗e3 ♛f6 lines having avoided 5 ♘b3 and 5 ♘f5. The immediate exchange on d4 allows White's queen to take up a dominating post in the centre, from which it is difficult for Black to dislodge, i.e. 4 ... ♘xd4 5 ♛xd4 and now:

a) 5 ... ♘e7 6 ♗c4 ♘c6 7 ♛d5 (7 ♛e3!?) 7 ... ♛f6 (Edinburgh – London [5] 1826/28) 8 0-0! and White is slightly better accord-

ing to Lewis.

b) 5 ... ♛e7 6 ♘c3 c6 7 ♗e3 ♛d6?! 8 0-0-0 ♛xd4 9 ♘xd4 b6 10 ♗c4 ♗b7 11 a3 ♘e7 12 ♗e5 f5 13 exf5 ♘xf5 14 ♖he1 ♗e7 15 g4 1-0 W. Hoogerwerf – Gischer, Virton 1992.

c) 5 ... d6 6 ♘c3 ♘f6 7 ♗g5 ♗e7 8 0-0-0 ♗e6 9 f4± Gobet – Nemet, Swiss Ch 1988.

d) 5 ... ♛f6 6 e5 ♛c6 7 ♘c3 ♘e7 8 ♗d3 ♘g6 9 ♗e3 ♗e7 10 0-0-0 0-0 11 h4 ♛e6 12 f4 c5 13 ♛e4 f5 14 exf6 ♛xe4 15 ♘xe4 ♗xf6 16 ♗c4+ ♔h8 17 ♗xc5 ♗e7 18 g3 b6 19 ♗xe7 ♘xe7 20 ♘d6 h6 21 ♖he1 ♘c6 22 b3 a5 23 ♘xc8 ♖axc8 24 ♖xd7 1-0 De Greef – Veloso, Novi Sad Ol 1990.

121
W

5	♘b3

White cuts across Black's

idea of transposing to the Classical Variation after 5 ♘e3 ♗c5 with this solid move. White can also play the aggressive 5 ♘b5 with similarities to the Steinitz Variation:

a) 5 ... ♗b4+ 6 ♘1c3 ♗xc3+ 7 ♘xc3 ♘ge7 8 ♗e3 a6 9 ♕d2 d6 10 0-0-0± Botterill - R. Miles, Welsh Ch.

b) 5 ... ♗c5 6 ♕e2 ♘b6 7 ♘1c3 ♘ge7 8 ♗e3 and now:

b1) 8 ... 0-0? 9 ♗xb6 axb6 10 ♘xc7 ♖a5 11 ♕f3 ♕g6 12 ♗d3 ♖h5 13 ♘7d5 ♖h6 14 0-0-0± Bednarski - Lombardy, Students Ol 1964.

b2) 8...a6 9 ♗xb6 axb5 10 ♗xc7 b4 (Zhdanov - Zhuravlev, Riga 1969) 11 e5! which gives White an advantage according to Keres.

b3) 8 ... ♔d8 9 0-0-0 a6 10 ♘a3 ♗xe3+ 11 ♕xe3 b5 12 ♘d5 ♘xd5 13 exd5 ♖e8 14 ♕g3 ♘d4 15 d6! cxd6 16 c3 and the stranded black king gives White the better chances, Borkowski - Meinsohn, Groningen 1974/75.

b4) 8 ... ♘a5 and now:

b41) 9 ♕d2 a6 10 ♘d4 ♘xd4 11 ♗xd4 ♕g6 12 0-0-0 0-0 13 ♕f4 d6 14 ♖d3 f6 15 ♖g3 ♕f7 16 ♘d5 ♘g6= Bruk - Flear, Tel Aviv 1989.

b42) 9 0-0-0 0-0 (9 ... a6!? 10 ♘d4 ♗xc3 11 bxc3 and White is slightly better according to Boleslavsky and Kapengut or 10 ♘d5 ♘xd5 11 exd5 axb5 12 ♗d4+ ♕e7 13 dxc6 dxc6! 14 ♕xe7+ ♔xe7 15 ♗xg7 ♖g8 16 ♗d4

♗b6= Kuprechik - Nei, USSR 1975) 10 ♘d5 ♘xd5 11 exd5 ♘e7 12 d6! cxd6 13 ♖xd6 ♕e5 14 ♗xa7 ♕f4+ 15 ♕e3 ♕xe3+ 16 ♗xe3 ♘f5 17 ♖d3 ♘xe3 18 fxe3 d5 19 a3 and White is a clear pawn up, Chiburdanidze - Miles, Palma 1989.

White also has two less forcing variations: 5 ♘f3 ♗c5 6 ♘c3 ♘ge7 7 ♗g5 ♕g6 8 h4 f6 9 h5 ♕f7 10 ♗f4 ♗b4 11 ♗xc7 d5 12 ♗d3 ♗g4 13 ♘g5! fxg5 14 ♕xg4 d4 15 a3 dxc3 16 axb4 cxb2 17 ♖b1 with an unclear position, Klovan - Ivanov, USSR 1975; and 5 ♘xc6 after which Black can either transpose to the 4 ... ♗c5 5 ♘xc6 ♕f6 lines (see chapter 6) with 5 ... ♗c5 or try the independent 5 ... dxc6 6 ♗c4 ♗d6 7 ♘c3 ♘e7 8 f4 ♗e6 9 ♗xe6 (9 e5? ♗xe5!) 9 ... ♕xe6 10 0-0 f5 11 ♕d4 fxe4 12 ♕xe4 ♕f7 13 ♕f3= Smagin - Hector, Valby 1991.

5 ... ♕g6

Black targets e4 and makes room for the knight to come to f6. White has generally done well after 5 ... ♗b4+ due to the exposed position of the black queen: 6 c3 ♗e7 7 g3 ♗e6 8 ♗g2 f5 9 0-0 fxe4 10 ♖e1 ♘f6 11 ♗f4 0-0 12 ♘1d2 d5 13 f3± Belousov - Klaman USSR 1970.

6 ♕e2

This serves a dual purpose of defending e4 and clearing the way to castle queenside. Of the alternatives, the most interesting possibility is to ignore the threat to the e4-pawn and concentrate on rapid development:

a) 6 ♗e2!? ♘f6 7 0-0 d6 8 ♘c3 ♗e7 9 f3 0-0 10 ♗e3 ♖e8 11 ♘c1! ♘e5 12 ♘d3 ♘xd3 13 cxd3 ♗d7 14 d4 c6 15 ♔h1 h6 16 ♗d3± Neiboolt - Rakitin, Corr 1978.

b) 6 ♕f3 ♘f6 7 ♘1d2 ♗e7 8 ♗b5 0-0 9 0-0 d5= Garcia Padron - Tseshkovsky, Las Palmas 1976.

6	...	d6
7	♘c3	♗e6
8	♗e3	

White continues with an easy plan of development involving queenside castling, realising that his opponent has a long-term problem in that his kingside is rather congested, whilst his queen is already looking misplaced.

| 8 | ... | ♗e7 |
| 9 | 0-0-0 | ♘f6 (122) |

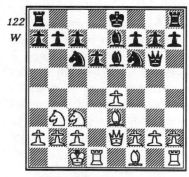

10 f3!

Now e4 is secured and Black cannot consider 10 ... 0-0 as this would walk into an advance of the white g- and h-pawns.

10	...	♘d7
11	♔b1	♘b6
12	♕f2	0-0-0
13	♘d5	

It is standard practice in such positions to station the knight on d5 and White quickly takes the opportunity of 'winning' the two bishops.

13	...	♗d7
14	♘xe7+	♘xe7
15	h4	f6

Black has adopted a passive stance and is relying on White to overstretch, but this is a dangerous policy and he should at least have tried 15 ... f5.

16	♘d4	♔b8
17	b3	♘c6
18	h5	♕f7
19	♘b5	♗e6
20	g4 (123)	

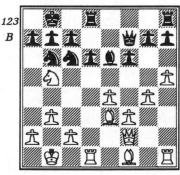

White is in total command of the board. His pawns severely limit the range of the opposing pieces and he can gradually build up the pressure using his space advantage. The knight on b5 is an immediate cause of concern for Black as it offers White several attacking options and cannot be removed by ... a6 due to ♘xc7!.

20	...	♖he8
21	c4	♘c8
22	♘c3	♘e5
23	♘b5	

White realises that 23 ♘d5 is met by 23 ... c6 and resorts to a slower approach, since Black has no active play.

23	...	♘c6
24	♕d3	♕g8
25	♘d4	♘xd4
26	♕xd4	h6

Black obviously feared 27 h6 to open the h-file and undermine his kingside pawns.

27	♕c2	b6
28	♖hg1	♘e7
29	f4	

The wave of pawns advance and Black has no way of stopping them.

29	...	♕f8
30	♕g3	♘g8
31	g5	♖e7
32	♕c3	♖f7
33	♕e3	♕c8
34	b4!	

Now that Black has been tied down on the kingside another avenue of attack is opened up with dramatic effect.

34	...	♕b7
35	gxh6	♘xh6
36	c5	dxc5
37	bxc5	♖fd7?
38	♖xd7	1-0

Black resigned in view of 38 ... ♖xd7 39 c6+-.

Now we turn to 4 ... g6.

Makarichev – Tukmakov
Palma 1989

1	e4	e5
2	♘f3	♘c6
3	d4	exd4
4	♘xd4	g6!?

The starting point of an unusual variation which has close similarities to the Pirc Defence. A variety of obscure moves has also been tested at this stage:

a) 4 ... ♗b4+!? 5 c3 ♗e7 6 ♘xc6 bxc6 7 ♕d3 d6 8 0-0 ♘f6 9 ♘d2 0-0 10 ♕a4 c5 11 ♖e1 ♖e8 12 ♘f1 ♗d7 13 ♕c2 ♗c6 14 b4 cxb4 15 cxb4 ♕d7 16 ♗b2 a5 17 a3 ½-½ van der Wiel – Tal, Brussels 1987.

b) 4 ... d5? 5 ♘xc6 bxc6 exd5 ♗b4+ (6 ... ♕xd5 7 ♕e2+ and 8 ♘c3 with advantage to White) 7 c3 ♗c5 8 ♕e2+ (8 dxc6?? ♗xf2+-+) 8 ... ♘e7 9 dxc6 0-0 10 ♕c4 ♕d6 11 ♗e2 ♕xc6 12 0-0 and White is a clear pawn up, A. Osborne – Bloodworth, Torquay 1985.

c) 4 ... d6 and now 5 ♗c4± transposes to a Hungarian Defence and 5 ♗b5± to a line of the Ruy Lopez, both of which are outside the scope of this book.

5	♘c3

Evans has suggested 5 c4!? to clamp down on the centre by preventing a later ... d5.

5	...	♗g7
6	♗e3	♘f6 (124)

When Karpov tested this

variation he chose a slightly different set-up in this position: 6 ... d6 7 ♕d2 ♘f6 8 0-0-0 (8 ♗b5 ♗d7 9 ♗xc6 bxc6 10 ♘h6 0-0= Karasev - Geller, USSR 1971) 8 ... ♘g4 9 ♘xc6 (9 ♗g5!?) 9 ... bxc6 10 ♗d4 ♗xd4 11 ♕xd4 ♕f6= 12 f3 ♕xd4 13 ♖xd4 ♘e3 14 ♘d1 ♘xd1 15 ♔xd1 with equal chances. A more convincing line for White is 7 ♗e2!? ♘f6 8 ♘xc6 bxc6 9 e5 dxe5 10 ♕xd8+ ♔xd8 11 0-0-0+ ♔e8 12 ♘f3 ♗d7 13 ♖he1 ♔f8 14 ♗c5+ ♔g8 15 ♖xe5 h5 16 ♗e7 ♖b8 17 ♖c5 ♘d5 18 ♗xd5 cxd5 19 ♖xc7+- S. Arkell - G. Flear, Hastings 1989/90.

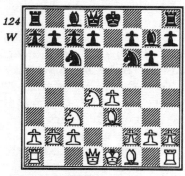

7 ♕d2

The sharpest method of play aiming for a rapid kingside attack. Other moves are slower and tend to justify Black's opening choice:

a) 7 g3 0-0 8 ♗g2 d6 9 h3 ♘e5!= Savon - Ree, Suhumi 1972

b) 7 f3 and now:

b1) 7 ... 0-0 8 g4 ♖e8 9 g5 ♘h5 10 ♘de2 ♘e5 11 ♘g3 ♘xg3 12 hxg3 d5 13 ♘xd5 c6 14 ♘f6+

♗xf6 15 gxf6 ♕xf6 16 ♗g2 ♘c4 17 ♕d4± Bellon - Mariotti, Rome 1977.

b2) 7 ... ♘e7! 8 ♗c4 d5 9 exd5 ♘fxd5 10 ♘xd5 ♘xd5∓ Zukertort - Steinitz, Vienna 1882.

c) 7 ♗e2 0-0 8 ♕d2?! (8 0-0 ♖e8 9 ♘xc6 bxc6 10 ♗f3 ♗b7 12 ♕d2 d6= Bagirov - Keres, Moscow 1963) 8 ... ♖e8 9 f3 d5! 10 ♘xc6 bxc6 11 exd5 ♘xd5 12 ♘xd5 cxd5 13 c3 (13 0-0-0?? ♕e7-+; 13 ♗g5 ♕d6 14 0-0? ♕e5-+) 13 ... c5 14 0-0 d4 15 ♘f2 (15 cxd4 ♖xe3!) 15 ... ♕a5 16 ♖fc1 ♗f5 17 ♗c4 ♖ad8 18 ♕g5 dxc3 19 bxc3 ♗xc3 20 ♖xc3 ♕xc3 21 ♖c1 ♕b2 22 ♘e1 h6! 0-1 Rossetto - Keres, Mar del Plata 1957.

d) 7 ♗c4 and now:

d1) 7 ... 0-0 8 ♘xc6 (8 0-0 ♖e8 9 ♖e1 d6 10 f3 a6= Hort - Keres, Moscow 1963) 8 ... bxc6 9 e5?! ♘e8 10 e6 fxe6 11 ♗xe6+ ♔h8∓ Prameshuber - Keres, Munich Ol 1958.

d2) 7 ... d6 8 f3 0-0 9 ♕d2 ♘e5 10 ♗e2 (10 ♘b3!= *ECO*) 10 ... d5! 11 f4 ♘eg4 12 e5 ♘xe3 13 ♕xe3 c5!∓ Corden - Littlewood, Hastings 1969/70.

e) 7 ♘xc6!? bxc6 8 e5 ♘g8 9 ♗d4! ♕e7 10 ♕e2 f6 11 exf6 ♘xf6 and White has a slight edge according to Keres.

7 ... 0-0

Instead 7 ... d6 8 0-0-0 ♘g4 transposes to Bellon - Karpov, (see note to Black's sixth move).

8 0-0-0

Another aggressive choice is

8 f3 d5 9 ♘xc6 bxc6 10 0-0-0
♗e6 11 ♗h6! ♖b8 12 ♗xg7 ♔xg7
13 ♕e3 ♕e7 14 exd5 cxd5 15
♘xd5 ♘xd5 16 ♖xd5 ♕f6 17 ♖e5
♖fd8 18 ♗e2+– Radulov – Planinc, Wijk aan Zee 1974.

8 ... ♘xd4

Black wishes to push for-
ward the queenside pawns, so
this trade on d4 is an essential
preliminary measure. The
attempt to exchange the bishop
on e3 fails after 8 ... ♘g4 9 ♗g5
f5 (9 ... ♗f6!? 10 ♗xf6 ♕xf6 11 f3
♕xd4 12 ♕xd4 ♘xd4 13 ♖xd4
♘f6 [13 ... ♘e3 14 ♘b5 c6 15
♘c7±] 14 e5 ♘e8 15 ♘e4 intending ♗c4±) 10 ♗f4 ♘xd4 11
♕xd4 f5 12 ♕c4+ ♔h8 13 ♗xc7
♕f6 14 ♕e2 and White has the
edge according to Makarichev.

9 ♗xd4 d6
10 f3

It should be noted that this
position can also arrive from a
Pirc move order, i.e. 1 e4 d6 2
d4 g6 3 ♘c3 ♗g7 4 ♗e3 ♗g7 5
♕d2 0-0 6 0-0-0 ♘c6 7 f3 e5 8
♘ge2 exd4 9 ♘xd4 ♘xd4 10
♗xd4.

10 ... ♗e6 *(125)*

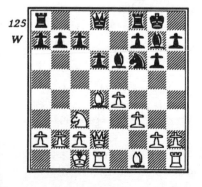

11 g4

This is intended to prevent
Black's freeing move ... d5
which would not be met by g5
when the knight must with-
draw its support. The text also
allows White to consider h4 as
the blockading ... h5 would
now be too hazardous. Also
possible is 11 ♗e3 ♖e8 12 ♗g5
♕e7 (12 ... c6?! 13 e5 dxe5 14
♕xd8 ♖cxd8 15 ♖xd8 ♖xd8 16
♘e4+–) 13 g4 ♕f8 14 ♔b1 a6 15
h4 with a powerful attack,
Chernin – Zaichik, Lvov 1987.

11 ... c5
12 ♗e3

Now White has a straight-
forward plan of 13 h4, h5, hxg6
♗h6, ♗xg7 and the ♕h6 when
the white pieces invade with
devastating consequences.
Black therefore has to create
counterplay as quickly as possible.

12 ... ♕a5
13 ♗h6!

White must continue actively
since 13 ♔b1?! (to defend a2)
simply moves the king into
danger after 13 ... b5 14 ♗xb5
♗xa2+! opening up lines against
the monarch. After 13 ♗h6 the
pawn is poisoned: 13 ... ♗xa2 14
♘xa2 ♕xa2 15 ♗xg7 ♔xg7 16
♕c3!+–.

13 ... ♗xh6
14 ♕xh6 b5!?

There is a sense of urgency
in Black's game since the capture on a2 fails: 14 ... ♗xa2?! 15
h4 ♗e6 16 h5 ♕a1+ 17 ♔d2 ♕xb2

18 ♖b1 ♕a3 19 hxg6 fxg6 20 g5 ♘h5 21 ♖xh5+-.

15	♗xb5	♖ab8
16	a4	a6 (126)

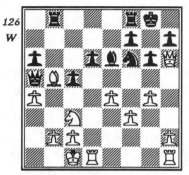

126
W

17   ♖xd6!

A remarkable idea; White gives up a piece in order to remove the defensive knight from f6. Less forcing play would allow Black to escape:

a) 17 ♗e2? ♖xb2 18 ♔xb2 ♖b8+ 19 ♔c1 ♕xc3 and Black has good attacking chances.

b) 17 e5?! dxe5 18 g5 ♘h5 19 ♘e4 ♔h8! with an unclear position according to Makarichev.

17	...	axb5
18	e5	♘xg4

The full force of the sacrifice is revealed after 18 ... ♘e8 19 ♘e4 (with the idea of 20 ♘f6+) 19 ... f5 20 ♘g5+-.

19	fxg4	♕b4!

The queen simultaneously prevents ♘e4 and opens up the possibility of 20 ... bxa4 with active play on the b-file.

20	a5	♕xg4
21	♖e1	♕f5

Black is hanging on by a thread; 22 ♘e4 can be met by 22 ... ♕xe5 which covers the vital f6-square.

22	♕h4	b4
23	♘e4	h5
25	♖d2!	

This clever switch threatens to bring the rook onto the vulnerable f-file.

24	...	♔g7!
25	♕f6+	♔h6
26	♘xc5	♖b5
27	♘xe6	fxe6
28	♕xf5	♖xf5?!

Black has defended excellently, but still faces a difficult endgame due to the outside passed pawn on a5. A better chance to confuse matters lay in 28 ... exf5 when the advance of the f-pawn must be considered, e.g. 28 ... exf5 29 a6 f4! 30 ♖d6 (30 e6 ♖a5! 31 ♖d6 f3 with an unclear position) when White threatens 31 ♖g1±.

29	a6	♖fxe5
30	♖xe5	♖xe5
31	♖d6	♔g5
32	c4!	♔h4

If instead 32 ... bxc3 33 b4 and the duo of passed pawns race through to promotion.

33	♔c2	♔h3
34	♔b3	♔xh2
35	♔xb4	♖e1
36	a7	♖a1
37	♖d2+!	1-0

Black resigned in view of 37 ... ♔g3 38 ♖d3+ ♔g2 39 ♖a3+-; or 37 ... ♔g1 38 ♖d1+! ♖xd1 39 a8(♕)+-. A well calculated game by Makarichev.

Conclusion

None of the variations considered in this chapter promise Black an equal game. However, White still needs to be prepared to meet them as they might be tried by an opponent wishing to avoid the well analysed 4 ... ♗c5, 4 ... ♘f6 and 4 ... ♕h4.

Index of Variations

1	e4	e5
2	♘f3	♘c6
3	d4	cxd4
4	♘xd4	

A) 4 ... ♗c5
B) 4 ... ♘f6
C) 4 ... ♛h4

4 ... ♘xd4 *134*; 4 ... ♛f6 *134*; 4 ... g6 *137*; 4 ... ♗b4+ *137*; 4 ... d5 *137*;
4 ... d6 *137*

A)

4	...	♗c5
5	♗e3	

5 ♘xc6 ♛f6 6 ♛d2 (6 ♛f3 *61*; 6 ♛e2 *61*; 6 f4 *61*) 6 ... bxc6 (6 ... dxc6
62; 6 ... ♛xc6 *62*) 7 ♗d3 *62*
5 ♘f5 g6 (5 ... d5 *54*; 5 ... d6 *55*; 5 ... ♛f6 *57*) 6 ♘e3 *55*
5 ♘b3 ♗b6 (5 ... ♗b4+ *50*; 5 ... ♗e7 *51*) 6 a4 (6 ♘c3 *51*; 6 c4 *51*) 6 ...
a6 (6 ... a5 *37*; 6 ... ♛h4 *42*; 6 ... ♛f6 *44*) 7 ♘c3 and now:

a) 7 ... d6
b) 7 ... ♛f6
7 ... ♘ge7 *39*; 7 ... ♘f6 *40*

a) 7 ... d6 8 ♗e2 (8 ♘d5 *42*; 8 ♛e2 *42*; 8 a5 *42*) 8 ... ♘f6 (8 ... ♛h4
42; 8 ... ♘ge7 *42*) 9 0–0 *40*
b) 7 ... ♛f6 8 ♛e2 ♘ge7 9 ♘d5 (9 a5 *48*) 9 ... ♘xd5 10 exd5+ ♘e7 11
a5 ♗a7 12 h4 h6 (12 ... 0–0 *45*; 12 ... d6 *45*; 12 ... ♛d6 *46*) 13 ♗d2 (13
♖a4 *46*; 13 g4 *48*) 13 ... 0–0 (13 ... ♛xb2 *46*; 13 ... d6 *48*) 14 ♗c3 *47*

5	...	♛f6

5 ... ♗xd4 *33*; 5 ... ♘b6 *33*

6	c3	♘ge7
7	♗c4	

7 ♗e2 *23*; 7 ♕d2 *23*; 7 f4 *23*; 7 ♘c2 *23*; 7 ♘d2 *23*; 7 ♗b5 *23*
7 g3 d5 (7 ... d6 *26*; 7 ... ♘xd4 *26*; 7 ... 0-0 *27*) 8 ♗g2 ♘xd4 (8 ... dxe4
27; 8 ... ♘e5 *30*; 8 ... ♗xd4 *30*) 9 cxd4 ♗b4+ (9 ... ♘b6 *30*) 10 ♘c3 *31*

7	...	0-0

7 ... b6 *20*; 7 ... ♕g6 *23*; 7 ... ♘xd4 *23*
7 ... ♘e5 8 ♗e2 (8 ♘b3 *14*) 8 ... ♕g6 (8 ... d5 *15*) 9 0-0 d5 (9 ... d6 *17*;
9 ... ♕xe4 *17*) 10 ♘b5 (10 ♘b5 *15*; 10 ♗f4 *15*; 10 ♔h1 *15*) 10 ... ♕xe4 *15*

8	0-0	♗b6

8 ... a6 *11*

9	♘c2	

9 ♘a3 *12*; 9 ♘b3 *12*; 9 ♔h1 *12*

9	...	d6 *13*

B)

4	...	♘f6
5	♘xc6	

5 ♘c3 ♗b4 (5 ... ♗c5 *64*; 5 ... ♘xe4 *64*) 6 ♘xc6 (6 ♗g5 *65*) 6 ... bxc6
7 ♗d3 (7 ♕d4 *67*; 7 ♗d2 *67*) 7 ... d5 (7 ... 0-0 *70*; 7 ... d6 *70*) 8 exd5
(8 e5 *65*; 8 0-0 *65*) 8 ... cxd5 (8 ... ♕e7+ *75*) 9 0-0 0-0 10 ♗g5 ♗e6
(10 ... ♗e7 *78*; 10 ... ♗xc3 *78*; 10 ... c6 11 ♘a4 [11 ♕f3 *79*; 11 ♘e2 *79*]
76) 11 ♘e2 (11 ♕f3 *70*; 11 ♘b5 *72*) 11 ... h6 (11 ... ♗d6 *70*; 11 ... ♗e7 *70*;
11 ... ♗g4 *70*; 11 ... ♖b8 *71*) 12 ♗h4 *67*

5	...	bxc6
6	e5	

6 ♗d3 *124*; 6 ♘d2 *124*; 6 ♕d4 *124*

6	...	♕e7

6 ... ♘d5 *120*; 6 ... ♘e4 *120*

	7	♕e2	♘d5
	8	c4	

8 h4 *89*

	8	...	♗a6

8 ... ♕b4+ *118*
8 ... ♘b6 9 ♘d2 (9 ♘c3 *86*; 9 b3 *86*; 9 ♗f4 *87*) 9 ... ♕e6 (9 ... a5 *89*; 9 ... ♗b7 *89*) 10 b3 a5 (10 ... ♗b4 *87*; 10 ... ♗e7 *87*) 11 ♗b2 *83*

	9	b3

9 ♕e4 *115*; 9 g3 *115*
9 ♘d2 ♘b6 (9 ... f6 *104*; 9 ... ♘f4 *105*; 9 ... g6 *107*; 9 ... 0-0-0 *108*; 9 ... ♘b4 *111*) 10 b3 *105*

	9	...	g6

9 ... 0-0-0 *97*; 9 ... ♕h4 *100*

	10	f4 *94*

C)

	4	...	♕h4
	5	♘c3	

5 ♘xc6 *128*; 5 ♘f3 *128*; 5 ♕d3 *128*; 5 ♗e3 *129*; 5 ♘f5 *129*; 5 ♘b5 *131*

	5	...	♗b4
	6	♗e2	

6 ♘b5 *129*; 6 ♘f3 *129*

	6	...	♕xe4

6 ... ♘f6 *129*; 6 ... ♘ge7 *129*

	7	♘b5 *129*